Chopsticks

Chopsticks have become a quintessential part of the Chinese, Japanese, Korean and Vietnamese culinary experience across the globe, with more than one fifth of the world's population using them daily to eat. In this vibrant, highly original account of the history of chopsticks, Q. Edward Wang charts their evolution from a simple eating implement in ancient times to their status as a much more complex, cultural symbol today. Opening in the Neolithic Age, at the first recorded use of chopsticks, the book surveys their use through Chinese history, before exploring their transmission in the fifth century to other parts of Asia, including Japan, Korea, Vietnam and Mongolia. Calling upon a striking selection of artwork, the author illustrates how chopstick use has influenced Asian cuisine, and how, in turn, the cuisine continues to influence chopstick use, both in Asia and across the globe.

Q. Edward Wang is Professor of History and Co-ordinator of Asian Studies at Rowan University and Changjiang Professor of History at Peking University, China.

Chopsticks

A CULTURAL AND CULINARY HISTORY

Q. EDWARD WANG

CAMBRIDGE
UNIVERSITY PRESS

University Printing House, Cambridge CB2 8BS, United Kingdom

Cambridge University Press is part of the University of Cambridge.

It furthers the University's mission by disseminating knowledge in the pursuit of education, learning and research at the highest international levels of excellence.

www.cambridge.org
Information on this title: www.cambridge.org/9781107023963

First published 2015
Reprinted 2018

Printed in the United States of America by Sheridan Books, Inc.

A catalog record for this publication is available from the British Library

Library of Congress Cataloging in Publication data
Wang, Q. Edward, 1958–
Chopsticks : a cultural and culinary history / Q. Edward Wang.
pages cm
ISBN 978-1-107-02396-3 (hardback)
1. Chopsticks. I. Title.
GT2949.W36 2014
394.1′2–dc23
2014021293

ISBN 978-1-107-02396-3 Hardback

To my mother who taught me to use chopsticks in China and for my son who is using them in the US, as the tradition lives on from past to present, China and beyond.

Contents

Acknowledgments

Researching and writing this book has been a pleasant experience for me. I also would like to express, with pleasure, my gratitude to the people who helped me in the process. I do not exactly remember when the idea of writing a book about the history of chopsticks first came to me. But I do remember that at the very early stage when I checked several major library catalogs online, trying to look for any book or article on the subject, I was quite surprised that essentially none had been written in English, save for a few children's books. This finding spurred me to take on the task. At the same time, I also realized that I would have less to draw on from existing scholarship. Fortunately, I received a prestigious fellowship from the Institute for Advanced Study (IAS) at Princeton in 2010, to work on a different (yet related) subject. With the kind agreement and encouragement of Nicola Di Cosmo, professor of Asian history at the IAS, I was able to pursue the initial research on this subject instead. The excellent research facility and friendly and capable staff at the IAS facilitated my work. The Gest Library at the neighboring Princeton University also offered me important access to many useful sources. Toward the end of my tenure at the IAS, I gave my first presentation on the research. I am grateful to Professor Di Cosmo and my fellow IAS members for their knowledge, help and comments, especially Daniel Botsman, Fa-ti Fan, Marie Favereau-Doumenjou, Sarah Fraser, Jinah Kim and Don Wyatt. During that period, I also sought advice and suggestions from Professors Ying-shih Yu, Benjamin Elman and Susan Naquin at Princeton University and Professors Paul Goldin, Xiaojue Wang and Si-yen Fei at the University of Pennsylvania. In the following academic year, while teaching as a visiting professor at the University of

Pennsylvania, I gave a presentation, entitled "Chopsticks: 'Bridging' Cultures in Asia."

I also presented my research for the book at Brandeis University and Rowan University (my home institution) in the US, and at Fudan University, Peking University, the Institute of Modern History, the Chinese Academy of Social Sciences and the National Library of Taiwan in Asia. Professor Aida Y. Wong, an art historian of China and Japan, arranged my talk at Brandeis University. A staunch supporter of the project from the beginning, Aida loaned me books and helped me in finding illustrations for the book. My talk at Fudan University in Shanghai was arranged by Professor Ge Zhaoguang, then the director of the Advanced Research Institute for the Humanities, and chaired by Professor Zhang Qing, head of the History Department at Fudan. Zhao Xiaoyang and her colleagues at the Institute of Modern History invited me to talk at the Chinese Academy of Social Sciences. Presided over by Huang Ko-wu, director of the Institute of Modern History, Academia Sinica, my presentation at the National Library of Taiwan was the first lecture of the series "Center for Chinese Studies Scholars Worldwide," introduced by Keng Li-ch'un, Jane Liau and the staff at the Center for Chinese Studies at the Library. Here I would like to express my deep appreciation for all the above invitations, which were a major encouragement for me in writing the book. I am also grateful to the audiences for their enthusiasm and questions, which helped me to explore more aspects of the history and culture of chopsticks.

I conducted the bulk of my research at Peking University where, since 2007, I have taught in summers and winters as Changjiang Professor in its History Department. As China's leading university, Peking University has a library which provided me with excellent access not only to its huge source collections but also to several key databases, including Zhongguo jiben gujiku and Hanji dianzi wenxian ziliaoku. When I gave my talk on chopsticks culture on the campus in June 2013, I received useful information and interesting queries from the audience. I would like to thank the faculty and students at Peking University for their support and assistance; especially Professors Li Longguo, Liu Qunyi, Luo Xin, Rong Xinjiang, Wang Xinsheng, Wang Yuanzhou and Zhu Xiaoyuan. Graduate students at Peking University, such as Zong Yu and Li Leibo, also provided help for my research.

In completing the book, I owe my greatest gratitude to the History Department at Rowan University. Before submitting my prospectus to Cambridge University Press, I first presented it in the Department and received warm encouragement and valuable suggestions from all my colleagues. Corinne Blake, James Heinzen, Scott Morschauser and Joy Wiltenburg kindly proofread several of the chapters and offered useful suggestions for improving the prose. Rowan colleagues in other departments also helped my work. Yuhui Li, a native of Northwest China, taught me a good deal about the dietary traditions and practices of the region, as did Hieu Heyuen, who answered my questions about the dining customs in Vietnam. Tomoyo Fukumori provided useful firsthand information regarding the eating etiquette in Japanese society. She also helped me gain a better understanding of the Japanese texts for my research. Her assistance, therefore, was much beyond her duty as a student worker, for which I am very grateful. At various stages, my writing of and research for the book received encouragement from Bill Carrigan, our current chair in the Department, and Cindy Vitto, dean of the College of Humanities and Social Sciences at Rowan.

For my research, I visited several museums and private collections, and interviewed food scholars in Asia, such as the special chopsticks collections at the Lüshun Museum in Lüshun, the Sanxia Museum in Chongqing, the Yangzhou Museum in Yangzhou, the Shanghai Chopsticks Private Collection in Shanghai, China, the National Folk Museum of Korea in Seoul, South Korea, the Museum of Chopsticks Culture in Kyoto, the Tokyo National Museum and the Edo-Tokyo Museum in Japan. I am indebted to the following individuals for those visits, as well as to the museums, which helped provide useful images for illustrating the book and enhancing my knowledge of chopsticks use: Ai Zhike, Chen Yunqian, Cui Jian, Han Junshu, Li Yujie, Liu Junyong, Liu Li, Liu Shilong, Luo Lin, Ouyang Zhesheng, Park Mihee, Wang Nan, Wang Rong, Xu Yue, Yu Xiaohang, Zeng Xuewen, Zhao Yi, Zhao Yifeng and Zhou Yiping. In particular, I would like to thank Mr. Lan Xiang for meeting and talking with me in June 2013. A chopsticks collector of many decades and owner of the Shanghai Chopsticks Private Collection, Lan is a prolific author on chopsticks culture and history. It was a pleasure to meet him and I obtained his permission for using some of the photos I took of his collection. Liu Jianhui, professor at the International Center for Japanese Studies in Kyoto, kindly accompanied me on my visit to the Museum of Chopsticks Culture in Kyoto in July 2013. Though the Museum was closed, we managed to find its owner Mr. Izu, with whom I had a brief conversation. Our subsequent visit to the Chopsticks Shop, Ichihara-Heibei Shoten in Kyoto, which has been in existence since 1764 and is one of the oldest chopsticks shops in Japan, was also very fruitful. I thank the shop owner for sharing with me an article featuring their store, which bears the interesting title "Chopsticks: A Tool that Bridges Food and Culture." It stresses that since chopsticks and bridge are pronounced the same in Japanese, chopsticks are a means for cross-cultural communication and exchange.

In addition, I would like to thank Han Jiang, Han Junshu (again!), Lim Jie-hyun, Okamoto Michihiro, Pan Kuang-che, Dennis Rizzo, Sun Weiguo, Xing Yitian, Zhou Bing and Zeng Xuewen who either helped me find research materials or provided clues and/or answers to my queries. On-cho Ng, Di Wang and two other anonymous readers reviewed my original prospectus for Cambridge University Press and offered valuable suggestions. Their ideas were useful for shaping and improving the structure of the book, for which I am thankful. Marigold Acland at Cambridge University Press, with whom I first discussed the idea of writing this book, was a strong supporter of the project from the outset. After completing the manuscript, I also received valuable help from Lucy Rhymer, Marigold's successor, and Amanda George at the Press. Without their professional knowledge and assistance, this book would not be the one it is now.

I essentially wrote this book for my mother and my son. To my mother, I owe a debt for her teaching me how to use the utensil correctly all my life. I also hope my son, who is old enough to use chopsticks, can carry on this tradition, and pass it on to his children. Last but not least, I thank my wife Ni who, a college professor herself, has a deep understanding of what it entails for me to complete a task like this one. My appreciation of her patience and support is beyond words.

Plates

1. Bone spoons unearthed at a Neolithic cultural site in Sichuan, China.
   (Courtesy of Ai Zhike, the Sanxia Museum, Chongqing, China)

2. Neolithic bone chopsticks found in Longqiuzhuang, a Neolithic
   cultural site in Jiansu, China.
   (Courtesy of the Yangzhou Museum, China)

3. Neolithic bone chopsticks (the two thin sticks in the lower part) in
   Longqiuzhuang.
   (Courtesy of the Yangzhou Museum, China)

4. This brick carving shows how chopsticks were used in early China,
   c. first century CE.
   *(Zhongguo huaxiangzhuan quanji [Complete collections of Chinese
   brick carvings], ed. Yu Weichao, Chengdu: Sichuan meishu
   chubanshe, 2006, p. 59)*

5. Eating customs in early China – sitting on the floor with foods placed
   on short-legged tables, shown on a brick carving, first to third
   centuries CE.
   *(Zhongguo lidai yishu: huihua bian [the Chinese art in different dynasties:
   painting], Beijing: Renmin Meishu Chubanshe, 1994, part 1, p. 72)*

6. Brick painting from the Fresco Tombs of the Wei and Jin Dynasty
   showing chopsticks used as utensils for cooking in early China,
   c. third–fifth centuries CE.
   *(Painting from the Fresco Tombs of the Wei and Jin Dynasty located
   in the Northwestern Gobi desert 20 km from Jiayuguan city.*

Color plates are located between pages 92 and 93.

Timeline

Time	China	Korea	Japan	Vietnam
To 4000 BCE	✓ Early humans ✓ Neolithic period (Yangshao) ✓ Crops ✓ Discovery of bone utensils	✓ Neolithic period	✓ Paleolithic and Neolithic periods (Jomon)	✓ Neolithic period
4000–1000 BCE	✓ Neolithic period ✓ Xia, Shang, Zhou dynasties ✓ Oracle bone inscriptions / Writing system ✓ Bronze Age (bronze utensils)	✓ Neolithic period ✓ Origin myths	✓ Neolithic period ✓ Origin myths	✓ Neolithic period ✓ Bronze Age
1000 BCE to 300 CE	✓ Zhou and Warring States periods ✓ Qin and Han dynasties ✓ Silk Road ✓ Confucianism and Daoism ✓ Millet as staple in north and rice in south ✓ Spread of wheat flour foods ✓ Shift from using fingers to utensils for foods	✓ Bronze Age ✓ Iron Age ✓ Chinese Han military commendaries ✓ Early Three Kingdoms period	✓ Neolithic period (Jomon) ✓ Yayoi Culture ✓ Origin myths	✓ Bronze Age ✓ Iron Age ✓ Conquest by Han dynasty of China
300–600 CE	✓ Fall of the Han dynasty ✓ Buddhism ✓ Period of Northern and Southern dynasties ✓ Tang dynasty ✓ Spoons and chopsticks used as a set of eating tools	✓ Three Kingdoms period ✓ Discovery of bronze utensils (spoons and chopsticks)	✓ Kofun (Tomb) period ✓ Asuka period ✓ Buddhism	✓ Bronze Age ✓ Iron Age ✓ Buddhism ✓ Chinese rule continued ✓ Use of utensils for food

Time	China	Korea	Japan	Vietnam
600–1000 CE	✓ Tang dynasty ✓ Spread of Buddhism ✓ Silk Road ✓ Wheat and millet were staples in North China and rice in South China ✓ Fall of the Tang dynasty	✓ United Silla ✓ Goryeo period ✓ Use of utensils for food	✓ Asuka period ✓ Nara period ✓ Heian period ✓ Spread of Buddhism ✓ Japanese missions to China ✓ Introduction of utensil use ✓ Discovery of wooden chopsticks	✓ Chinese rule continued
1000–1450 CE	✓ Song dynasty ✓ Liao dynasty ✓ Jin dynasty ✓ Xixia dynasty ✓ Introduction of Champa rice ✓ Mongol conquest and Yuan dynasty ✓ Neo-Confucianism ✓ Ming dynasty ✓ Development of communal eating style ✓ Chopsticks became exclusive eating tool	✓ Goryeo dynasty ✓ Joseon dynasty ✓ Neo-Confucianism ✓ Mongol conquest ✓ Meat consumption ✓ Metal utensils	✓ Late Heian period ✓ Kamakura and Muromachi periods ✓ Chopsticks for food	✓ End of Chinese rule
1450–1850 CE	✓ Ming dynasty ✓ Qing dynasty ✓ Porcelain soup spoon	✓ Joseon dynasty ✓ Ming China and Joseon against Japanese invasion ✓ Spoon and chopsticks as a set of eating tools	✓ Muramachi period ✓ Unification of Japan ✓ Tokugawa period ✓ Edo period	✓ Independent period ✓ Le dynasty against Champa

1. Map of East Asia.

I

Introduction

Over one and a half billion people eat food with chopsticks daily. This is the first book in English that traces the history of the utensil from ancient times to the present day. The aim of this book is threefold. The first is to offer a comprehensive and reliable account of how and why chopsticks became adopted by their users and continued, as a dining habit, through the centuries in Asia and beyond. The second is to discuss the culinary impact of chopsticks use on Asian cookeries and cuisines and vice versa: how the change of foodways in the region influenced people's choice of eating tools to aid their food consumption. And the third is to analyze the cultural meanings of chopsticks and chopsticks use in the respective cultures of their users. Chopsticks are distinctive in that though mainly an eating implement, they also have many other uses. A rich and deep cultural text is embedded in the history of chopsticks, awaiting our exploration.

Over many centuries, chopsticks have helped distinguish their users in Asia from those in the rest of the world. So much so that some Japanese scholars have identified a distinct "chopsticks cultural sphere" vis-à-vis the other two spheres on the globe: those who feed with fingers, which was a dining tradition for the people in the Middle East, South Asia and some parts of Southeast Asia, and those who eat with forks and knives, or the people who live in today's Europe, North and South America, Australia, etc.[1] Other scholars, such as Lynn White, have also noticed this tripartite division among

---

[1] Isshiki Hachirō, *Hashi no Bunkashi: Sekai no Hashi Nihon no Hashi* (A cultural history of chopsticks: world chopsticks and Japanese chopsticks) (Tokyo: Ochanomizu Shobō, 1990), 36–40; and Mukai Yukiko & Hashimoto Keiko, *Hashi* (Chopsticks) (Tokyo: Hōsei daigaku shuppankyoku, 2001), 135–142.

the finger-feeders, the fork-feeders and the chopsticks-feeders in the world.[2] Centering on China, where the utensil originated, the chopsticks cultural sphere encompasses the Korean Peninsula, the Japanese archipelago, certain regions of Southeast Asia, the Mongolian Steppe and the Tibetan Plateau. Thanks to the increasing global popularity of Asian foods in recent decades, this sphere is expanding – people outside the zone have increasingly adopted chopsticks while eating Asian foods. Indeed, in Chinese and other Asian restaurants throughout the world, many non-Asian customers attempt the use of chopsticks, with some showing admirable dexterity. In Thailand and Nepal, where the traditional dining method is to use one's right hand, it is now increasingly common to see people use chopsticks to convey foods.

For many chopsticks users, employing this Asian eating utensil does not just continue a time-honored dietary practice. They also believe its use brings myriad benefits besides conveying food. Kimiko Barber, a Japanese-English author living in London, wrote *The Chopsticks Diet* (2009), in which she argues that while Japanese food is by and large healthier than Westerners', the key to a healthy diet is not what you eat, but *how* you eat. Chopsticks, she claims, bring such a benefit. "Eating with chopsticks slows people down and therefore they eat less," she writes. And eating less is not the only benefit. Since one eats more slowly with chopsticks – by as much as twenty more minutes per meal – by her calculation, "it also has," Barber proclaims, "the psychological benefit of making you think about the food and the enjoyment you get from it."[3] In other words, eating with chopsticks helps you to appreciate food and turns you into a gourmet!

Others argue that there are even more benefits. Isshiki Hachirō, one of the Japanese writers who coined the term "chopsticks cultural sphere," maintains that since chopsticks use requires brain–hand coordination (perhaps more so than using other implements), it improves not only one's dexterity but ultimately also the development of one's brain, especially among children. And Isshiki is not the only one who holds this belief.[4] Scientists in recent years have conducted experiments exploring,

[2] Lynn White, a professor of history at UCLA, gave a speech, entitled "Fingers, Chopsticks and Forks: Reflections on the Technology of Eating," at the American Philosophical Society meeting in Philadelphia on July 17, 1983, in which he discussed these different dining habits. *New York Times* (Late Edition – East Coast), July 17, 1983, A-22.

[3] Kimiko Barber, *The Chopsticks Diet: Japanese-Inspired Recipes for Easy Weight-Loss* (Lanham: Kyle Books, 2009), 7.

[4] Isshiki, *Hashi no Bunkashi*, 201–220. In their study of chopsticks, Mukai and Hashimoto also describe how learning to use chopsticks helps children's development of fine motor skills. *Hashi*, 181–186.

among other questions, whether or not habitually using the eating device improves one's deftness. Psychologists too have examined whether chopsticks manipulation among children could promote a higher level of independence in eating. The findings in both cases are positive. In the meantime, scientific research also suggests that while helping to develop fine motor skills among children, lifetime chopsticks use might result in a higher risk of osteoarthritis in hand joints among the elderly.[5]

To investigate and explain the various benefits as well as possible harms associated with chopsticks use is certainly a worthwhile scientific undertaking. Yet my goals are limited to the three I set out at the beginning; as a historian, I shall mainly discuss the advantages and disadvantages of chopsticks use in history and base my discussion on historical and archaeological evidence. To describe the multiple functions of chopsticks as a social token, literary symbol, cultural artifact and religious object, I will rely on literary sources, folklore and religious texts.

As an eating implement used across Asia for several millennia, chopsticks have shown their continuing utility and persistent appeal, even though it requires some practice to wrap one's fingers around them properly and put the tool to effective use. In the chopsticks cultural sphere, such training usually begins in childhood. In more recent years, reflecting Western cultural influence, forks and knives have increased their presence in Asian countries, not only in restaurants frequented by Western customers. Meanwhile, the level of skillfulness among young Asians in proper chopsticks use also is said to have declined. Having failed to receive adequate instruction at home, where one traditionally learned how to use chopsticks, many children nowadays simply apply the utensil in their own way, however inelegantly. Nonetheless, compared to the other parts of the world where many now depend on Western cutlery to transport food, the base of the chopsticks cultural sphere remains intact and solid – the utensil is indispensable to people in their day-to-day life. Moreover, those living in the zone also expect outside visitors to use the implement, as

---

[5] Sohee Shin, Shinichi Demura & Hiroki Aoki, "Effects of Prior Use of Chopsticks on Two Different Types of Dexterity Tests: Moving Beans Test and Purdue Pegboard," *Perceptual & Motor Skills*, 108:2 (April 2009), 392–398; Cheng-Pin Ho & Swei-Pi Wu, "Mode of Grasp, Materials, and Grooved Chopsticks Tip on Gripping Performance and Evaluation," *Perceptual & Motor Skills*, 102:1 (February 2006), 93–103; Sheila Wong, Kingsley Chan, Virginia Wong & Wilfred Wong, "Use of Chopsticks in Chinese Children," *Child: Care, Health & Development*, 28:2 (March 2002), 157–161; David J. Hunter, Yuqing Zhang, Michael C. Nevitt, Ling Xu, Jingbo Niu, Li-Yung Lui, Wei Yu, Piran Aliabadi & David T. Felson, "Chopsticks Arthropathy: The Beijing Osteoarthritis Study," *Arthritis & Rheumatism*, 50:5 (May 2004), 1495–1500.

it is the only utensil put on the table in most eateries. In Chinese and other Asian restaurants outside Asia, simple illustrations on how to use the eating device are often printed either on the chopsticks' sleeves or on the paper tablemat, encouraging all their patrons to experiment with it.

When were chopsticks invented and how were they originally used in ancient China? Archaeological finds have yielded samples of bone sticks in various Neolithic cultural sites in China, which suggests that prototype chopsticks had appeared as early as 5000 BCE, if not before. Yet if they were indeed chopsticks, they might have not been used exclusively for conveying food. Rather, those proto-chopsticks probably had a dual function: either as a cooking or as a dining utensil, or as both. This, interestingly, remains the case in many Asian households; that is, chopsticks are a convenient kitchen utensil to this day. For instance, when boiling food, one can use (chop)sticks as stirrers and/or mixers. One, too, can use them, in pairs, to pick up food contents in a cooking vessel in a pincer movement. When one also transports the foodstuffs from the vessel to the mouth, then the sticks one uses become an eating tool, or chopsticks. This is how food experts generally believe chopsticks originated in ancient China. Historical texts and research have shown that from the fourth century BCE, eating with utensils (chopsticks included), rather than fingers, gradually became the preferred dining custom among the Chinese.[6]

Once invented, both cultural and culinary factors played, distinctly or relatedly, a part in enhancing chopsticks use, and utensil use in general. To the Chinese and other Asians, using utensils to convey foods represents cultural advancement, a point we will return to throughout the book. But utensil use may also be essential if food is cooked and eaten hot. During the Shang dynasty (1600–1046 BCE), or China's Bronze Age, bronze vessels in the form of cauldrons and tripods were commonplace. Without a doubt, these utensils were made for cooking, especially for boiling. Of course, one can eat cooked food with fingers. But if the contents are immersed in the broth, as is common with boiled food, then it is difficult. Moreover, it seems the early Chinese not only preferred boiled foods, but they also liked to eat them hot. To avoid scalding or soiling their hands, utensil use thus became necessary. No definitive explanation, however, has been given as to how and why this food habit – eating hot food – became favored among

---

[6] Ōta Masako, *Hashi no genryū o saguru: Chūkoku kodai ni okeru hashi shiyō shūzoku seiritsu* (Investigation into the origin of chopsticks: the establishment of the habit of chopsticks use in ancient China) (Tokyo: Kyūko Shoin, 2001), 1–23; and Liu Yun et al., *Zhongguo zhu wenhuashi* (A history of chopsticks culture in China) (Beijing: Zhonghua shuju, 2006), 70ff.

the Chinese, and remains so more or less to this day. The climate of North China might be a factor, as it was (and is) mostly cold and dry except in the summer, which made hot food gastronomically more agreeable. Stew (*geng* in Chinese) was recorded as the most popular dish in historical texts from ancient China. Meat consumption, which seems to have been more prevalent in earlier times than in later periods, might be another, for cooked meat becomes less palatable when it becomes cold.

Once utensil use became a dietary custom and accepted as a form of culture, it appealed to peoples across various geographical zones. The Japanese, for instance, do not necessarily prefer eating hot food as do the people in North China, but they have been committed chopsticks users since the seventh century. Vietnamese cookery features some hot dishes, even though the region's climate is much more warm and humid than North China's. It can be argued that the Japanese and the Vietnamese turned to utensil use in eating mostly because of Chinese cultural influences. In the case of Vietnam, which was ruled by imperial China for a millennium, this cultural factor is particularly salient since most of their neighbors in Southeast Asia traditionally consumed food with hands. By contrast, the Vietnamese have adopted chopsticks as a utensil for many centuries.

If one decides to use a utensil to eat, does it have to be a pair of chopsticks? Not necessarily. Indeed, although the chopsticks cultural sphere has existed in Asia from approximately the fifth century to the present, the eating device was *not* the only one invented and used by the people in the zone. Indeed, spoons and ladles, as well as knives and forks, all appeared in the continent and were used as either cooking or eating utensils. Moreover, according to archaeological finds and historical texts, though invented early, chopsticks were *not* the earliest nor, for a long time, the primary eating tool, even in ancient China, their birthplace. Spoons were. More precisely, it was a dagger-shaped spoon, known as *bi* 匕 in Chinese, that was used as the essential implement for eating among the ancient Chinese (Plate 1).

To understand why the spoon was initially a more important eating tool than chopsticks, one needs to consider the types of food the Chinese and other Asians consumed historically. Food historians tend to divide human foods into two categories: grain and nongrain food. The former, apparently, is more important because in many places, consuming a meal is often equivalent to eating a grain cereal, be it rice, wheat, millet or maize. Asians are no exception. In the Chinese language, *fan* is a rubric word for all cooked grain food, even though in modern times, it usually means "cooked rice." Pronounced *bap* in Korean, *[go]han* in Japanese and *co'm* in Vietnamese, the word conveys the same meaning in those Asian languages as well. As such, eating a meal in Chinese is simply *chifan*, which literally means "eating cooked grain (rice)," even though the meal most likely also consists of nongrain food dishes, which are referred to as *cai*. Likewise, *gohan o taberu* carries the same dual meaning in Japanese, rather than just meaning feeding oneself with cooked rice. These similar expressions suggest the importance of grain food in a meal. In fact, nongrain food dishes – *cai* – in colloquial Chinese are sometimes called *xiafan*, or "rice downers," revealing that their principal function is to help people ingest the grain food.

The spoon was the main eating utensil in ancient China because the Chinese used it to transport grain food (not soup as in later times). By comparison, chopsticks were the device designed initially for carrying nongrain foods. As a dual set, these two instruments were termed *bizhu*, or "spoon and chopsticks" in parallel, in Chinese literature for many centuries. That the spoon precedes chopsticks in the word compound suggests its primacy, extending the *fan* and *cai* relationship in food intake. A reflection of this dining tradition can still be observed today, in the Korean Peninsula, where the people use both a spoon and chopsticks as a set in eating a meal. Like the dining custom of ancient China, the recommended practice among Koreans is to apply the spoon in transporting grain food, or rice, whereas chopsticks are used for nongrain dishes.

Yet the Koreans' eating etiquette reflects more a cultural decision than a culinary need, for as rice increased in popularity as a grain staple across Asia, chopsticks became an effective tool to convey it in clumps to one's mouth. This is what most chopsticks users usually do these days, including many Koreans on less formal occasions, such as in family dining. But from ancient to Tang times (618–907), the dominant grain in North China (and the Korean Peninsula) was millet, a hardy crop suitable for the region's climate. Unlike cooked rice, which is sticky and can be moved in globs, millet is best cooked as porridge, which, as recommended by Chinese ritual texts, made the spoon a better tool in transporting it. Chopsticks, by comparison, were then mostly used to pick up foodstuffs from a soupy dish, such as a stew.

If chopsticks were used as a secondary eating implement in ancient China because their assigned function was to transfer only the nongrain food, or the foodstuffs in a stew, this role soon changed. In fact, the change began as early as the Han dynasty (206 BCE to 220 CE), due to the growing appeal of floured wheat foods, or noodles, dumplings and pancakes. Archaeology has shown that the Chinese had long learned how to grind grains on mortars and pestles to make noodles. Indeed, the world's earliest sample of noodles has been discovered in Northwest China; made of millet grains, it is over 4,000 years old. During the Han period, powered either by humans or by animals, stone mills became widespread. And besides millet, the Chinese also milled wheat, possibly due to the cultural influences from Central Asia. Before milling became a widely accepted method in processing wheat, the Chinese had consumed wheat whole by boiling it. Yet without question, it was flour that turned wheat into a more popular grain; by the end of the Tang dynasty, or the early tenth century, wheat indeed had become important enough to shake the predominance of millet in North China.

In addition to pancakes and buns, noodles and dumplings are two well-liked forms of wheat foods, in Asia as well as in other parts of the world. For eating these two foods, chopsticks were considered a better tool than the spoon. In other words, thanks to the appeal of wheat foods, chopsticks began to challenge the spoon's primacy from approximately the first century in China. Interestingly, food experts in the West have observed that the pasta noodle's popularity also caused Europeans, much later, to use the fork and eventually other table utensils from the fourteenth century onward. According to an Italian story, the fork had been introduced to Europeans as an eating implement – as opposed to its being a kitchen tool in Roman times – by a Turkish princess after she married a wealthy nobleman from Venice in the early eleventh century. Yet it only became widely used once Europeans grew accustomed to pasta. Indeed, according to some research, medieval Turks not only used the fork but, at one time, also chopsticks to eat pasta.[7] In any case, if the fork is the tool for handling noodles among Europeans and others, chopsticks are the choice for Asians, including those outside the bounds of the chopsticks cultural sphere. In such countries as Thailand in Southeast Asia, people also tend to use chopsticks to convey noodles whereas for other foods they use either fingers or other utensils.[8]

Noodles are a grain food. Yet more often than not, people do not eat noodles by themselves. They tend to mix them with something else, be it a

---

[7] See Giovanni Rebora, *Culture of the Fork*, trans. Albert Sonnenfeld (New York: Columbia University Press, 2001), 14–17; James Cross Giblin, *From Hand to Mouth, Or How We Invented Knives, Forks, Spoons, and Chopsticks and the Table Manners to Go with Them* (New York: Thomas Y. Crowell, 1987), 45–46; and Peter B. Golden, "Chopsticks and Pasta in Medieval Turkic Cuisine," *Rocznik orientalisticzny*, 49 (1994–1995), 71–80.

[8] Penny Van Esterik, *Food Culture in Southeast Asia* (Westport: Greenwood Press, 2008), xxiv; 54–55.

soup, a sauce or sometimes meat and vegetables. In so doing, noodles become a meal. In this mixture, the supposed *fan* and *cai*, or grain and nongrain food dichotomy, comes unraveled. A good example in Asia is the *lamian* (*ramen* in Japanese), a type of soup noodle that originated in China but gained wide popularity throughout Asia in more recent centuries. The noodle in the *lamian/ramen* is made by stretching, or "pulling" as the word *la/ra* suggests, the wheat dough many times into strands and strips, by hand or by machine. But its appeal is due as much to the accompanying soup, which is flavored with meat, vegetables, green onions, soy sauce and other condiments. The Japanese *ramen* also typically has seaweed, *kamaboko* (a fish cake sliced into pieces) and sometimes an egg. All of this suggests that once seasoned, a noodle dish coalesces and blends grain and nongrain foods into one. Similarly, a Chinese dumpling, which wraps ground meat and vegetables with a thinly rolled dough skin, also transcends the traditional grain/nongrain food divide. When these wheat foods were consumed with the aid of chopsticks, the eating device effectively rivaled the spoon (Plate 24).

But the spread of wheat foods probably was only the story of North China. In such regions as South China, where rice had been the staple grain from time immemorial, the inhabitants probably had used chopsticks to carry both the grain starch and the accompanying nongrain dishes for a long time. In the Song period (960–1279), rice production grew considerably in both North and South China, thanks to the adoption of a new – early ripening – rice variety from Vietnam. The growth continued well into the Ming period (1368–1644) and expanded also into Korea. The increase of rice consumption during those periods reinforced and solidified the foundation of the chopsticks cultural sphere. From the fourteenth century, historical and literary sources reveal that chopsticks became the exclusive eating implement for many. This change was especially notable among the Chinese, since their dining tradition before had been to employ both spoon and chopsticks together. Likely reasons for the exclusive use of chopsticks in China were myriad, one being the broad adoption of the communal eating style, with all diners sitting together at a square table. Once chopsticks were used in transporting both the grain and nongrain foods, the utensil became the primary eating tool in the chopsticks cultural sphere. As a result, the spoon was relegated to use for soup, with a modified design (Plate 26). It remains so in China, Vietnam and Japan today.

Besides rice consumption, tea drinking, another distinct cultural tradition with an Asian/Chinese origin, might have also increased the appeal of chopsticks as a table utensil. For although many tea experts like to savor the beverage by itself, it was/is also customary among tea drinkers to nibble on some snacks or small dishes to go with the drink. These snacks and appetizers are called either *xiaoshi* (lit. small foods) or *dianxin*; the latter is more commonly spelled as "dim sum" in English, meaning appetizers. Both terms appeared in Tang China, thanks to the growing trend of tea drinking. The custom of drinking tea while sampling a variety of small dishes was to intensify and expand in the following centuries and continues to this day. Most of these small dishes – pancakes, meat, shrimp or fish balls, etc. found commonly nowadays in Cantonese restaurants around the world – are best and customarily eaten with chopsticks. And chopsticks are indeed often the most common utensil found in inns as well as in teahouses in Asia (Plate 19).

Since chopsticks can be inexpensive (if made of bamboo or cheap wood) compared to other utensils, chopsticks have become the most used utensil in Asia also because they are cost-effective. In a sense, both tea drinking and chopsticks use are habits that can be enjoyed by people of different social backgrounds. Undeniably, class differences do exist in practice. The rich, for example, can afford expensive tea and chopsticks whereas the poor cannot. But whether rich or poor, one can drink tea to relax and use chopsticks to eat. Indeed, as will be argued in this book, the exclusive use of chopsticks as the eating tool, as well as the development of communal eating, probably began with the lower social classes in Chinese and other neighboring societies. As they are casual and informal, these customs are more likely to be practiced first among the ordinary people and gradually move upward to the members of the upper social strata. That some Koreans use chopsticks – instead of the ritual-required spoon – to transport rice in family dining and on other similarly relaxed occasions might also help illustrate the point.

What about the knives and forks that had once appeared almost in tandem with spoons and chopsticks in ancient China? In the Han tombs unearthed by modern archaeologists, there are several cooking and eating scenes portrayed on the walls. These stone paintings and carvings show that knives and forks were then used as kitchen utensils, but not as eating implements. And in the subsequent centuries, knives, or cleavers, and forks retained this function without any change, till their being (re) introduced as tableware by Europeans in modern times. In other words, unlike chopsticks, which began as a cooking tool but later became a table utensil, forks and knives failed to undergo such a metamorphosis in China and neighboring regions. Again, culinary and cultural factors played their part.

Culinarily speaking, the popularity of the stew in early China is something worth our attention. A stew is generally made by boiling and simmering solid food ingredients in liquid and is served together with the gravy or the sauce. Both historical texts and archaeological finds from Han China suggest that during this period, if not before, the solid ingredients in the stew were already cut into bite-size morsels before cooking. The knife used to cut the meat thus could stay in the kitchen, since there was no need for it to be on the table. As the morsels were small and in a broth, chopsticks were a more effective tool than, say, a fork to pick them up.

One could, of course, say that meat was pre-cut into bite-size portions because people preferred to use chopsticks. Roland Barthes (1915–1980), the French linguist and literary critic who visited Japan during the 1960s, indeed made such an observation, stressing that the food and the utensil were complementary to each other:

There is a convergence of the tiny and the esculent: things are not only small in order to be eaten, but are also comestible in order to fulfill their essence, which is smallness. The harmony between Oriental food and chopsticks cannot be merely functional, instrumental; the foodstuffs are cut up so they can be grasped by the sticks, but also the chopsticks exist because the foodstuffs are cut into small pieces; one and the same movement, one and the same form transcends the substance and its utensil: division.[9]

Having observed closely how chopsticks were used in carrying the food, Roland Barthes also speculated on the cultural significance of chopsticks use by comparing it to that of the knife and the fork, the cutlery to which he was more accustomed:

For the chopsticks, in order to divide, must separate, part, peck, instead of cutting and piercing, in the manner of our implements; they never violate the foodstuff: either they gradually unravel it (in the case of vegetables) or else prod it into separate pieces (in the case of fish, eels), thereby rediscovering the natural fissures of the substance (in this, much closer to the primitive finger than to the knife). Finally, and this is perhaps their loveliest function, the chopsticks *transfer* the food, either crossed like two hands, a support and no longer a pincer, they slide under the clump of rice and raise it to the diner's mouth, or (by an age-old gesture of the whole Orient) they push the alimentary snow from bowl to lips in the manner of a scoop. In all these functions, in all the gestures they imply, chopsticks are the converse of our knife (and of its predatory substitute, the fork): they are the alimentary instrument which refuses to cut, to pierce, to mutilate, to trip (very limited gestures, relegated to the preparation of the food for cooking: the fish seller

---

[9] Roland Barthes, *Empire of Signs*, trans. Richard Howard (New York: Hill and Wang, 1982), 15–16.

who skins the still-living eel for us exorcises once and for all, in a preliminary sacrifice, the murder of food); by chopsticks, food becomes no longer a prey to which one does violence (meat, flesh over which one does battle), but a substance harmoniously transferred; they transform the previously divided substance into bird food and rice into a flow of milk; maternal, they tirelessly perform the gesture which creates the mouthful, leaving to our alimentary manners, armed with pikes and knives, that of predation.[10]

This long rumination serves well for discussing the cultural factors influencing how and why chopsticks were turned into a table utensil from early China. According to Roland Barthes, chopsticks are not "predatory" in that their users do not treat food as "violently" as do those using knives and forks. Barthes is not the only one who has put forward this opinion. Upon seeing chopsticks on their trips to Asia in the sixteenth century, many Westerners developed a similar impression, commending the use of the utensil by Asians as a (more?) civilized dining custom.

Among the Chinese, this has become a cherished cultural belief. Raymond Dawson, a sinologist who had a long career at Oxford, made a pithy statement that for the Chinese,

No line so definitely divided civilized people from barbarians as that which separated men who consume their food with chopsticks from those who used their fingers or in later times such inferior instruments as knives and forks.[11]

Needless to say, this notion has not been entertained only by the Chinese, but also by other Asians in the chopsticks cultural sphere, as they all leave the knife in the kitchen rather than bring it to the table. A simple way to trace the origin of this practice culturally is to look at the remark made by Mencius (372–289 BCE), a major follower of Confucius (551–479 BCE), when he discussed one of the qualities of a "gentleman" or a "superior man" (the term used in Confucianism to stand for an upright, humane and often educated person):

"There is no harm in their saying so," said Mencius. "Your conduct was an artifice of benevolence. You saw the ox, and had not seen the sheep. So is the superior man affected towards animals, that, having seen them alive, he cannot bear to see them die; having heard their dying cries, he cannot bear to eat their flesh. Therefore he keeps away from his slaughter-house and cook-room."[12]

---

[10] Ibid., 17–18.

[11] Raymond S. Dawson, ed., *The Legacy of China* (Oxford: Oxford University Press, 1971), 342.

[12] Mencius, *The Works of Mencius*, trans. James Legge (New York: Dover Publications, Inc., 1970), 141.

We do not know how this comment contributed to the overall meager presence of animal meat in traditional Asian cookery. But Mencius' injunction that a true gentleman ought to stay away from the kitchen was proverbial, not only in China but also around Asia, or at least within the reaches of Confucian influence. To follow it through, knives were to be used only by the cook in the kitchen to slice the meat into small morsels before presenting it on the table. And this seemed exactly what Confucius, Mencius' master, had demanded when he was presented with a meat dish.[13] Compounded by Buddhist influence, which is thought to have developed in China around the first century, animal meat made even rarer appearances in Asian foods because Buddhism shunned any killing. If meat was used in cooking a dish, its main function, according to Frederick Mote, the late professor of Chinese history at Princeton, was "more often as flavoring for vegetables and as the basis of a sauce than as the principal component of a dish."[14] This culinary tradition thus effectively kept the knife inside an Asian kitchen for centuries. The absence of the knife also made the fork less useful, for the latter's utility, among others, was to stabilize the meat for cutting.

Although the Chinese and other chopsticks users in Asia traditionally believed their dining style to be more civilized than others', it must be noted that whether one eats food with utensils or with fingers is only a reflection of cultural preference, rather than an indication of cultural sophistication. Indeed, a refined dining style is more dependent on how one brings food to the mouth than on whether and what instruments are applied. That is, in every dietary tradition, there is a way to demonstrate an elegant eating style vis-à-vis a coarse one; and how the two are differentiated often varies from one place to another. In many regions where people eat with their hands, for instance, they are often required to use only their right hand, as the left hand is deemed unclean. Moreover, a refined style in dining with hands, practiced in some places, is such that the diner only employs three fingers (the thumb, the index and the middle fingers) instead of the whole hand. In regions where Western cutlery is employed, sophistication in dining is shown in how one applies the suitable utensil(s) to the desired dish, be it salad, soup or the main course, accordingly and appropriately.

---

[13] Confucius, it was said, "did not dislike to have his rice finely cleaned, nor to have his mince meat cut quite small." *Confucian Analects, The Great Learning and The Doctrine of the Mean*, trans. James Legge (New York: Dover Publications, Inc., 1971), 232.

[14] Frederick Mote, "Yuan and Ming," *Food in Chinese Culture: Anthropological and Historical Perspectives*, ed. K. C. Chang (New Haven: Yale University Press, 1977), 201.

Over the millennia when chopsticks have been employed in transferring foods, a rule of etiquette has also been developed about how one should hold and use them, properly and gracefully. The rules of etiquette are surprisingly similar across the entire chopsticks cultural sphere. First, chopsticks users generally believe that the most effective and elegant way to hold the sticks is to place the lower one at the base of the thumb and secure this position by resting it between the ring and middle fingers in order to keep the stick stationary. Then the upper stick is to be held like a pencil, using the index and middle fingers for movement and the thumb for stabilization. In conveying food, the two sticks are worked together to grasp the food for transportation and delivery. Second, once one learns how to hold chopsticks, there is also general agreement as to how the device is applied in clasping and carrying the food. For instance, as nimble and flexible as they are, chopsticks are not used to mine or dig for food in the bowl in search of a particular item, nor to spear a food item (e.g. a meatball) even if it may be hard to pick up in the pincer movement. It usually is a *faux pas* if the food item drops or drips in the process of transfer. Since chopsticks are a widely used utensil, their proper and skillful use has become an essential part of good table manners in Asia.

Table manners develop to prevent distasteful dining behavior, lest others' appetite be affected. The development of the chopsticks etiquette described above essentially stems from the same interest and concern. In fact, one may argue that the invention and use of chopsticks has in part been intended to prevent messiness in eating. In the modern Western world, in addition to tableware, napkins are used to wipe one's mouth and hands as needed. When Europeans went to Asia in the sixteenth century, they found that Asians used chopsticks instead to deliver bite-size food morsels from the bowl to the mouth, without soiling their hands.[15]

Yet again, what is considered a neat and refined dining style certainly varies to a degree from people to people, culture to culture. In the chopsticks cultural sphere, for instance, since dropping food from the chopsticks is generally frowned upon, chopsticks users have developed various ways to prevent it from happening. One common approach is

---

[15] Francesco Carletti, an Italian merchant, visited Japan in the late sixteenth century and made such an observation: "With these two sticks, the Japanese are able to fill their mouths with marvelous swiftness and agility. They can pick up any piece of food, no matter how tiny it is, without ever soiling their hands." Quoted in Giblin, *From Hand to Mouth*, 44.

to reduce the distance of the transportation. While eating rice with chopsticks, therefore, the Chinese, the Japanese and the Vietnamese customarily raise the rice bowl up to their mouths and push the grain inside. But to Koreans and some of the Europeans who saw chopsticks used for the first time, this dining custom looked much less elegant. Koreans recommend instead the use of the spoon to transport rice, for this reason as well as for preserving an ancient rite.

Whether used skillfully or not, chopsticks need to be operated together in a pair. This unique quality, or the sticks' inseparableness, together with their design, color and material, have long helped the utensil to become a popular gift, a cultural symbol and even a literary metaphor across Asia. That is, chopsticks are not merely an eating implement. For their inseparableness, for instance, chopsticks have had a broad appeal across Asia as a wedding gift, and a token for exchanging affection between lovers and expressing good wishes for couples. Chopsticks are used as a primary, sometimes essential, item in wedding ceremonies among many peoples across Asia. Love stories featuring chopsticks also appear in Asian folklore and legends. In fact, as recorded in the stories and practiced still today at weddings, chopsticks do not merely appear, but are an effective tool for gesticulation. As such, literary writers have coined certain phrases, specific to the ways chopsticks are used, and employed them in poems and stories for vivid and graphic illustration. Lastly, the materials from which chopsticks are made also carry important social and even political meanings. The wealthy, for example, tend to prefer expensive chopsticks, made of gold, silver, ivory, jade, ebony and rare wood, to reflect and boost their status – although ivory chopsticks, for historical reasons, were traditionally a symbol of decadence and corruption. As they are fragile, jade chopsticks have not been used as a daily utensil. But they have appeared frequently in literary texts, where the color and shape of jade chopsticks are often compared figuratively to women's tears!

As an ancient utensil with a long history, therefore, chopsticks have evolved over time to become an adaptable tool, conveniently and creatively used on both eating and non-eating occasions. This adaptability has become their distinct characteristic, unmatched by other eating instruments. Tsung-dao Lee, a Nobel Prize Laureate in Physics, made an interesting comparison between chopsticks and fingers:

As early as the Warring States period Chinese invented chopsticks. Although simple, the two sticks perfectly use the physics of leverage. Chopsticks are an extension of human fingers. Whatever fingers can do, chopsticks can do, too. Moreover, their great talent is not even affected by high temperatures or freezing cold.[16]

In more recent centuries, chopsticks have experienced yet more significant changes. Thanks to modern technology, for instance, plastic chopsticks have become most common, surpassing the other varieties, as they are both durable and economical. But wooden and bamboo chopsticks remain popular, as do metal ones. In fact, durability sometimes is not the only quality one desires today. Modern consumerism, which touts consumption rather than saving and preservation, coupled with a heightened sense of hygiene, have made the use of disposable chopsticks – mostly of cheap wood but sometimes also of bamboo – a new and rising trend in Asia and around the world. No doubt, the popularity of plastic and disposable varieties has made chopsticks use a global experience, adding to the cross-cultural appeal of Asian foods, and Chinese food in particular (Plate 28). The chopsticks cultural sphere, therefore, is growing, reaching corners outside Asia and around the globe. At the same time, the overuse of plastic and wooden materials has also given rise to environmental concerns. As one of the world's oldest utensils, chopsticks are sure to retain their appeal for years to come.

---

[16] Lee supposedly expressed this opinion on the use of chopsticks when he was interviewed by a Japanese reporter. See www.chinadaily.com.cn/food/2012-08/02/content_15640036. htm.

2

Why chopsticks? Their origin and original function

If the stew be made with vegetables, chopsticks should be used; but not if there be no vegetables.

Do not use chopsticks in eating millet.

Classic of Rites (Liji)

On April 5, 1993, an archaeological team from the Institute of Archaeology of the Chinese Academy of Social Sciences launched a series of excavations of Neolithic ruins in Longqiuzhuang in present-day Gaoyou, Jiangsu. By December 1995, the team had completed its fourth and last dig of the 1,335-square-meter site. From the ruins, dated between 6600 and 5500 BCE, they unearthed over 2,000 objects, mostly tools and utensils made of animal bones. Hailed as one of the ten new archaeological discoveries of 1993, what distinguished this excavation from other archaeological discoveries in Neolithic China was that forty-two bone sticks were uncovered from the site – these sticks, Chinese scholars believe, were the earliest chopsticks (Plates 2 and 3)!

Were they really chopsticks? What did they look like? According to the team's report, these objects were between 9.2 and 18.5 cm in length and 0.3–0.9 cm in diameter. The sticks were thicker in the middle, with a square-shaped top, and their bottom tapered off into a point.[1] Though coarse, their appearance does indeed resemble chopsticks used today.

[1] Longqiuzhuang yizhi kaogudui (Archaeological team of the Longqiuzhuang ruins), *Longqiuzhuang: Jianghuai dongbu xinshiqi shidai yizhi fajue baogao* (Longqiuzhuang: Excavation report on the Neolithic ruins in the east of Jiangsu and Huai River) (Beijing: Kexue chubanshe, 1999), 346–347.

However, similar bone sticks had been found at other Neolithic sites, and scholars generally regarded them as hairpins. In fact, the Longqiuzhuang excavation originally ruled that the bone sticks were to be classified in this fashion.

Nevertheless, Liu Yun, chief editor of *A History of Chopsticks Culture in China* (Zhongguo zhu wenhuashi), believes that these bone sticks were indeed chopsticks for two reasons. One is that the bone hairpins were more polished and largely uniform in length and shape, while the Longqiuzhuang sticks vary one from another. Though thicker in the middle, their two ends are either round, oblate, square or flat, as well as differing in size. The other is that, whereas the hairpins were usually positioned near the head at burial, these sticks were placed down near the hands, along with other daily utensils such as pots and farming tools. Liu suggests that these bone sticks were used as feeding instruments, i.e. chopsticks. This assumption led Liu and others to reexamine some other Neolithic bone and wooden sticks found elsewhere. These scholars concluded that though originally deemed hairpins, like the Longqiuzhuang sticks, they, too, were placed around the body, rather than the head, and thus were more likely to be used as utensils for food.[2] Still, questions remain: even if these sticks were used in handling food, were they actually chopsticks? More precisely, were they used in pairs and held by one hand to clasp food and carry it to the mouth as in later times? It is hard to know for sure, and more evidence is needed to ascertain whether the Longqiuzhuang finds are the world's earliest examples of chopsticks.

It is in the Bronze Age, or during the Shang dynasty (*c.* 1600–1046 BCE), that there seems to be clearer evidence that the Chinese began using chopsticks to prepare and eat meals. During the 1930s, archaeologists excavating in the Henan Province of North China uncovered six bronze sticks, together with spoons and ladles, in the Shang capital ruins of Anyang. Their number and placement suggest that they had been used in pairs like tongs, although at about 1.3 cm in diameter, they were thicker than later chopsticks. Moreover, archaeologists are less sure if they were used exclusively for eating; some suspect that the sticks could well have been made for metallurgical work.[3] But more assume that these bronze pieces were employed in cooking – stirring and mixing foodstuffs in a pot, or arranging charcoals or firewood and poking the flame (Plate 6). In his *The Food of*

[2] Liu, *Zhongguo zhu wenhuashi*, 52–55.
[3] Chen Mengjia, "Yindai tongqi" (Bronze vessels in the Shang dynasty), *Kaogu xuebao* (Journal of archaeology), 7 (1954); and Liu, *Zhongguo zhu wenhuashi*, 92–93.

China, E. N. Anderson observes that few tools are needed to cook Chinese food: besides a cleaver, a chopping board, a wok or a pot, a wok shovel or turner and a pair of chopsticks are sufficient. Chopsticks, in his words, are used as "tongs, stirrers, whisks, strainers, rearrangers, and so forth."[4] Based on traditional practices, then, the idea that the Shang materials were chopsticks seems to be reasonable, as they remain an essential cooking tool in East and Southeast Asia, with people using them as whisks (for beating eggs) and mixers (for blending ground meat and vegetables as dumpling fillings).

From other Bronze Age sites in South and Southwest China, archaeologists have uncovered sticks that they believe were, in fact, feeding tools. In Changyang, Hubei (located in the middle reach of the Yangzi River), for example, a dig in the 1980s yielded two bone chopsticks that also belonged to the Shang period. Likewise, a pair of ivory chopsticks – the earliest examples of this type – dated in the Zhou period (1045–256 BCE) was uncovered in the same area. Additionally, bronze chopsticks were found in Anhui (South China) and Yunnan (Southwest China). Between 0.4 and 0.6 cm in diameter, these objects were much slimmer than those found in Anyang. Thicker and square-shaped on the top and thinner and rounded at the bottom, these chopsticks look almost exactly like those in current usage. Wang Shancai, an archaeologist who participated in the excavation in Changyang, remarked:

> The shape and design of the ancient spoons and chopsticks discovered in Changyang are almost identical with the ones that we use today. The chopsticks were quite polished, whose surface was even decorated with carvings. As of today, the earliest chopsticks found by archaeologists were from the mid-Shang period, proving that the Chinese had used chopsticks about 3,300 years ago and that the level of technology in making them was also quite high.[5]

Significantly, Wang Shancai indicates that the spoon was another feeding instrument used in ancient China. Both archaeological evidence and literary sources have proven that the spoon indeed was the primary tool the early Chinese used to handle food. Like chopsticks, spoons could allow one to stir items cooking in a pot and convey them to the mouth. Thus, when (chop)sticks first appeared during the Neolithic Age, the spoon, or more precisely a dagger-shaped spoon – referred to as the *bi* or *chi* in Chinese historical texts – had been well known in China. This type of spoon, along with flint and bone knives, has been discovered in various

---

[4] E. N. Anderson, *The Food of China* (New Haven: Yale University Press, 1988), 150.
[5] Liu, *Zhongguo zhu wenhuashi*, 92–96; quote is on 94.

Neolithic deposits throughout China. To date, the earliest *bi* has been found in Peiligang in Wuyang, Henan, in North China, in 1977. Dated between 8000 and 7500 BCE, these *bi* were made of animal bones, and are believed to have been used variously as a tool to cut meat, or to scoop cooked food from the pot or bowl. Besides these *bi* spoons, two pottery spoons were also present at the site. Compared with the *bi*, whose bottom is pointed and looks like a tongue, the pottery spoon – called *shao* or *si* in ancient Chinese – is rounder and oval in shape, more like a ladle. Both the *bi* and the *shao* have a narrow handle at the top. To this day, archaeological digs have yielded more dagger-shaped *bi* spoons than the oval-shaped *shao* type. While the *bi* was mostly made of animal bone, the *shao* could be made of other materials, including jade and ivory. They have surfaced elsewhere, such as in Banpo, Xi'an, in the mid-1950s.

Knives and forks – made of bones and metals – have also been discovered in Neolithic China, though in a much smaller quantity. With the progress of time, fewer and fewer knives and forks were found in historical sites, indicating that the Chinese gradually turned away from using them (especially the knives) to eat food. The role of knives became limited to food preparation from the late Zhou period on. Forks, mostly with two tines instead of three or more, remained in use till the Han dynasty (206 BCE to 220 CE) and later. The fork then was a kitchen utensil, primarily for serving rather than for eating food.[6] Chinese archaeologists have offered an explanation for why knives and forks were not used as feeding tools in traditional China. "The use of the fork had a close relationship with the consumption of meat," observes Wang Renxiang of the Institute of Archaeology, Chinese Academy of Social Sciences, "because different from the spoon and chopsticks, the fork allows one to use strength to convey food [meat]. In ancient China, the fork was not so common because those who used it, or the 'carnivores,' were limited to the upper class whereas most people were 'herbivores.' As the latter's food seldom contained meat, they did not need the fork."[7] While Wang's point can be qualified by the fact that the fork can be an effective tool for eating both

---

[6] This ought not to be so surprising because in ancient Rome, the fork too was a kitchen tool. Table forks were not introduced to Europe until the fourteenth century, and the earlier table forks were two-pronged, like those used in the Roman kitchen, rather than three- or four-pronged as we see today. Shū Tassei, *Chūgoku no Shokubunka* (Food culture in China) (Tokyo: Sōgensha, 1989), 125–131; and Giblin, *From Hand to Mouth*, 45–56.

[7] Wang Renxiang, "Shaozi, chazi, kuaizi: Zhongguo jinshi fangshi de kaoguxue yanjiu" (Spoon, fork, and chopsticks: an archaeological study of the eating method in ancient China), *Xun'gen* (Root searching), 10 (1997), 12–19.

vegetables – such as a tossed salad – and meat, his statement about the culinary habits of the ancient Chinese (and Asians) is supported by both archaeological finds and historical studies. Not unexpectedly, the type of food people eat determines the eating tools employed. There is good reason to believe that the invention of utensils was related to one's desire to cook and eat food. That the Chinese – past and present – use chopsticks as both a cooking and feeding tool offers a good example of this phenomenon.

In the development of human civilization, if one's ability to control fire constituted an epoch-making achievement, then the use of fire for cooking marked another. In his survey of the history of food, Felipe Fernandez-Armesto considers the invention of cooking the very first revolution humans made regarding their changing eating habits.[8] Likewise, eating cooked food, Harald Brüssow reckons, enabled *Homo erectus* to become *Homo sapiens*: the habit of eating cooked food "not only contribute[d] substantially to food safety but it also reduced the advantage of big teeth." Besides the nutritional benefits for the development of the brain, "cooked food requires much less cutting, tearing, and grinding than raw food," hence the reduction of tooth size among *Homo sapiens*.[9]

Eating cooked food, of course, does not necessarily mean eating hot food. But if one intends to eat food hot, then using instruments becomes a necessity, a point already made in the Introduction.[10] Specifically, spoons and chopsticks were invented and adopted in ancient China because the people desired to eat hot food without scalding their hands. With an implement, the Chinese could taste and eat food hot; the latter has become an entrenched dining habit from ancient times to the present. While entertaining their guests, many Chinese today prepare several dishes to show their hospitality. But they usually would not, observes Zhao Rongguang, an expert on Chinese culinary culture, cook them before the guests' arrival because the host wants his/her guests to eat food hot, "right off the grill," or *chengre chi* (lit. to eat while it is hot), as the common Chinese phrase goes.[11] By comparison, in parts of the world where people traditionally use

---

[8] Felipe Fernandez-Armesto, *Food: A History* (London: Macmillan, 2001), 1–24.

[9] Harald Brüssow, *The Quest for Food: A Natural History of Eating* (New York: Springer, 2007), 608.

[10] Lynn White, the historian who observed the different dining methods around the world, also believed that utensils are adopted because one intends to handle hot food. "Some Reflections on the Technology of Eating," *New York Times*, July 17, 1983, A-22.

[11] Zhao Rongguang, "Zhu yu Zhonghua minzu yinshi wenhua" (Chopsticks and Chinese food and drink culture), *Nongye kaogu* (Agricultural archaeology), 2 (1997), 225–235. This phrase has become a common expression of the Chinese while treating their guests to a meal. A famous example is that when Henry Kissinger accompanied Richard Nixon

their hand to transfer food, it is not customary to eat food hot. South and Southeast Asians, for instance, often prefer meals at room temperature, as do the people in the Middle East.[12] And though some have turned to utensils on certain occasions, in South Asia, using the hand to move food has been a long tradition well into this era. Consequently, climate and ecology likely played a part in how a particular food culture developed.

From the Neolithic Age, China's political and culture center was located in North China, whose climate may be described as arid or semi-arid; the winter being cold, while the rest of the year is dry, except in the summer. This climate might have contributed to the abovementioned Chinese preference for eating hot and juicy food, cooked either by boiling or by stewing. The great number of bronze – as well as pottery – vessels from Shang China and their shapes and sizes helped shed light on how the early Chinese prepared and transported food. The most common food vessels in the Shang were *ding* (tripod or quadripod), *li* (tripod with hollow legs), *zeng* (steamer), *fu* (cauldron) and *yan* (steamer). As their names indicate, these vessels were for boiling, stewing and steaming. If these were the primary ways of cooking, then utensils (ladles, spoons and chopsticks) might be quite useful, even essential, to mix, turn and stir the foodstuffs cooked in these vessels, as some of them are quite large in size. Once the cooking was done, utensils were again needed to serve the cooked food. Chopsticks might not be the most convenient tool to serve food, but they were quite useful in checking, stirring and tasting the food during cooking and, of course, eating it afterwards. Another use of sticks in the kitchen was to employ them as pokers or tongs for arranging the firewood underneath these vessels. Referred to as "fire-sticks" in China and Japan (Plate 8), this is an early example of chopsticks used on a non-eating occasion (cf. below).

It was said that King Zhou (1105–1046 BCE), the last ruler of the Shang dynasty, used a pair of ivory chopsticks to eat his fancy meals. This was one of the earliest references, and also the most well-known, to the utensil's

to China in 1972, Zhou Enlai, China's then premier, entertained them with a state dinner and suggested to Kissinger that he first taste the Beijing Duck before it became cold. J. A. G. Roberts, *China to Chinatown: Chinese Food in the West* (London: Reaktion Books, 2002), 117.

[12] Zhao, "Zhu yu Zhonghua minzu yinshi wenhua." In her study of the export of Chinese food to areas outside China, Kosegi Erino observes that the Filipinos often like to eat lukewarm food. "'Osoroshii aji': taishū ryori ni okeru Chuka no jyuyou sarekata: Filipin to Nihon no rei wo chūshinni" ("Terrible Taste": the acceptance of Chinese food as a daily food in the Philippines and Japan), *Di 6 jie Zhongguo yinshi wenhua xueshu yantaohui lunwenji* (Proceedings of the 6th academic symposium of Chinese food and drink culture) (Taipei: Zhongguo yinshi wenhua jijinhui, 1999), 229–230. The same is true among the Arabs and others in the Middle East, observes Bee Wilson in his *Consider the Fork*, 203.

existence in ancient China. Elephants and other large animals had once roamed the warmer and more humid region of North China in ancient times. But archaeological digs have yielded ivory chopsticks only from the Zhou dynasty (1046–256 BCE) rather than from the Shang period. The text that described King Zhou's use of ivory chopsticks also comes from the Zhou period, attributed to Han Feizi (281–233 BCE), a philosopher and political strategist:

> Of old, Zhou made chopsticks of ivory. Thereby was the Viscount of Ji frightened. He thought: "Ivory chopsticks would not be used with earthen-wares but with cups made of jade or of rhinoceros horns. Further, ivory chopsticks and jade cups would not go with the gruel made of beans and coarse greens but with the meat of longhaired buffaloes and unborn leopards. Again, eaters of the meat of long-haired buffaloes and unborn leopards would not wear short hemp clothes and eat in a thatched house but would put on nine layers of embroidered dresses and move to live in magnificent mansions and on lofty terraces. Afraid of the ending, I cannot help trembling with fear at the beginning."
>
> In the course of five years, Zhou made piles of meat in the form of flower-beds, raised roasting pillars, walked upon mounds of distiller's grains, and looked over pools of wine. In consequence ended the life of Zhou. Thus, by beholding the ivory chopsticks, the Viscount of Ji foreknew the impending catastrophe of All-under-Heaven. Hence the saying: "Who beholds smallness is called enlightened."[13]

In other words, if there were ivory chopsticks in ancient China, they were regarded as extremely precious, or as a symbol of an extravagant lifestyle. In King Zhou's case, as reckoned by Han Feizi, his luxurious taste caused his dynasty's fall. Indeed, Han Feizi's allegorical reference to King Zhou's flaunting his "ivory chopsticks" (*xiangzhu*) also impacted the historical memory of Koreans. The scholars in Joseon Korea (1392–1897) – the period which witnessed a high level of Chinese influence in the Korean Peninsula – considered King Zhou's use of ivory chopsticks a stigma, symbolizing a profligate, decadent lifestyle and wicked, corrupt government.[14]

Paradoxically, ivory chopsticks became a symbol of lavishness – and thus more desirable – unlike other types in early China, which were made

---

[13] Han Feizi, *Han Feizi*, "Yulao" (Illustrations of Lao Zi's teachings), translations, with modifications, see www2.iath.virginia.edu/saxon/servlet/SaxonServlet?source=xwomen/texts/hanfei.xml&style=xwomen/xsl/dynaxml.xsl&chunk.id=d2.21&toc.depth=1&toc.id=0&doc.lang=bilingual.

[14] A search in the Database of Korean Classics (http://db.itkc.or.kr/itkcdb/mainIndexIframe.jsp) yields fourteen mentions of *xiangzhu* appearing in official histories and other writings from the Joseon dynasty.

of less precious materials. Save for Koreans' preference for metal chop-sticks, implements of wood and bamboo have continued more or less to this day in the chopsticks cultural sphere. However, archaeological digs so far have not yielded many bamboo wooden chopsticks in ancient China. One pair of bamboo chopsticks was uncovered in the Tomb of Marquis Yi of Hubei in 1978. About 37–38 cm long and 1.8–2.0 cm wide and dated *c.* mid-fifth century BCE, the chopsticks were connected at one end, thus looking more like pincers.[15] From the same region of Dangyang, Hubei, another pair, about 18.5 cm long and composed of two separate sticks, was discovered, dating to the fourth century BCE.[16] More quantities of bamboo or wooden chopsticks were found in the Han period (206 BCE to 220 CE), which will be discussed in the next chapter. The archaeological scarcity of bamboo and wooden chopsticks may be explained by the fact that they decay much more easily than those made of bones, ivory, rhi-noceros horn and metals (bronze, copper, gold, silver and iron).

Yet, historical texts from the Zhou to the Han period offer clear evidence that bamboo and wood were the primary materials with which chopsticks were made in early China. All the Chinese characters standing for chopsticks, written either as 箸 and 筯 (both pronounced *zhu*), or 梜 and 筴 (both pronounced *jia*), found in these texts have either the bamboo or wood radicals, suggesting their absolute popularity as chopsticks ma-terials. The pictography of these characters also tells us a good deal about the use of chopsticks and their status as a tool. The first *zhu* contains the meaning of "something bamboo" whereas the second *zhu* suggests that it is a supplementary/assistant tool made of bamboo. The two *jia* likewise show that chopsticks, like pincers, were applied to clutch and hold food-stuffs. Despite the dearth of strong archaeological evidence, all these characters, with their bamboo and wood radicals, clearly reveal that like today, earlier chopsticks were made of more accessible and less expensive materials such as wood and bamboo, rather than ivory, gold and bronze.

The frequency with which chopsticks appear in these texts suggests that the utensil had become commonly used among the Chinese. Due to their ubiquity, chopsticks were referenced conveniently to make a point, such as the case of Han Feizi's discussion of the alleged role ivory chopsticks played in the downfall of the Shang. In the *Xunzi*, attributed to Xun Zi

---

[15] Mukai & Hashimoto, *Hashi*, 3–4. It is worth noting that pincer-like chopsticks have also been found in ancient Japan, though from a later period.

[16] See Zhou Xinhua, *Tiaodingji* (Collection of food essays) (Hangzhou: Hangzhou chu-banshe, 2005), 75.

(340–245 BCE), a contemporary of Han Feizi, chopsticks are further used to help illustrate the importance of "Dispelling Obsession" (one of the themes in the book). Xun Zi states:

> If you look up at a forest from the foot of a hill, the biggest trees appear no taller than chopsticks, and yet no one hoping to find chopsticks is likely to go picking among them. It is simply that the height obscures their actual dimensions.[17]

This passage indicates that it was commonplace for people to break off twigs from lower parts of the tree and turn them into chopsticks. Indeed, according to Chinese legends, chopsticks were first made by Da Yu, founder of the Xia dynasty (2100–1600 BCE), in exactly this way. As he was in a hurry to fight the Flood, by which he would be selected as the ruler, Da Yu supposedly seized a pair of twigs to help down his meal. Although a fairytale, it illustrates that chopsticks indeed could be easily made with makeshift materials. A similar account occurred several millennia later, when the ruling Qing court (1644–1911) was defeated by Western powers in 1900. Empress Dowager Cixi (1835–1908), the dynasty's then *de facto* ruler, fled Beijing. In her escape, while passing a village, she was presented with a bowl of porridge. Unable to find her utensils, a servant in her entourage made a pair of makeshift chopsticks using two small sorghum stalks with which the Dowager managed to finish her meal.[18] Thanks to the ease of making chopsticks, the Empress Dowager was saved from an otherwise awkward moment. The Empress's embarrassment would have been due to the fact that it had long been a tradition for the Chinese to eat food with utensils.

It is difficult to pin down the exact time when chopsticks were adopted widely by the Chinese as an eating utensil. Given the recurrent mentions of chopsticks in various texts from the Warring States period (475–221 BCE), one might reasonably guess that the utensil had become commonly used in those centuries. Having drawn on the readings of those texts, Ōta Masako, a Japanese scholar who wrote a detailed study of the origin of chopsticks in ancient China, agrees that it was during the late Zhou, or between the sixth and third centuries BCE, that using spoons and chopsticks gradually became habitual among the Chinese.[19] If so, this transition seemed to take a long time to complete. For historical texts show that long after the utensil

---

[17] Xun Zi, *Hsün Tzu: Basic Writings*, trans. Burton Watson (New York: Columbia University Press, 1963), 134.

[18] The story derives from Wu Yong, *Gengzi xishou congtan* (The flight of the Qing court) (Beijing: Zhonghua shuju, 2009).

[19] Ōta, *Hashi no genryū o saguru*, 1–19.

had been invented and adopted into daily use, the early Chinese continued using their hands to convey food. The *Classic of Rites* (Liji), a compendium of rituals and etiquette for the upper social class, contains important information on this transitional process. It is generally believed that the *Classic* was first compiled by Confucius and his disciples in the late Zhou and continuously edited and annotated by Confucian scholars through the Han dynasty. Two dining instructions in the *Classic of Rites* deserve special attention:

> When eating with others from the same dishes, one should not try to eat [hastily] to satiety. When eating with them from the same dish of the *fan*, one should not have to wash his hands.
> Do not roll *fan* into a ball; do not bolt down the various dishes; do not swill down [the soup]. Do not make a noise in eating; do not crunch the bones with the teeth; do not put back fish you have been eating; do not throw the bones to the dogs; do not snatch [at what you want]. Do not spread out *fan* [to cool]; *do not use chopsticks in eating millet* [emphasis added]. Do not [try to] gulp down soup with vegetables in it, nor add condiments to it; do not keep picking the teeth, nor swill down the sauces. If a guest adds condiments, the host will apologize for not having had the soup prepared better. If he swills down the sauces, the host will apologize for his poverty.[20]

According to the first quote, *fan*, or cooked grain, was to be taken by hand, not by a utensil, since the first sentence of the second quote also states "Do not roll *fan* into a ball." Obviously, one can only roll it with the hand. But in this regard, why should one not wash one's hands, as instructed by the first quote? Zheng Xuan (127–200), a prominent Confucian scholar of the Han period, when Confucianism became a form of learning, offered his explanation, which was agreed with by Kong Yingda (574–648), another renowned expert on Confucian teaching in the Tang dynasty. Zheng and Kong both believed that instead of asking one not to wash one's hands, the *Classic of Rites* actually meant that one should carry *fan* in dry and clean hands, not rub off dirt, sweat and water from the hands in front of guests, lest such behavior affect their appetite.[21]

A more intriguing issue, relevant to the original function of chopsticks, is why the *Classic of Rites* teaches one to use hands to carry *fan*, but not chopsticks. In other words, why did the early Chinese use both fingers and

---

[20] *Liji* (Classic of rites) – "Quli I" (Summary of the rules of property part 1), CTP, 47 & 48.
[21] But in more recent years, scholars have challenged this interpretation. See Wang Renxiang, *Wanggu de ziwei: Zhongguo yinshi de lishi yu wenhua* (Tastes of yore: history and culture of Chinese foods and drinks) (Ji'nan: Shandong huabao chubanshe, 2006), 47–51.

utensils to consume meals? While the question deserves some explanation, one may say at this juncture that it is common to see this mixed use (fingers and utensils) in many cultures, even today. For example, while Europeans, probably in the fourteenth century, began conveying meals with utensils, they used their fingers to transport certain types of food as the occasion demanded, as is still done today. The term "finger food" in English is a case in point. That "finger food" covers a wide variety (ranging from miniature pies, sausage rolls, sausages on sticks, cheese and olives on sticks, to chicken drumsticks or wings, miniature quiches, samosas, sandwiches and asparagus) shows that the custom of using the hand during meals in the West is not only viable but also popular. In addition, it is commonplace for most peoples in the world to bring bread to their mouth with the hand, even on formal occasions. The people in the chopsticks cultural sphere, indeed, might be an exception in that most of them nowadays are accustomed to using a utensil to eat. They tend to only use fingers to eat snacks such as nuts (e.g. peanuts), even though many of them are skillful enough to accomplish such tasks with chopsticks.

In other words, whether one employs one's fingers or a utensil to consume a meal often depends on the type of food one eats. In ancient China, chopsticks were not used to transfer millet. But why? From the context, one can tell that millet was a type of *fan*. Was millet the only *fan* consumed at the time? It seems not, for in early Chinese historical texts from the Zhou period, there are terms like *baigu* (hundred grains), *jiugu* (nine grains), *liugu* (six grains) and the most common, *wugu* (five grains). These terms clearly suggest that as a cooked grain, *fan* could be made of other cereals. What were they?

A famous reference to the "five grains" is found in the *Analects*, a text in which Confucius' disciples recorded his words and deeds. It reads as follows:

Zi Lu [a disciple of Confucius], following the Master, happened to fall behind, when he met an old man, carrying across his shoulder on a staff a basket for weeds. Zi Lu said to him, "Have you seen my master, sir?" The old man replied, "Your four limbs are unaccustomed to toil; you cannot distinguish the five kinds of grain – who is your master?" With this, he planted his staff in the ground, and proceeded to weed.

However, the *Analects* does not specify what was included in the "five grains." "Five grains" also appears several times in the *Classic of Rites* and the *Rites of Zhou* (*Zhouli*), another important ritual text from the Zhou times, but again with no taxonomic classification. About a century or so later, Mencius (372–289 BCE), a leading Confucian of the age, vaguely mentions "five grains" in the *Mencius*: "The Minister of Agriculture taught the people to sow and reap, cultivating the five kinds of grain. When the five kinds of grain were brought to maturity, the people all obtained a subsistence."[22]

Efforts to define the "five grains" were made first in the Han. The Han dynasty was founded on the ruins of the Qin dynasty (221–206 BCE) that had ended the Warring States period of the late Zhou and unified China proper (centering on North China) in 221 BCE. However, the Han definitions of the "five grains" were inconsistent. In his explanation of the "five grains" in the *Mencius*, for example, Zhao Qi (*c.* 108–201), the leading Han commentator on the *Mencius*, stated that they comprised "rice, foxtail millet (*Setaria italica*), broomcorn millet (*Panicum miliaceum*), wheat, and legumes." By comparison, in annotating the ritual texts like the *Rites of Zhou* and the *Classic of Rites*, Zheng Xuan, Zhao's contemporary whom we mentioned above, believed that the "five grains" referred instead to "hemp, broomcorn millet, foxtail millet, wheat, and beans." Zheng here substituted hemp (*ma*) for rice. While hemp was a fiber crop, its seeds were edible and indeed were eaten by the early Chinese in the north and northwest where Zheng spent his life.[23] But when explaining the term "six grains" in the *Rites of Zhou*, Zheng Xuan did not include hemp among them, causing more confusion.[24] Some modern scholars thus have questioned Zheng Xuan's definition. They have argued that even if rice were not part of the "five grains," the word *ma* would not refer to hemp, but possibly to sesame, which too was written and pronounced *ma* in Chinese. As a Central Asian crop, sesame entered China via the northwest regions in Zheng's time.[25]

Despite the variation, it remains clear that millet was a main cereal crop in North China, in addition to wheat, legumes and perhaps also rice.

[22] Mencius, *The Works of Mencius*, 251.

[23] Cf. He Julian, *Tianshan jiayan: Xiyu yinshi wenhua zonghengtan* (Dining on Mt. Tianshan: discussions of food cultures in the Western regions) (Lanzhou: Lanzhou daxue chubanshe, 2011), 58, which discusses how hemp seeds were eaten in Turpan, or modern Xinjiang, in ancient times.

[24] N. A., *Xianqin pengren shiliao xuanzhu* (Annotated pre-Qin historical sources of culinary practices) (Beijing: Zhongguo shangye chubanshe, 1986), 58.

[25] Xu Hairong, *Zhongguo yinshishi* (A history of Chinese food and drink culture) (Beijing: Huaxia chubanshe, 1999), vol. 2, 15. In modern Chinese, sesame is called *zhima*. Shinoda Osamu, a Japanese scholar of Chinese food history, notes that "five grains" appeared most often in Chinese texts because of the Daoist concept of "five elements/phases," which made "five grains" more popular than the "six grains" or "nine grains." In other words, "five grains" was a figurative term, defying a definitive taxonomy. Shinoda Osamu, *Zhongguo shiwushi yanjiu* (Studies of Chinese food), trans. Gao Guilin, Sue Laiyun & Gao Yin (Beijing: Zhongguo shangye chubanshe, 1987), 6–7.

Millet, especially the foxtail millet, soybeans and rice are believed to have been first cultivated in China. Rice, or *Oryza sativa* (Asian rice), was long believed to be indigenous to South and Southeast Asia until the recent archaeological excavation in Diaotonghuan Cave in South China found the earliest domesticated rice remains, dating as far back as 10000 and 9000 BCE. Others might be imports – wheat is native to Central Asia but entered China during the Bronze Age, if not earlier, for its character appeared in the inscriptions on the bronze vessels of the Shang dynasty.[26] In addition to Diaotonghuan, located in modern Jiangxi Province, the archaeological site in Hemudu of Zhejiang Province had rice remains that were dated around 8000 BCE. Then in Longqiuzhuang of Jiangsu Province, where the first bone chopsticks surfaced, fossilized rice deposits, dated between 6500 and 5500 BCE, were also evident.[27] These archaeological discoveries prove that South China, or the regions of the Yangzi River with plenty of rainfall, is the origin of Asian rice cultivation. But rice was mainly, and remains so to this day, a southern crop in China, hence Zheng Xuan, a northerner, excluded it in defining the "five grains."

As a cereal, millet's popularity is well documented. The *Classic of Odes*, arguably the oldest literary source from ancient China that has survived, describes millet, the foxtail, the broomcorn and other varieties, a total of thirty-seven times, making it the most mentioned cereal crop in the text. For example:

> The Descendant's stacks
> Are high as cliffs, high as hills.
> We shall need thousands of carts,
> Shall need thousands of coffers
> For broomcorn and foxtail millet, rice and spiked millet.[28]

In fact, the Chinese god of agriculture was called Houji, or Lord Millet. The *Classic of Odes* recorded a poem dedicated to Houji, which reads:

> ... He planted the yellow crop ...
> It nodded, it hung ...
> The black millet, the double-kernelled,
> Millet pink-sprouted and white.

---

[26] Francesca Bray, *Science and Civilization in China: Biology and Biological Technology. Part 2, Agriculture* (Cambridge: Cambridge University Press, 1986), vol. 6, pt. 2, 434–449; 459–489.

[27] Longqiuzhuang yizhi kaogudui, *Longqiuzhuang: Jianghuai dongbu xinshiqi shidai yizhi fajue baogao*, 440–463.

[28] Bray, *Science and Civilization in China*, vol. 6, pt. 2, 435.

Millet was also the most highly regarded grain food of the age. When invited to a banquet, it was said, Confucius decided to eat the millet before anything else, even though the host had actually intended him to use the millet only to clean the skin of a peach. Confucius' explanation was that "millet is the most noble among the five grains and in sacrifices to the ancestors it is an offering of supreme standing." By comparison, he said, "Among the six kinds of fruits, however, the peach is the lowest sacrificial offering."[29]

Millet was so important and popular in ancient China with reason: compared with other crops, it was most dry and drought-resistant, well suited to the northern Chinese climate in the reaches of the Yellow River. Indeed, although millet might originally have grown in semi-tropical areas such as South China and Southeast Asia, it is almost certain that it first became domesticated in North China. Ping-ti Ho, an expert on early Chinese agriculture, has argued strongly that millet is native to the region, or the high and low grounds around the Wei and Yellow Rivers which he calls "the loess" and identifies as the cradle of Chinese Neolithic civilization.[30] K. C. Chang (1931–2001), the late professor of archaeology and anthropology at Harvard who edited the first study of Chinese food culture in English, also stated that species of foxtail millet (*Setaria italica*) "grew natively in north China and were utilized by the Chinese from the Neolithic period to the Chou [Zhou]."[31] Since the early twentieth century, archaeological excavations in the region, such as from the Yangshao Neolithic cultural site in Banpo, Xi'an, have yielded many samples of millet deposits.

There was a wide variety of millet cultivated in ancient China. In the *Essential Techniques for the Peasantry* (Qimin yaoshu), a key text on Chinese agriculture written by Jia Sixie (*c.* 386–543), there is a detailed description of the variety of millets grown at the time:

There are all sorts of millet: they ripen at different times, they vary in height and yield, in the strength of their straw, in flavour, and in the ease with which they shed their grain. (The varieties that ripen early have short stems and give a good yield; those which ripen late have longer stems and yield less grain. The strong-strawed varieties belong to the class of short yellow millets, and those with weaker straws belong to the class of tall green, white and black millets. Those

[29] Han Feizi, *Han Feizi jishi* ("waichushuo zuoxia"), quoted in Roel Sterckx, *Food, Sacrifice, and Sagehood in Early China* (New York: Cambridge University Press, 2011), 12.
[30] Ping-ti Ho, "The Loess and the Origin of Chinese Agriculture," *American Historical Review*, 75:1 (October 1969), 1–36.
[31] Chang, "Ancient China," *Food in Chinese Culture*, 26.

which yield a light crop are delicious but shed their grain easily; the large yielders are unpalatable but productive.)[32]

The proliferation of millet cultivation was also shown by the fact that in Chinese writing, millet was referred to by multiple terms. The most common ones, appearing in Shang oracle-bone inscriptions and the historical documents from the Zhou period, were *shu*, *su*, *ji* and *liang*, though the character *liang* could also refer to sorghum at a later time. But what varieties of millet they actually stand for – it is generally believed that *shu* refers to broomcorn millet whereas *su* to foxtail millet – and how they relate to one another (e.g. whether or not *su* and *ji* both stand for foxtail millet) remain uncertain.[33] Confusing as it is in nomenclature, the proliferation of millet in terminology attests to the crop's popularity. Indeed, all evidence points to millet being a dominant crop in North China for at least a millennium, or from antiquity to about the eighth century.

The above discussion gives us enough reason to believe that the *fan* mentioned in the *Classic of Rites* was most likely millet, alone or mixed with beans, wheat and other cereals.[34] Still, the question remains: why could not one eat millet with chopsticks? The answer seems to have much to do with how millet was (is) cooked. From ancient times to the present, most Chinese have usually prepared millet either by boiling or by steaming, due to its small grains (smaller than rice). Once heated, they stick together rather tightly, making it hard for air to pass through them. Consequently, millet cannot be cooked like rice – which is brought to the boil by applying high heat to the right amount of water, and then using low heat to simmer it until the rice becomes soft and fluffy. Had millet been cooked this way, or without sufficient water, the grains at the bottom of the pot would have been burnt while those in the middle would remain undercooked.

In classical Chinese, steamed millet seems referred to more as *fan* whereas boiled millet – porridge or gruel – was *zhou*. This distinction was already drawn in Zhou literature and reiterated from the Han onward. "It was the Yellow Emperor [the legendary progenitor of the

---

[32] Bray, *Science and Civilization in China*, vol. 6, pt. 2, 441.

[33] Ibid., 440. The *liang* millet was known for its large grain. It might be equivalent to German millet in European languages.

[34] A keyword search in the texts from the Zhou to the Tang in ZJGK finds that *shufan* (broomcorn millet) and *sufan* (foxtail millet) appear ninety-two and seventy-three times, respectively, whereas *maifan* (wheat steamed whole) appears 107 times, showing that millet was the staple.

Chinese people]," so says a late Zhou text, "who began to steam grains into *fan* as well as boil them into *zhou*."³⁵ The character *zhou* appears in Shang and Zhou oracle-bone and bronze inscriptions whereas *fan* is mentioned later in Zhou historical texts onwards. That *zhou* preceded *fan* suggests that boiling was perhaps a more popular cooking method. Studies of Shang bronze vessels also find that boilers, cauldrons and tripods were invented before steamers. Modern scholars believe that the designs of the steamers, such as *zeng* and *yan*, were an improvement on the *fu*, or the cauldron, a widely found boiler among Shang and Zhou bronze and pottery vessels. Both the *zeng* and *yan* have two parts; the top part holds the food while the bottom is for applying heat and producing steam. That is, these steamers were made by simply adding a steamer basket onto the cauldron. Historical records reveal that the *zeng*, which was small in size, was mainly used for steaming grain food.³⁶

It is quite possible that when the *Classic of Rites* instructed one to eat *fan* with one's hands, the *fan* was steamed millet, but not boiled millet: compared with the latter, steamed millet was more solidified, allowing transfer by hand. Accordingly, steamed millet was less economical, as it took more time to cook and once ready, it was smaller in quantity. But this seems to fit exactly with the nature of the *Classic of Rites*, which was written mainly for the upper class. By contrast, the ordinary people prob-ably could only afford boiled millet (*zhou*), porridge or gruel (with legu-minous seeds and/or vegetables), to fill up their stomachs. But on festive occasions, common people also liked to prepare grain food by steaming, for making cakes and buns – still a practice in many Asian food cultures.

Using hands to convey food appears easy, but it actually requires more etiquette. South Asians, for example, mostly use fingers to eat, reflected in several dining taboos in their culture, most of which aim to prevent messy dining and disgusting others. Thus, the *Classic of Rites* in ancient China

---

³⁵ The quote was said to be from *Zhoushu*, or *Yi Zhoushu*, which was possibly from the late Zhou, or the Warring States, period. It was quoted by Gao Cheng, a Song scholar, in his *Shiwu jiyuan* (Origin of things), *juan* 9, ZJGK, 208. But Wang Chong, a Han philosopher in his *Lunheng* (Discussive weighing), writing in the first century, also used the phrase "to steam grain into *fan*," *Lunheng* – "Jiyan" (Auspicious portents), *juan* 2, ZJGK, 10.

³⁶ Xu, *Zhongguo yinshishi*, 51–55. That *zeng* was traditionally used to steam grain, such as millet and wheat, was recorded in texts. See Wang, *Lunheng* – "Liangzhi" (The valuation of knowledge): "The ripened grain is called *su* [foxtail millet]. After grinding it on the mortar, then one steams it in *zeng* on fire to make it eatable." *Juan* 12, ZJGK, 121. Tuo Tuo, *Songshi* (Song history) – "Hu Jiaoshiu" (Biography of Hu Jiaoxiu) recorded: "there was steamed wheat in the *zeng*" HDWZK, 11677.

gave such meticulous and fastidious instructions about how one should use one's hands to handle cooked (steamed) millet. It is believed that as ritual experts, Confucius and his disciples mostly used hands to eat their meals, knowing how to do it properly. In the age of Confucius, aristocrats seemed also accustomed to using hands to bring food to the mouth. A famous example is Prince Song of Zheng State around the early seventh century BCE; he is remembered in history for habitually moving his fingers whenever he saw an exotic and enticing dish.[37] In the Chinese language, the index finger is known as the "food finger," or *shizhi*, reflecting the residual influence of the ancient dining custom.

But for many others, it might have been more convenient to use a utensil, as they were mostly eating boiled grains anyway. In the *Guanzi*, attributed to Guan Zhong (*c.* 723/716–645 BCE), a political strategist, advice is given that when eating in front of a teacher, a pupil should, among others, use hands only to carry the grain, but not other foods.[38] That is, since a youngster might not have mastered the techniques of using his hands to convey food, it was better for him to limit their use, lest his improper method be chastised by the teacher.

The *Classic of Rites* does not specify how one eats *zhou*, or boiled millet. But Kong Yingda, the Confucian annotator, believed that instead of hands, one was supposed to employ a spoon. While annotating the sentence "do not use chopsticks in eating millet," he stated that the *Classic* recommended one use a spoon, or *bi*. Living in a much later time than the

---

[37] The story is found in the *Zuo Commentary* (Zuozhuan), a historical text emerging around the same time as did the *Classic of Rites* and the *Book of Etiquette and Ceremonial*. It records that during the fourth year of Duke Xuan (605 BCE), someone from the Chu State (located in the Middle Yangzi River region, or in South China) presented a turtle to Duke Ling of Zheng State, just at the time when Prince Song and his friend Zijia came to pay the Duke a visit. Seeing the turtle, Prince Song's index finger moved and he joked that: "If you see it move again another time, it means that I shall taste something special." However, after the turtle was cooked into a stew, Duke Ling invited all the others to taste it, except Prince Song. Humiliated, Prince Song went up and put his index finger in the tripod, tasted its soup, and stormed out. His act angered Duke Zheng who vowed that he would kill Prince Song. However, a year later, it was Prince Song and Zijia who conspired to have Duke Zheng murdered. Intriguing and dramatic as it was, the story has evolved into a proverb/phrase in later ages. Prince Song's decision to dip his finger into the tripod and taste the food is abbreviated as *ranzhi yuding* (lit. to soil one's finger in the tripod), or simply *ranzhi*, which means that one is not supposed to meddle in things without invitation. Zuo Qiuming, *Chunqiu zuozhuan* (Spring and Autumn Annals and Zuo commentary) – "Xuan'gong sinian" (Prince Xuan, 4th year), CTP, 2.

[38] Guanzi, *Guanzi* – "Dizi zhi" (Duties of the student): "Don't use the hand to eat *geng*," CTP, 4.

first writing of the *Classic of Rites*, Kong noted that millet was cooked in two ways: steaming and boiling, and that millet cooked the former way was eaten with hands and the latter by a spoon, for it was soggy.[39] Of course, one could eat watery food – e.g. porridge – with the aid of chopsticks. To do this, however, one needs to raise the bowl to the mouth and gulp down the food, using chopsticks to shovel it when necessary. Needless to say, this dining behavior was far from refined, resulting in the *Classic of Rites* ruling against it. Undoubtedly, it had been done before (hence the injunction), just as some still do it today.[40] All the same, a spoon is a better tool for eating millet porridge more elegantly, by scooping the food from the bowl, without the need to raise the bowl to the mouth.

People turned to utensils, therefore, for several reasons: necessity, expedience and modishness. In ancient China, without a doubt, boiling was a more popular way of cooking than steaming, as it was more economical and convenient. Archaeologists have uncovered more boilers than steamers among the bronze and pottery vessels from the Shang through the Han dynasties. They have also discovered that in addition to *fu* (cauldron) and *ding* (tripod), *li*, a smaller and more personal tripod, was another common item. Compared with the bronze *ding*, which was used mainly to cook meat, *li* were mostly made of pottery. Given its small size, archaeologists believe, *li* was used by individuals to prepare cereal, or millet. Since the early twentieth century, a great many *li* pottery fragments have surfaced in Yinxu, Henan, the ruins of the Shang dynasty capital. These finds suggest that *li* was a popular cooking utensil among the commoners, and is further proof that more people boiled millet into porridge in early China.[41]

According to historical records, boiled millet took various forms, depending on how watery it was and whether other ingredients were used. It ranged from *zhan*, a thick gruel, to *zhou* or *yu*, both meaning a thin

---

[39] Kong explained that since chopsticks were not recommended for eating millet, then one should use a spoon. Wang Renxiang, a modern scholar, believes that Kong Yingda contradicted himself by stating that in ancient China, one used hands to transport *fan* whereas here he said one should use a spoon. See Wang's *Wanggu de ziwei*, 50. But I do not see any inconsistency because steamed millet could be picked up by hands whereas boiled millet required with a spoon, for it was in a more liquid form.

[40] While eating the popular *Miancha* (lit. noodle tea) in modern Beijing, a millet porridge mixed with sesame, sesame oil and salt, it is customary and also recommended that one sip the liquid directly from the bowl beneath the gel formed on the top that keeps its warmth and taste. Using utensils would break the gel. See Cui Daiyuan, *Jingweier* (Beijing taste) (Beijing: Sanlian shudian, 2009), 71.

[41] Hu Zhixiang, "XianQin zhushi pengshi fangfa" (Study of the ways staple [grain] food was cooked in the pre-Qin period), *Nongye kaogu*, 2 (1994), 214–218.

congee. Again, the *Classic of Rites* records: "Zeng-zi said, 'I have heard from my father that the sorrow declared in the weeping and wailing, the feelings expressed in the robe of sackcloth with even or with frayed edges, and the food of grain made thick or in congee, extend from the son of Heaven to all.'"[42] Besides steamed millet, which was the noble's and festive food, how one cooked and ate millet might well have registered class differences: the thick porridge was possibly more for the rich whereas the thin one was for the less affluent. But this difference could not be absolute, for porridge was (is) a suitable food for the dry and cold weather of North China.

As boiled grain was most common and best eaten with a spoon, it became the primary utensil in ancient China. By comparison, chopsticks seemed secondary, as they were not supposed to carry cooked grain. In early Chinese, one character for chopsticks was *zhu* 箸, which had the bamboo radical on top and the word "assistance/help/supplement" at the bottom, revealing the supplementary role of chopsticks. The *Classic of Rites* specifies the exact – and only? – occasion for one to use chopsticks: "If the stew be made with vegetables, chopsticks should be used; but not if there be no vegetables."[43] Stew – *geng* in Chinese – is made by first boiling the ingredients in water. Like boiled millet porridge, a stew was cooked in various ways in China. It could be a meat stew with a thick sauce or a thin soup with only vegetables. The character *geng* 羹 (with the lamb radical) indicates that in its original form, *geng* must have contained lamb or mutton. The *Erya*, the oldest Chinese dictionary, explains that "meat (*rou*) could be called *geng*." Besides lamb, ingredients in making a *geng* also included beef, pork, chicken, duck and dog. These varieties were indicated with a prefix, such as *yanggeng* (lamb stew), *quangeng* (dog stew) and *tungeng* (pork stew). There was also *xinggeng*, which was believed to be a meatless, vegetarian stew or broth. Yet a meat *geng* might contain vegetables and other spices for better taste, making chopsticks a useful tool in eating many types of *geng*.[44]

These many varieties suggest that *geng* was a popular dish in ancient China. Indeed, the *Classic of Rites* observes: "*geng* (stew) and *fan* (grain)

---

[42] *Liji* – "Tangong I," CTP, 14. Similarly, Mencius also confirmed the popularity of porridge: "The ceremonies to be observed by the princes I have not learned, but I have heard these points: that the three years' mourning, the garment of coarse cloth with its lower edge even, and the eating of congee, were equally prescribed by the three dynasties, and binding on all, from the sovereign to the mass of the people." *The Works of Mencius*, 236.

[43] *Liji* – "Quli I," CTP, 53.

[44] Kong Yingda explained that if the *geng* had no vegetables, then people could drink it directly. Cited and discussed in Wang, *Wanggu de ziwei*, 50.

were eaten by all, from the princes down to the common people, irrespective of status." In other words, the early Chinese not only boiled grains into porridge and gruel, but they also liked to boil nongrain foods, making stew the most common form of *cai* (nongrain food). The stew's popularity helped render chopsticks an important eating implement, for the Chinese preferred to eat food hot. Besides a large number of cauldrons and tripods, archaeologists have unearthed a variety of food warmers, or *wending*, among Zhou bronze and pottery vessels.[45] These food warmers confirm the Chinese dietary preference. One could imagine that chopsticks were used to stir, mix, clasp, try and eat the contents of the vessels.[46] Indeed, Chinese food scholars have postulated that it was due to the need to make and eat *geng* that chopsticks were invented, first as stir sticks and then chopsticks and more.[47]

But what about in areas where millet was not the grain staple – as in South China? Were chopsticks only used to transport nongrain dishes? Actually, even in ancient times, diverse culinary traditions and food cultures seemingly developed on the Asian mainland. The *Classic of Odes* describes many eating occasions, as the following excerpt demonstrates:

> The five grains are heaped up six ells high, and corn of zizania set out;
> The cauldrons seethe to their brims; their blended savours yield fragrance;
> Plump orioles, pigeons, and geese, flavoured with broth of jackal's meat;
> O soul, come back! Indulge your appetite!
> Fresh turtle, succulent chicken, dressed with a sauce of Chu;
> Pickled pork, dog cooked in bitter herbs, and zingiber-flavoured mince.
> And sour Wu salad of Artemisia, not too wet or tasteless.
> O soul, come back! Indulge in your own choice!
> Roast crane is served up, and steamed duck and boiled quails,
> Fried bream, stewed magpies, and green goose, broiled.
> O soul, come back! Choice things are spread before you.
> The four kinds of wine are all matured, not rasping to the throat;
> Clear, fragrant, ice-cooled liquor, not for base men to drink;
> And white yeast is mixed with must of Wu to make the clear Chu wine.
> O soul, come back and do not be afraid![48]

[45] Wang Renxiang, *Yinshi yu Zhongguo wenhua* (Foods and drinks in Chinese culture) (Beijing: Renmin chubanshe, 1994), 16–17.

[46] Zhao, "Zhu yu Zhonghua minzu yinshi wenhua."

[47] "If one intends to investigate the origin of chopsticks," Wang Renxiang states, "one must study the development of stew [as a popular dish]." Wang, *Yinshi yu Zhongguo wenhua*, 270. Also, Zhao, "Zhu yu Zhonghua minzu yinshi wenhua" and Hu, "XianQin zhushi pengshi fangfa tanxi."

[48] Chang, "Ancient China," *Food in Chinese Culture*, 32–33.

Depicting a variety of foods and prevalent cooking methods, this poem shows that Wu and Chu cookeries were markedly different. Wu and Chu referred to the reaches of the Yangzi River in South China – the Chu being the middle part and the Wu the lower part. Yet, what was food culture really like in South China? Unfortunately, neither the poem, except by stressing its exoticness, nor most of the historical texts of the late Zhou period, describe it in detail. Indeed, most of the historical literature from ancient China surviving today was originally written, as well as annotated, by the people in the north, which invariably resulted in a certain bias.

Modern archaeological and anthropological studies have shown that a north–south divide had already appeared in Chinese agriculture and agronomy from ancient days. This divide resulted from the geographical and ecological differences between the northern confines around the Yellow River and those further south around the Yangzi River. The two great rivers exerted a considerable influence in shaping the agriculture and foodways in the two regions – and respective sub-districts – throughout Chinese history. In Joseph Needham's magisterial *Science and Civilization in China*, contributor Francesca Bray offers a succinct observation: "we have distinguished two main agricultural traditions in China, the dry-cereal cultivation of the North and the wet-rice agriculture of the South, each characterised by distinctive crops, tools and field-patterns . . ."[49]

If rice cultivation distinguishes the agriculture of South China from that of North China, this is not manifested in extant historical literature. In such ancient texts as the *Classic of Odes*, rice is mentioned about a dozen times, much fewer than the appearances of millet. But in South China, rice seems to have been the staple grain from antiquity. The archaeological finds from Diaotonghuan, Hemudu and Sanxingdui, Sichuan (discovered in the 1980s) all yielded convincing evidence that rice had long been a leading crop in the Yangzi River regions. Moreover, the findings there show that South China achieved a similar level of cultural development as did North China in Neolithic times. "Even the earliest cultural stratum," comments Francesca Bray on the Hemudu Culture, "shows signs of considerable technological sophistication, including well-made, finely decorated pottery and complex carpentry work, and the sheer volume of the rice remains shows that the inhabitants were not proto-farmers but relied heavily on cultivated rice as a food supply."[50]

Since rice played such a crucial part in advancing Chinese civilization in the south, a brief overview of its role as a grain crop is in order.

[49] Bray, *Science and Civilization in China*, vol. 6, pt. 2, 557.   [50] Ibid., 485.

Throughout history, rice has been one of the most cultivated, as well as most diverse, grains. "This grain," exclaims Margaret Visser, an award-winning author, "is the main sustenance of half the population of the earth. If at this minute some catastrophe were to kill off all the rice crops of the world," she continues, "at least a billion and a half human beings would suffer acute hunger, and millions would die of starvation before anything could be done to save them."[51] As indispensable as rice is in today's world, it seems to have played an even more important role in pre-modern times. "For most of history – until the scientific recrafting of wheat strains to produce today's staggeringly efficient varieties – rice," writes food historian Felipe Fernandez-Armesto,

was *hors de pair* the world's most efficient food: with traditional varieties, one hectare of rice supports, on average, 5.63 persons, compared with 3.67 per hectare of wheat and 5.06 for maize. For most of history, the rice-eating civilizations of east and south Asia were more populous, more productive, more inventive, more industrialized, more fertile in technology and more formidable in war than rivals elsewhere.[52]

This is certainly the case in China. And if millet nurtured early Chinese civilization in the north, rice played a similar role in developing the culture in the south. As time went on, rice would occupy an even greater position in Chinese agriculture and its food system.

Chinese historical texts mention rice's importance in South China. The *Rites of Zhou*, for example, acknowledges that "rice was a suitable crop" for both Jingzhou and Yangzhou, which were located in the middle and lower parts of the Yangzi River. In his *Records of the Grand Historian* (Shiji), Sima Qian (*c.* 145–87 BCE), the great Han historian who had travelled widely throughout the land, concurs that "In States Chu and Yue [in the middle and lower parts of the Yangzi River], where land was vast and people were few, *rice was the chief grain and fish stew the main dish* [emphasis added]." Sima's description pits the foodway of South China against North China's.

Was it the consumption of rice that turned the Chinese in the south to use chopsticks more? Archaeology seems to suggest that there might be some correlation, since more of these objects have surfaced in the historical sites of South China. Longqiuzhuang, the site of the earliest chopsticks, is located in Jiangsu Province, or the lower Yangzi River. And the

[51] Margaret Visser, *Much Depends on Dinner: The Extraordinary History and Mythology, Allure and Obsessions, Perils and Taboos, of an Ordinary Meal* (New York: Grove Press, 1986), 155–156.
[52] Fernandez-Armesto, *Food: A History*, 105–106.

Longqiuzhuang Culture was more closely related to those along the Yangzi and Huai Rivers than to those along the Yellow River. Thus, it is likely no coincidence that rice remains also surfaced in Longqiuzhuang. As mentioned above, from the Bronze Age through the Han dynasty, the majority of chopsticks (bronze and bamboo) uncovered by archaeologists have been in southern and southwestern Chinese sites, where rice was grown more widely. These findings lead one to suspect that in South China, chopsticks would have been a more practical means of eating as opposed to northern traditions. That is, the people in South China possibly used chopsticks not only to pick out foodstuffs in a stew, they also used them to eat rice – their grain food.[53]

Compared with other grains, then, cooked rice can be more easily held and moved in clumps by chopsticks (Plate 25). One could thus speculate on the possible bond between eating rice and using chopsticks. Of course, rice is a diverse crop. The most common types consumed in East and Southeast Asia are the non-glutinous *sinica* (*japonica*) and *indica*, which are regarded as ordinary. The glutinous rice, known in Chinese as *nuo*, in Vietnamese as *nep* and in Thai as *nieo*, is more customarily used to make rice cakes and other kinds of confectionery during festivals. Both *sinica/japonica* and *indica*, which have relatively translucent grains as opposed to the round and opaque grain of glutinous rice, have appeared in Neolithic sites across China proper but notably were more present along the Yangzi River.[54] Among other things, the two varieties are differentiated by their ripening period, grain size and shape, and cooking characteristics. The *sinica/ japonica*, for instance, is softer and stickier than the long-grain *indica*. Like millet, rice can be eaten whole or milled into flour: the ancient Chinese used both methods.

But in contrast to millet, including its glutinous varieties, rice becomes much more integrated once cooked, as its larger grains allow air to pass through the boiling water. As a result, rice has a shorter cooking time than

---

[53] Longqiuzhuang yizhi kaogudui, *Longqiuzhuang: Jianghuai dongbu xinshiqi shidai yizhi fajue baogao*. For the nature of Longqiuzhuang Culture, see discussions in Zhang Jiangkai & Wei Jun, *Xinshiqi shidai kaogu* (Neolithic archaeology) (Beijing: Wenwu chubanshe, 2004), 173–176. Given that more chopsticks were discovered in the south, Shen Tao hypothesized that the utensil originated in Yunnan of Southwest China, which is cited, sympathetically, in Ōta, *Hashi no genryū o saguru*, 248–249, and Mukai & Hashimoto, *Hashi*, 4–6.

[54] Te-Tzu Chang, "Rice," *Cambridge World History of Food*, eds. Kenneth F. Kiple & Kriemhild C. Ornelas (Cambridge: Cambridge University Press, 2000), vol. 1, 149–152. In Chinese historical sources, *sinica/japonica* and *indica* rice are referred to as *geng* 粳 and *xian* 籼, respectively.

millet, whether by boiling or by steaming. Though called non-glutinous rice, both *sinica/japonica* and *indica* are more cohesive than millet after preparation, making it much easier for one to hold small chunks with chopsticks. Given the gluey nature of cooked rice, it would be inconvenient to transport it by hand like steamed millet, for its grains would stick to the skin. In some parts of the world where people do use their fingers to eat rice, a basin of water is immediately available for washing. Admittedly, another way to deal with the problem is to cook rice with oil; but this would present the nuisance of having to wipe away accumulated grease. Using chopsticks to eat rice, therefore, presents a solution to such inconvenience. Of course, even if chopsticks can deliver grains efficiently to the mouth, rice can stick on them, too. But it is easier to remove rice from chopsticks, since they are smaller and thinner in size. As time went on, they became pointed and polished, further eliminating such dining problems.

However, as stated in the Introduction, both cultural and culinary factors play roles in determining whether or not one uses a utensil – and which kind – to eat a meal. Consuming rice does not necessarily mean having to use a utensil, nor must it be chopsticks. In Southeast Asia where rice has long been the staple, only the Vietnamese have used chopsticks to eat it; all others prefer using either their hands or a spoon and a fork. In Thailand, for example, where in the past rice was eaten by hand, most people now use a spoon to first scoop it from the bowl, and then push it with the back of a fork held in the other hand, before finally bringing it to the mouth. As for glutinous rice, which is difficult to eat with a fork and spoon, people usually use their right hand to take a lump and form a small ball, with a thumb-size indentation being made to hold sauces, condiments and side dishes, before placing the prepared ball into the mouth.[55] This demonstrates that many ways of eating rice have developed. Using chopsticks is one of them, which is adopted more because of cultural influences than practical needs.

In sum, drawing on both archaeological evidence and literary sources, one can make some general observations about food culture in ancient China, in relation to the story of chopsticks. First, although eating utensils had been invented during the Neolithic Age, the early Chinese continued to eat food with their hands (though preferably only the right hand per custom). Indeed, this juxtaposition between using one's hand and utensils

---

[55] See Leedom Lefferts, "Sticky Rice, Fermented Fish, and the Course of a Kingdom: The Politics of Food in Northeast Thailand," *Asian Studies Review*, 29 (September 2005), 247–258. Also, Van Esterik, *Food Culture in Southeast Asia*, 21.

to convey food persisted for quite some time. Second, boiling was the most prevalent cooking method, followed by steaming, even though other ways of cooking also appeared in early China.[56] The Chinese boiled not only grain, but also nongrain foods; the former took the form of porridge (*zhou*), and the latter stew (*geng*). These forms determined whether and what kind of utensils were used for eating. Third, the spoon was invented first in early China to consume boiled food, since it contained sufficient liquid. Shaped like a dagger with sharp edges, the spoon, or *bi*, would also have been useful for cutting the meat in the stew. As such, the spoon was the primary feeding tool, whereas chopsticks played a supplementary role. Their main function was to grasp vegetables in a stew or a broth, but they were not recommended for boiled grain food – such as millet. As for steamed millet, people generally used their hands instead. Thus, the original use of chopsticks was limited to eating *cai* (nongrain food), but not *fan* (grain food); the latter was and still is the main type of food consumption in China and elsewhere. However, in South China where chopsticks were introduced as a utensil, people possibly used them to eat not only nongrain foods, or the stew, as they were intended to, but also rice, the staple in the region. Since most of the historical sources come from North China, it is difficult to ascertain when this dining habit began; namely, how chopsticks became a widely used, and even the exclusive, eating implement that one sees in present-day Vietnam, Japan and most of China. But it certainly would not take long for people to discover the effectiveness of chopsticks in conveying cooked rice. From the Han period onward, as culinary traditions experienced a marked change in North and Northwest China, chopsticks would demonstrate even more versatility – a topic to be covered in the next chapter.

---

[56] See the instruction given by the *Classic of Rites*: "When the child was able to take its own food, it was taught to use the right hand." *Liji* – "Neize" (The pattern of the family), CTP, 76. For cooking methods in ancient China, see Chang, "Ancient China," *Food in Chinese Culture*, 31.

3

Dish, rice or noodle? The changing use of chopsticks

At your birth when they first hung out the bow, I was the most honored guest at the birthday feast. Wielding my chopsticks I ate boiled noodles, and composed a congratulatory poem on a heavenly unicorn.

Liu Yuxi (772–842)

The discovery of a new dish does more for the happiness of mankind than the discovery of a star.

Anthelme Brillat-Savarin, *Physiologie du Gout* (1825)

In his masterpiece, *Records of the Grand Historian*, Sima Qian relates many fascinating episodes happening during the Han dynasty (206 BCE to 220 CE), a great era in early imperial China. Some of them, interestingly, feature chopsticks. In his biographical account of Liu Bang (256–195 BCE), Sima records that while preparing to seize power, Liu, who grew up in northern Jiangsu near Longqiuzhuang and later became Emperor Gaozu after founding the dynasty, once considered a strategic plan by a counselor over a meal. But Zhang Liang (256–186 BCE), his main and most trusted advisor, opposed it. In order to persuade Liu, Zhang borrowed several chopsticks and made a strong counterargument. And he prevailed in the end; Liu decided to adopt his plan instead.[1] Sima does not tell exactly how Zhang used chopsticks to explain his objection. But the story has been well remembered in history ever since. It reveals that Liu and his staff, among others, used chopsticks in eating their food.

Chopsticks appear in another biography in the *Records of the Grand Historian*. Its protagonist is Zhou Yafu (199–143 BCE), a distinguished

---

[1] Sima, *Shiji* – "Liuhou shijia" (Biography of Zhang Liang), HDWZK, 2040.

and capable general under Han Emperors Wen (r. 176–157 BCE) and Jing (r. 157–141 BCE), son and grandson of Emperor Gaozu. Thanks to his remarkable accomplishments, Zhou became trusted by both emperors during most of their reigns. But in the end, perhaps due to his arrogance, Zhou lost Emperor Jing's trust. Sima records an episode in which one day Zhou was summoned to court to dine with the Emperor and found a big chunk of meat in his food tray with no sliced pieces, nor chopsticks. He turned around asking for chopsticks, only to be mocked by the Emperor: "Was this treatment not good enough for you?" Feeling insulted and humiliated, Zhou thanked the Emperor and left the court without touching the food. Seeing him leave, Emperor Jing sighed: "With that kind of attitude, how can you continue to be my advisor?" A few years later, Emperor Jing indeed found an excuse to have Zhou executed.[2]

These two stories demonstrate that by Han times, chopsticks had become customary. Yet two issues seem worthy of more exploration. One is that in both the stories, Sima Qian does not mention whether spoons were also used or provided. As established in the previous chapter, spoons were the primary eating tool among the early Chinese. The other issue is that when Zhou Yafu saw the uncut meat in front of him, he turned around looking for chopsticks, but according to the instruction of the *Classic of Rites*, chopsticks were supposed to be only used for picking up vegetables in a stew. The answer to the first question seems somewhat easier to find: until then the Chinese still used their fingers to bring some types of grain food to their mouths, not always using the spoon. As for the second issue, a possible explanation might be that the Chinese had begun using chopsticks to handle all nongrain foods. This chapter will discuss these two subjects – when the Chinese adopted the custom of eating only with utensils and when they used chopsticks to convey all food items in dishes – in detail, covering the period from the Han to the Tang dynasty (618–907).

Over the past several decades, Chinese archaeologists have discovered a number of tombs from the Han period. These excavations offer valuable information on how the people then consumed their daily meals. The Mawangdui Tombs, near Changsha, capital of Hunan Province, are an important case. Unearthed between 1972 and 1974, the Mawangdui tombs consist of three, which contain three members of one family headed by Li Cang, the first Marquis of Dai in Changsha during 193–186 BCE. Of the three tombs, the first tomb discovered in 1972 was the most spectacular because the body buried therein, identified as the Marquis'

---

[2] Sima, *Shiji* – "Jianghou Zhou Bo shijia" (Biography of Zhou Yafu), HDWZK, 2078.

wife Xin Zhui – Lady Dai, who died around the age of fifty – remained quite well preserved. Forensic archaeologists found that Lady Dai likely died of a heart attack, triggered possibly by eating musk melons whose seeds were found in her esophagus, stomach and intestines. Equally interesting finds from the tomb were forty-eight bamboo cases and fifty-one pottery vessels of various types that contained a variety of foodstuffs, indicating that Lady Dai loved food in life. The grains found in the cases and vessels included rice, wheat, broomcorn millet, foxtail millet and lentil. Besides food containers, Lady Dai was surrounded by many lacquered dinnerware and drinking vessels, and on top of one lacquered bowl, lo and behold, lay a pair of bamboo chopsticks (Plate 7)![3]

Besides the chopsticks, lacquered wooden spoons and ladles, which had an oval-shaped deep bowl and a long handle, were also uncovered in the tombs. The spoons look more refined whereas the chopsticks, with some lacquered paint, seem rather simple. Mukai Yukiko and Hashimoto Keiko, authors of a study of chopsticks in Japan, surmise that Lady Dai used the chopsticks in life, but the more delicate spoons, bowls and other utensils were possibly burial goods, or spiritual objects. They also suggest that Lady Dai may have continued the custom of eating some foods with the hands.[4] The Mawangdui Tombs, of course, are not the only place where spoons, chopsticks and other utensils have surfaced together. Archaeologists have made similar discoveries in other Han tombs. Their being placed together has made scholars believe that spoons and chopsticks became increasingly employed as a set of tools for meals through the period.[5] But if this were the case, the relationship between the two utensils seems still not as close and collaborative as that of forks and knives – one holds down the food and the other does the cutting. The Chinese could use only either one of them in conveying a meal.

Some of the Han tombs also contained stone reliefs and painted stones in their chambers and passageways that portray cooking and eating scenes. The stone relief found in Xindu, Sichuan, for instance, depicts a feast scene: three men sitting on the floor with the man in the center holding a pair of chopsticks pointed toward the food being presented by the person on the left. On top of the food in the bowl held by the person on the left is a pair of chopsticks (Plate 4). Moreover, two additional pairs of chopsticks are placed on the big mat at the center of the floor.

[3] Hunan Sheng Bowuguan (Hunan Museum), *Changsha Mawangdui yihao Hanmu* (The first tomb of Mawangdui, Changsha) (Beijing: Wenwu chubanshe, 1973).
[4] Mukai & Hashimoto, *Hashi*, 9–10.   [5] Liu, *Zhongguo zhu wenhuashi*, 125–135.

The famous Wuliang Shrine in Jiaxiang, Shandong, features another eating scene painted on the wall. Named "Xing Qu bufu" (Xing Qu feeding his father), the mural portrays Xing Qu, holding food with a pair of chopsticks in his left hand and a dipper or ladle in his right, presenting food to his father. A servant behind him holds another bowl of food, indicating more food was prepared for the father. Without question, this painting served to promote the Confucian ideal of filial piety, which the Han dynasty officially endorsed.

These feast and feeding scenes confirm what the *Records of the Grand Historian* suggests: chopsticks were a main eating tool in the Han period. They also illustrate that although often buried together, chopsticks and spoons were not necessarily used together in conveying food. The dipper held by Xing Qu to feed his father could well contain the grain food for his father to grasp with his own hand and deliver to his mouth, for it was larger than the usual size of a spoon intended to bring food to the mouth. The lacquer-painted spoons found in the Mawangdui Tombs also seem to support the idea that some of them were not for personal use. Most of the spoons were over 18 cm long (bowl + handle) and 6 cm wide (bowl), which might be more suitable as a serving tool. In addition, the Mawangdui Tombs contained a number of small bowls, which were oval-shaped, shallow, with two "ears" or wings, one on each side. Archaeologists have suspected that this type of bowl was used to hold ale/wine, soup or watery food, for the two wings were obviously designed for one to grip by hand and deliver whatever was inside the bowl to the mouth. In other words, using these winged bowls to transport food, e.g. millet porridge, one did not need a spoon.

If during the early Han period the dining custom in China remained more or less unchanged from the previous ages – the Chinese used utensils and hands alternately in transporting foods – a notable change occurred toward the end of the Han, beginning in the second century.[6] This change led to the increased use of utensils, which eventually replaced fingers. In Chinese literature, feeding utensils were referred to as *bizhu* (spoon and chopsticks). One of the earliest mentions of *bizhu* is in Chen Shou's (233–297) *History of the Three Kingdoms* (San'guozhi), a

---

[6] H. T. Huang states that during the Han, "fingers were used for rice, chopsticks for viands and spoons for soups." See his "Han Gastronomy – Chinese Cuisine in *statu nascendi*," *Interdisciplinary Science Reviews*, 15:2 (1990), 149. Though largely correct, this statement overlooks the fact that spoons were also used for eating such loose grains as millet before and during this period.

historical account of the fall of the Han and the rise of the Kingdoms of Wei, Shu and Wu in its ruins during the third century. Chen begins by describing the decline of the Han dynasty, attributing it to the manipulation of young emperors by both eunuchs and military strongmen. Dong Zhuo (?–192), a powerful general, is recorded as an early example of the latter. According to Chen, to intimidate his opponents and exercise full control of the Han court, Dong once invited other ministers to a dinner party, at which he punished a group of war prisoners by cutting out their tongues and eyes and amputating their limbs in front of everyone. Having witnessed such horror, many "dropped their spoons and chopsticks as they were trembling with fear," while Dong calmly ate his food and drank his wine.[7] Chen's graphic description reveals that at the time, or toward the end of the Han, spoons and chopsticks were used more as a set in transferring food.

This is not the only time Chen Shou mentions spoons and chopsticks in the same breath. A more proverbial incident occurred at another dining occasion, or between Cao Cao (155–220) and Liu Bei (161–223), future founders of the Kingdom of Wei and Kingdom of Shu. Cao, a military strongman who exercised power and influence at the Han court after Dong Zhuo, invited Liu to a dinner meeting. Though a member of the Han royal family, Liu at the time was Cao's junior both in age as well as in power. Before the meeting, Liu had been given a secret decree by the reigning Han emperor to find a way to kill Cao. At the dinner just as Liu was ready to eat, Cao toasted him: "Well, as I see it, you and I are the only two heroes in the country. All others are really nobody." Afraid that Cao had discovered his conspiracy, wrote Chen, "Liu dropped both his spoon and chopsticks on the floor," out of shock and fear.[8]

It is unclear from these stories whether or not the people involved employed spoons and chopsticks exclusively in conveying food, or still used their hands on occasion. But from then – the third century – to the early twentieth century, *bizhu* or *chizhu*, its variation (*chi* is shaped more like a modern spoon, with a shallow bowl and a long and curved handle, usually longer than the one on the *bi*), became a stock phrase in Chinese texts, used in many texts across various genres whenever an eating occasion was depicted or recorded.[9] (Details are omitted here to save space but some examples are given in later chapters.) This suggests that from no later

---

[7] Chen Shou, *San'guozhi* (History of the Three Kingdoms) – "Dong Zhuo, Li Cui, Guo Fan" (Biographies of Dong Zhuo, Li Cui and Guo Fan), HDWZK, 176.

[8] Chen, *San'guozhi* – "Liu Bei" (Biography of Liu Bei), HDWZK, 875.

[9] *Bizhu* appears a total of 1,232 times and *chizhu* 492 times in the texts in ZJGK.

than the third century, eating with utensils, shunning one's hands, had become a preferred custom, or a social norm, among the Chinese.

As chopsticks were effective extensions of the fingers, their flexibility was instrumental in helping the Chinese to cease using their hands for eating meals during this era. Sima Qian's story of Zhou Yafu disclosed that in Han times, the function of chopsticks had already extended beyond picking up just vegetables in soups as had been prescribed by the *Classic of Rites*. But for chopsticks to become an efficient tool to carry all foodstuffs in the nongrain dishes, it was necessary to cut the food into small morsels for the utensil to clasp and pinch and for the mouth to bite and chew. As some Shang bronze vessels were large in size, one could assume that in the Bronze Age, the early Chinese had cooked large lumps of meat. Once cooked, the meat could be bitten off, though more delicately when guests were present. Hence the *Classic of Rites* suggests that while eating with guests, "meat that is wet [and soft] may be divided with the teeth, but dried flesh cannot be so dealt with."[10] This shows that biting off cooked meat was socially acceptable, but gnawing on large pieces of dried meat was not.

During the twilight years of the Zhou period, a new culinary practice seems to have appeared, appealing first to the cultured class: cutting and slicing meat into desirable portions and arranging them properly for a better visual presentation and dining experience. Confucius, as a cultural master, was known for being meticulous about whether or not meat was minced into the right size. "He did not eat meat," his students observed, "which was not cut properly, nor what was served without its proper sauce." In fact, Confucius' eating preference is best characterized as follows: "He did not dislike to have his rice finely cleaned, nor to have his mince meat cut quite small."[11]

Could the new culinary practice of cutting meat into small pieces have arisen because of the scarcity of animal meat at the time? It is hard to know one way or another. But historical texts reveal that the Zhou government did discourage meat consumption, especially beef, for cattle and water buffalo were valuable in helping with farm work. Other land animal meats, such as lamb, pork and even dog, were also reserved for special occasions.[12] The *Classic of Rites*, therefore, contains the following injunction:

---

[10] *Liji* – "Quli I," CTP 48.   [11] Confucius, *Confucian Analects*, 232.
[12] Xu, *Zhongguo yinshishi*, 29–36.

Without sufficient cause, a prince did not kill an ox, nor a great officer a sheep, nor another officer a dog or a pig, nor a common person eat delicate food.

The advice given by the *Mencius* appears more stringent:

Let mulberry trees be planted about the homesteads with their five *mu* [a unit in measuring land], and persons of fifty years may be clothed with silk. In keeping fowls, pigs, dogs, and swine, let not their times of breeding be neglected, and *persons of seventy years may eat flesh* [emphasis added].

As consuming the meat of larger land animals became regulated, the Chinese turned to smaller ones, such as chicken, pheasant and ducks whose meat hardly required much cutting. Thus the practice of slicing meat into bite-size morsels might also be the default choice, besides being the cultural preference. But the latter was undoubtedly important. During the Han dynasty as Confucianism gained ascendancy to become an official ideology, the general populace perhaps also adopted Confucius' dining preferences as the norm for demonstrating cultural refinement.

The finds at Mawangdui Tombs again help to shed light on culinary customs during Han times. A total of 312 inscribed bamboo slips, or proto-books in ancient China, were uncovered from the burial sites. Some of these "books" were indeed recipes, offering information not only on cooked food but also on cooking methods. We know from them that "roasting, scalding, shallow-frying, steaming, deep-frying, stewing, salting, sun-drying, and pickling" were ways of cooking practiced during this age. But the recipes also show that stewing – or cooking *geng* – was most popular. The *geng*/stews described on the bamboo slips were broken down into two groups: meat stew and mixed stew. The former included nine different recipes, made respectively of ox, sheep, deer, pig, suckling pig, dog, wild duck, pheasant and chicken. The latter, mixing meat with grains and/or vegetables, such as beef and rice, had even more variety: "deer meat–salted fish–bamboo shoots, deer meat–taro, deer meat–small beans, chicken–gourd, crucian carp–rice, fresh sturgeon–salted fish–lotus root, dog meat–celery, crucian carp–lotus root, beef–turnip, lamb–turnip, pork–turnip, beef-sonchus (a wide grass), and dog meat–sonchus."[13] Specific as they were, these recipes did not detail whether, in stewing larger animal meats, one should slice them into small portions as with other, smaller meats (chicken, duck, pheasant, etc.). But possibly people did, as almost all the stews mixed many ingredients, which would work better if they were in similar sizes.

[13] Ying-shih Yu, "Han," *Food in Chinese Culture*, 57–58.

"The whole culinary art of China," summarized Lin Yu-tang, a famous writer of twentieth-century China, "depends on the art of mixture."[14] When food items were prepared in similar sizes and cooked together in a pot, chopsticks became the best tool for eating them, irrespective of whether they were meat, vegetable or something else. This culinary art seems already well established in the Han. Thus upon seeing a big piece of uncut meat, Zhou Yafu looked for a pair of chopsticks, but not a knife or a dagger-shaped *bi*, even though chopsticks clearly were not the right tool to help him eat the meat. Zhou had possibly already become accustomed to eating nongrain foods, including meat dishes, with chopsticks.

Since the Chinese had eschewed knives and forks very early on, it could be daunting and awkward for them to handle a huge piece of animal meat. In Sima Qian's *Records of the Grand Historian*, another story in the biography of Liu Bang is worth citing here. When Liu Bang was still gathering his forces, Xiang Yu, then his chief rival, invited him to a banquet at Hongmen, near modern Xi'an. But it was a trap because Xiang, whose force then was larger than Liu's, intended to annihilate Liu and his entire entourage. Having realized the dangerous situation, Fan Kuai, Liu's bodyguard, burst onto the scene. Xiang challenged him by giving him a half-cooked pig leg. Unfazed, Fan carved the leg with his sword on his shield and devoured it. His courage intimidated Xiang. As Xiang hesitated, Liu Bang seized the moment and found an excuse to escape from the situation, saving his life. In the end, it was Liu who turned around and defeated Xiang, establishing the Han dynasty.[15] The banquet at Hongmen, therefore, became the most remembered one in Chinese history, for Xiang's failure in killing Liu at the site tipped the balance of power against him, resulting in his ultimate defeat and death. Interestingly, Fan Kuai's heroism was displayed by overcoming a big piece of meat!

Handling big pieces of meat in the Han became heroic and courageous because during this period, it had gradually become a custom to cook meat in small, bite-size morsels. One story recorded by Fan Ye (398–445), a post-Han historian, helps illustrate this point. A person named Lu Xu was involved in a conspiracy against the court and was arrested. His mother sent a meal to him in jail. Passing it to Lu, the warden did not tell him who had cooked it. As Lu Xu was eating the stew, he broke down in tears and told the warden that the meal had to be cooked by his mother. Asked how he knew, Lu answered: "When my mother cooks a stew, she dices meat into exact cubes and cuts scallions into the same inches. So I know this stew must be made by her."[16] All these charming stories help establish that in Han China, as cooked items were cut into bite size pieces, chopsticks had extended their utility and were used to convey all nongrain foods, no longer just the vegetables in the stew.

But the expansion of the utility of chopsticks did not stop here, for in the Han, a new and different "culinary revolution" also occurred, pertaining to the grain food people then ate. This "revolution" was powered and characterized by milling wheat into flour and cooking doughy foods.[17] As noted before, the earliest sample of noodles has so far been discovered in China. In the Neolithic cultural sites across North China, archaeologists have located saddle querns and rubbing stones, suggesting the people had ground grains. However, in the middle and late Neolithic Age, the Yangshao Culture (5000–3000 BCE) near Xi'an and the Dawenkou Culture (4040–2240 BCE) in Shandong failed to produce a stone grinder. Food historians have speculated that by that time, people had turned to steaming and boiling cereals whole, instead of grinding them.[18]

Boiled or steamed wheat was called *maifan* in Chinese. It denotes the fact that wheat, like rice and millet, was cooked whole. But *maifan* was known to be coarse and unpalatable.[19] As a result, *maifan* symbolized a simple and frugal lifestyle. For instance, if *maifan* was an official's daily food, it would help establish him as an upright moral person, even receiving accolades from the emperor.[20] There were ways to improve the taste of boiled whole wheat. One was to mix it with other foods, such as red beans, soybeans and vegetables, in cooking. And the other was to flavor it with certain seeds and flowers. The blossoming pagoda tree flowers, for example, were often

---

[16] Fan Ye, *HouHanshu* (Late Han history) – "Lu Xu" (Biography of Lu Xu), HDWZK, 2683.

[17] Yu, "Han," *Food in Chinese Culture*, 81ff; and Zhang Guangzhi (Chang Kuang-chih), "Zhongguo yinshishi shangde jici tupo" (Several breakthroughs in the Chinese food and drink history), *Di 4 jie Zhongguo yinshi wenhua xueshu yantaohui lunwenji* (Proceedings of the 4th academic symposium on Chinese food and drink culture) (Taipei: Zhongguo yinshi wenhua jijinhui, 1996), 3.

[18] Ishige Naomichi, "Filamentous Noodles, '*Miantiao*': Their Origin and Diffusion," *Di 3 jie Zhongguo yinshi wenhua xueshu yantaohui lunwenji* (Proceedings of the 3rd academic symposium on Chinese food and drink culture) (Taipei: Zhongguo yinshi wenhua jijinhui, 1994), 118.

[19] Xu, *Zhongguo yinshishi*, 475–476.

[20] Xu Pingfang, "Zhongguo yinshi wenhua de diyuxing jiqi ronghe" (Regions and cross-regional development in Chinese food and drinking culture), *Di 4 jie Zhongguo yinshi wenhua xueshu yantaohi lunwenji* (Proceedings of the 4th academic symposium on Chinese food and drinking culture) (Taipei: Zhongguo yinshi wenhua jijinhui, 1996), 96–97.

mixed in when cooking wheat. It made *maifan* fragrant and even enticing, hence easier to swallow. But its texture remained not as soft as that of rice or millet, especially the *huangliang* (lit. yellow millet; ordinary Setaria) variety of millet.

But once wheat is milled into flour and made into doughy food, its taste becomes dramatically improved. This is also how most people consume the grain today. The Chinese had discovered the method from the Han period. Both archaeology and history have shown that around the first century BCE, the Chinese not only resumed using saddle querns, but they also turned to rotary querns to grind wheat into flour, which became fine enough to make dumpling wrappers and noodles. In the Han tombs of Shaokou of Henan Province, for example, archaeologists found three millstones in 1958. Then a decade later in 1968, an archaeological excavation unearthed another rotary millstone in a well-preserved Han tomb in Mancheng, Hebei Province. In addition, Huan Tan's (23 BCE to 50 CE) *New Essays* (Xinlun) provides the best textual evidence about the variety of mills used in his time:

After Mi Xi [Fu Xi, an agricultural god] invented the pestle and mortar, the invention benefited numerous people. Over time, people improved its use and learned how to grind [the grain] with the help of their body weight. The result was ten times better than before. Further on, they invented devices that allowed them to use the ox, horse, donkey and mule as well as to use water to power the mill. Then the result was improved a hundred times.[21]

The existence of these animal mills and watermills indicates that grinding had become common for processing wheat and other grains during this era.

Thanks to milling, floured wheat foods became popular in Han China. In Chinese, the term *bing* refers to either dough or dough-based foods. While it had appeared in the *Mozi*, attributed to Mo Zi (470–391 BCE), the term appeared much more frequently in Han texts.[22] Liu Xi's *Shiming*, a lexicon from the second century CE, for example, registers six types of floured wheat foods distinguished by different prefixes that describe either their texture or shape. *Bing*'s popularity also entered historical records. Before Han Emperor Xuan (r. 74–49 BCE) was chosen as the successor to the throne, according to the record, he often purchased *bing* from street

---

[21] Huan Tan, *Xinlun* (New essays) (Shanghai: Shanghai renmin chubanshe, 1967), 44.

[22] Mozi, *Mozi* – "Gengzhu," CTP, 18. Combining the radical "*shi*" (food) and the verb "*bing*" (to blend), *bing* described how wheat flour dough was made by adding water to the flour – the word *bing* 并, without the food radical, means "to blend" whereas its homonym *bing* 餅, with the food radical, refers to a food that blends – mixes – wheat flour with water.

food stands. Another Han ruler, Emperor Zhi (r. 145–146 CE) also loved *bing*, which unfortunately caused his tragic death; an evil minister put poison into the "boiled *bing*" (*zhubing* – noodles?) for him to eat.[23]

Not only did Han rulers like floured wheat products, but they also designed policies to encourage wheat farming, especially in areas around the Han capital in today's Xi'an. Fan Shengzhi, a minor official under Han Emperor Cheng (r. 32–7 BCE), was put in charge of the project. For his success, Fan received promotion. Drawing on his experience, Fan also wrote a book, one of the first food histories in China, which describes the techniques of growing both winter and spring wheat. The *Monthly Ordinances for the Four Peoples* (Simin yueling), another Han agricultural text by Cui Shi (105–170), further instructs that spring wheat should be sown in the first month (February) of the year, winter wheat in the eighth month (October).[24] And the trend to grow more wheat continued in the following centuries. During the Tang dynasty, wheat rivaled millet as the leading cereal crop in North China, a subject to be discussed below.

If the improved milling technology made it easier to produce flour from wheat, the craze for doughy foods among the Chinese reflected influences from Central and South Asia. That is, although the nomadic or semi-nomadic tribal peoples on the Han empire's northern borders presented a perennial concern for the Han government, cultural exchanges invariably took place between the Han Chinese and the so-called *huren*. *Huren* was a disparaging term then coined by the Chinese to refer to all nomadic inhabitants in the *Xiyu* (lit. Western regions), which was a sweeping concept for the vast regions stretching from Northwest China to Central and South Asia in Chinese texts. In an article on the food culture in Han and post-Han China, David Knechtges, professor of Chinese at the University of Washington, points out that "the foods of the western regions can often be identified by the presence of the prefix *hu*, which in the early medieval period refers to the peoples of Central Asia, India, and 'more particularly to peoples of Iranian extraction.'"[25] *Xiyu* was at times a

---

[23] Fan, *HouHanshu* – "Li Du Liezhuan" (Biographies of Li Gu and Du Qiao), HDWZK, 2085.

[24] Fan Shengzhi, *Fan Shengzhi shu* (Fan Shengzhi's book), annotated Shi Shenghan (Beijing: Kexue chubanshe, 1956), 8–20; Cui Shi, *Simin yueling jiaozhu* (Annotated *Monthly Ordinances for the Four Peoples*), annotated Shi Shenghan (Beijing: Zhonghua shuju, 1965), 13, 60–64.

[25] David R. Knechtges, "Gradually Entering the Realm of Delight: Food and Drink in Early Medieval China," *Journal of the American Oriental Society*, 117:2 (April–June 1997), 231.

troublesome area for the Han Empire where assaults on its borders originated, but it was also a crucial pathway for the Empire to explore trade relations with its nomadic neighbors. The famed Silk Road, which passed through the region, is a prime example. Zhang Qian (164–114 BCE), a Han official who led a decade-long mission sent by Han Emperor Wu (r. 141–87 BCE) to the *Xiyu*, was a prominent figure in trailblazing the Silk Road. In Han historical records, Zhang was credited with bringing back many fruits, vegetables and grain crops, in addition to horses.[26] The most well known were alfalfa, peas, onion, broad bean, cucumber, carrot, walnut, grapes, pomegranate and sesame; all of them later became well integrated in the Chinese food system.

In fact, *bing* became a popular food in Han China also because of Central Asian influences. Toward the end of the third century, a writer named Shu Xi (263–302) wrote "Rhapsody on Pasta" (Bingfu), describing vividly a variety of *bing* available at that time. It gives a glowing and saliva-inducing description of how these *bing* were made – e.g. with or without meat – and what they tasted like when seasoned with different condiments and how to consume them. Jia Sixie's *Essential Techniques for the Peasantry*, the sixth-century agricultural encyclopedia, also includes a dozen recipes for making *bing*. These recipes reveal that some types of *bing* were made similarly to doughy foods such as baked pancakes (*shaob-ing*), hand-pulled noodles (*lamian*) and wonton (*huntun*), which are still consumed daily by many today.

At the outset of his beautifully rhymed essay, Shu Xi makes an interesting observation. "The making of the *bing*," he writes, "was something quite recent. It might, as I was told, have come from the common folks or even *originated in a foreign land* [emphasis added]." Shu was probably right in noting the *bing*'s origin, for in Han China, *hubing*, with the prefix *hu* for its Central Asian influence, seems to have been the quintessential *bing* of the age. The Han Emperor Ling (168–189 BCE), it was recorded, liked "*hu* clothes, *hu* tent, *hu* seat, *hu* [way of] sitting, *hu* food, *hu* harp, *hu* flute, and *hu* dances." And because of his interest in the exotic, "royal relatives and nobles at the capital all tried to follow suit." As a result, a "*hu* craze" swept over the entire Empire, which included hiring *hu* soldiers in the Han army. Dong Zhuo, the powerful warlord in the late Han, was known for bolstering his military prowess by using *hu* cavalry.[27] Without

---

[26] Sima, *Shiji* – "Dawan liezhuan" (Biography of Great Wan), HDWZK, 3166–3168; Ban Gu, *Hanshu* – "Dawan guo" (Kingdom of Great Wan), HDWZK, 3895.
[27] Fan, *HouHanshu* – "Fuyao" (Subdue the demon), HDWZK, 3272.

question, *hubing* was a doughy food, made of floured wheat. When Liu Xi described the six most common wheat foods in the second century, *hubing* was the first on the list. Liu described *hubing* as "a big flatbread with sesame seeds on top."[28] As such, it resembles *naan* bread, a daily starchy food of Central Asia then and now. The Uyghurs (a Turkic people) in Xinjiang, which is part of the *Xiyu*, call *naan* bread *nang* and still consume it daily.[29] In other parts of China, the popular *zhima shaobing* (baked sesame seed bread/pancakes) might be its variation.

Eating *hubing*, or baked bread and pancakes in general, does not usually require the use of utensils. This perhaps further proves that in most of Han China, spoons and chopsticks were not necessarily used together in eating a meal – particularly if the grain food was bread. As a craze, the once prevalent influence of Central Asian food began to taper off toward the late Han. For instance, despite *hubing*'s popularity, baking never became a leading cooking method in Chinese communities. The other common wheat foods described in Liu Xi's dictionary are early forms of noodles and dumplings, cooked by either boiling or steaming, the two more traditional Chinese methods. By the third century, when Shu Xi heaped his praise on wheat foods, most of them were already made and cooked in traditional Chinese ways. For instance, in place of baking, the Chinese steamed dough into *mantou* (steamed buns), or lightly pan-fried it into *mianbing* (pancakes). Then there were noodles, called *tangbing* (lit. dough in the soup) by Shu. Shu Xi also made specific recommendations on how to eat these varieties in tandem with seasonal changes. *Mantou* was best for a warm spring, he said, whereas *tangbing* was for the summer because it was cooked in water, which is needed for the body as it perspires in the heat. For the winter season, Shu suggested eating *mianbing* hot to cope with the cold weather.[30] Of these varieties, it seems Shu Xi personally preferred *mantou*, or steamed buns, which can be dubbed "Chinese bread." Over time, *mantou* became a daily food across

---

[28] Liu Xi, *Shiming* (Interpretation of names) (Taipei: Shangwu yinshuguan, 1965), *juan* 4, 62.

[29] Cf. Zhu Guozhao, "Zhongguo de yinshi wenhua yu sichou zhilu" (Chinese food and drink culture and the Silk Road), *Zhongguo yinshi wenhua* (Chinese food and drink culture), ed. Nakayama Tokiko, trans. Xu Jianxin (Beijing: Zhongguo shehui kexue chubanshe, 1990), 228–231. A more extensive discussion of the *naan* bread as *hubing* in ancient China is in He, *Tianshan jiayan*, 75–84.

[30] See Liu, *Zhongguo zhu wenhuashi*, 180–181. David Knechtges translates some of Shu Xi's rhapsody in his "Gradually Entering the Realm of Delight: Food and Drink in Early Medieval China," *Journal of the American Oriental Society*, 117:2 (April–June 1997), 236.

China, along with *baozi*, wheat dough with a filling (meat, vegetables, red bean paste, etc.) wrapped inside.

Baozi is made similarly to *jiaozi*, or Chinese dumplings, for both wrap food inside a thin flour skin. Also like *baozi*, *jiaozi* can be steamed, though boiled *jiaozi* seems to have been more common. A more significant difference lies in the way one eats them: *jiaozi* is transported by chopsticks whereas *baozi* is held by the hand. Chopsticks are also a convenient tool for eating noodles, another popular doughy food. As an expert on wheat foods, Shu Xi already observed in his time that chopsticks were most suitable for eating noodles.[31] In the following ages, these two forms of wheat foods became more popular than other varieties. Yan Zhitui (531–595), a prominent writer of his time, made a remark, exclaiming that the dumpling – which he called *huntun*, or wonton – had become so popular that it was indeed "a food for everyone in the world!" If this were the case, then it also continued in the centuries after.[32] The *Ennin's Diary*, written by Ennin (793–864), a Buddhist monk from Japan, chronicled his trip in Tang China during 838–847. When they traversed China, Ennin and his associates were at times offered *huntun* by the Chinese. They also ate noodles as often as – if not more than – wonton while in Tang China.[33]

Thanks to the popularity of noodles and dumplings in Han and post-Han China, chopsticks, perhaps for the first time, became employed also in conveying grain food, and the mixed form of both grain and nongrain food in particular. As discussed in the Introduction, once these forms of floured foods were created, then the traditional *fan-cai*, or grain and nongrain food, divide became irrelevant, for in making dumplings one blends the grain and nongrain foods in one unity, while in eating noodles one also tends to mix them with some sauce or broth. Chopsticks are quite adequate for conveying both dumplings and noodles. While drinking the broth in a soup noodle dish, a spoon can be of assistance, though it is not indispensable because one can raise the bowl to the mouth and drink the soup directly. In fact, this is even a recommended way among the Japanese: consuming the broth amounts to the final act in finishing the noodles. One is also

---

[31] Liu, *Zhongguo zhu wenhuashi*, 181.

[32] Duan Gonglu, *Beihulu* (Gazetteers of Guangdong), *juan* 2, ZJGK, 20. Many recipe books from the period, especially those written in the Tang, registered the popularity of dumplings in China. There were as many as twenty-four varieties of dumpling fillings, according to one recipe. See Nakayama, *Zhongguo yinshi wenhua*, 165.

[33] *Ennin's Diary: The Record of a Pilgrimage to China in Search of Law*, trans. Edwin Reischauer (New York: Ronald Press, 1955), 107, 141, 209, 295–296.

supposed to drink *miso* soup this way in Japan, after using chopsticks to pick up the foodstuffs therein.

Since dumplings and noodles are so important to the increased use of chopsticks, a brief review of their history perhaps is in order. Legend attributes the invention of dumplings to Zhang Zhongjing (150–219), a Han pharmacologist. The earliest example of dumplings, however, had appeared much earlier; it was found in a grave dating back to the fourth century BCE.[34] The Chinese term for dumplings – *jiaozi* – did not enter popular use until the Song dynasty (960–1279), but *huntun* appeared earlier. In *Guangya*, a comprehensive lexicon compiled by the philologist Zhang Yi in the early third century, *huntun* is described as a ball of dough shaped like the miniature crescent moon. Since the earliest noodle samples were discovered in China, the Chinese might take the credit as their inventor. Like pasta, noodles have several varieties, with *lamian* being the most well known. In classical Chinese, soup noodle was called either *suobing* (string noodle), or *tangbing*, or *shuiyinbing* (lit. noodle drawn/floated in the water) – the former refers to its shape and the latter to the way it is cooked in boiling water.[35] *Suobing* thus is thinner, more like vermicelli; it is called *sōmen* in Japanese and *somyeon* in Korean.

The popularity of noodles also extended beyond regions in East Asia westward, along the Silk Road, to Central Asia and beyond. That is to say, while the Han Chinese imported a number of plants and fruits from Central Asia, they also exported noodles to their neighbors through *Xiyu*, including today's Xinjiang. Ishige Naomichi, a Japanese expert on food cultures in East Asia, has noted that the Uyghur word *lagman/legman*, meaning filamentous noodles, which is commonly used by the peoples from Xinjiang to Central Asia, was derived from the Chinese term *lamian*.[36] And the spread continued further. In his philological study of medieval Turkish, Peter B. Golden discusses the "pasta complex,"

---

[34] Wang Renxiang, "Cong kaogu faxian kan Zhongguo gudaide yinshi wenhua chuantong" (Traditions of food and drink culture in ancient China shown in archaeological finds), *Hubei jingji xueyuan xuebao* (Journal of Hubei economics college), 2 (2004), 111. But Wang also notes that better shaped dumplings, resembling more the modern ones, were found in Xinjiang in the seventh century. Cf. Xinjiang Weiwuer zizhiqu bowuguan (Uyghur autonomous district in Xinjiang), "Xinjiang Tulufan Asitana beiqu muzang fajue jianbao" (Brief report on the excavation in the tombs of northern Astana, Turpan, Xinjiang), *Wenwu* (Cultural relics), 6 (1960), 20–21. Also, He, *Tianshan jiayan*, 85–86.

[35] See Jia Sixie, *Qimin yaoshu* (Essential techniques for the peasantry), http://zh.wikisource.org/zh/齊民要術, *juan* 9, "Bingfa" (methods in making doughy foods).

[36] Ishige, "Filamentous Noodles, '*Miantiao*': Their Origins and Diffusion," 122.

spreading from East Asia to the Mediterranean through the migration of such nomads as the Xiongnu and the Mongols from the first to the fourteenth centuries. Golden also notes the intrinsic relationship between eating noodles and chopsticks use. In medieval Turkish, he finds, chopsticks were glossed as "two sticks of wood with which macaroni is eaten."[37]

As chopsticks gained broader appeal as an eating implement, they also came to be made of more expensive and durable materials. To be sure, wooden and bamboo chopsticks remained the most common throughout the period, as they were more likely used by the masses. But archaeological digs in China have recorded a significant increase in metal chopsticks from the first century onward and, in particular, a great number of silver chopsticks between the sixth and the tenth centuries. Having looked over the unearthed samples of chopsticks, Liu Yun remarks that from the Neolithic Age, chopsticks were always made of different materials, ranging from bone and brass or bronze to bamboo and wood. In early Han tombs, such as in Mawangdui, bamboo chopsticks were common whereas toward the late Han, more brass utensils were found. "But in the Sui and Tang periods," Liu notices, "a significant change occurred," as many chopsticks were made of precious metals, jade and rare animal bones.[38]

Of the chopsticks unearthed in China from 1949 to the present, silver chopsticks have been found most frequently, totaling eighty-seven pairs, all dating between the sixth and the tenth centuries, or the Sui and Tang periods. The earliest sample of silver chopsticks in the group was unearthed near Xi'an, capital of the Sui dynasty (581–618),[39] but others appeared across the land. In fact, more silver chopsticks were discovered in the south, or the Yangzi River regions, than in the north. Of the eighty-seven pairs of silver chopsticks, thirty-six of them surfaced in Dantu, Jiangsu, and thirty were found in Changxing, Zhejiang.[40]

The uneven distribution of these unearthed silver chopsticks could be coincidental. But without question, the unprecedentedly large number of metal chopsticks, and the silver variety in particular, found from the Sui

---

[37] Peter B. Golden, "Chopsticks and Pasta in Medieval Turkic Cuisine," *Rocznik orientalisticzny*, 49 (1994–1995), 71–80.

[38] Liu, *Zhongguo Zhu wenhuashi*, 215.

[39] Zhongguo shehui kexueyuan kaogu yanjiusuo (The Institute of Archaeology, Chinese Academy of the Social Sciences), *Tang Chang'an chengjiao Suimu* (The Sui tombs near the Tang capital Chang'an) (Beijing: Wenwu chubanshe, 1980).

[40] Liu, *Zhongguo zhu wenhuashi*, 215–219.

and Tang periods suggests that they were in vogue at the time. Multiple reasons might account for this new phenomenon. One could be the concern for durability, as mentioned above, since chopsticks now took on more duties – transferring not only nongrain but also grain food. The other might be due to the common belief that silver could detect arsenic poisoning in food, hence making silver chopsticks desired by the rich and powerful in China and beyond. The third factor, to be discussed below, might have something to do with the increased consumption of meat, lamb and mutton in particular, among the northern Chinese in the Tang period.

Additionally, Liu Yun and his cowriters argue that improved living standards and metallurgical technology in the Tang made metal chopsticks more available in that period. Their argument is based on the finding that some of the silver and other metal chopsticks had exquisite carvings on top or were even plated with fine gold; both had not been seen before. In other words, during the Tang, crafted or artistic chopsticks – *gongyi zhu* in Chinese and *kogei bashi* in Japanese – appeared (Plate 27).[41] Demonstrating advanced technology, these crafted chopsticks also attest to the improved life under the Tang as well as the elevated status of chopsticks, which began to be exchanged as gifts.

The Tang dynasty was another golden age in Chinese imperial history, rivaling the previous Han dynasty in importance. The Tang Empire occupied a large territory; the part on the west stretched to Inner Asia during most of its rule. As such, the Tang kept open the channel for Central and South Asian influences to filter into China proper. Some ancestors of the Li family who founded the Tang dynasty originally came from the prairieland. After establishing their government, Tang rulers designed and promoted policies to encourage trade and commerce between the Han Chinese and their nomadic neighbors to the north and northwest. They also allowed the practice of different religious faiths and fostered cultural exchanges in the region. Thus the period under Tang rule is commonly called an era of cosmopolitanism in East Asian history. It was during this cosmopolitan age that the chopsticks cultural sphere took deeper roots and also expanded in Asia (e.g. into Japan).

Tang rulers' open-mindedness encouraged diverse culinary practices to coexist among the different peoples under its rule. To some extent, this was the default choice for the Tang government because after the fall of the Han dynasty, North China had become overrun by several nomadic groups, causing massive migration: Chinese farming communities from

[41] Ibid., 222–225.

the region moved southward, mostly to the Yangzi River regions. In Chinese history, this post-Han period is usually referred to as the "period of southern and northern dynasties" because as the nomads established their regimes in North and Northwest China, the émigré groups who retreated from the north (re)created their governments in South and Southwest China. In both the north and south, the kingdoms were short-lived; none was able to conquer the others and unify the land until the rise of the Sui dynasty in the late sixth century, followed by Tang rule in the early seventh century. All this meant that the northern and southern divide in foodway and cookery continued. Given the nomadic influence, the people in the north, for example, consumed more meat and dairy foods, whereas the people in the south took rice, fish and vegetables as their daily foods. This difference in food intake and taste is well reflected in literature. Yang Xuanzhi's *Records of Buddhist Temples in Luoyang* (Luoyang qielanji), an expansive literary and historical text written in the mid-sixth century, described how when Wang Su, a southerner, worked for the Northern Wei dynasty (386–534), a nomadic regime in North China, he retained his habit of eating rice and fish stew and drinking tea, instead of taking lamb and drinking milk as most others around him did. Indeed, while Wang Su was disgusted by the northern diet, the northerners also disliked and mocked his eating habits.[42]

The interregnum between the fall of the Han and the rise of the Tang also saw the commencement of the formative period of Buddhist influence in East Asia. But interestingly, Buddhist influence too was received differently in China. Even though Mahayana Buddhism, the prevalent sect in East Asia, is generally believed to have entered China through the northern route, and Buddhism frowned upon animal killing, the people in the north still consumed more meat than did their southern counterparts. While discussing the Buddhist culinary influence in East Asia, Yao Weijun observes that since meat and dairy foods had been so essential among the Mongols, the Tibetans and their peers, their Buddhists, past and present, have never practiced meat prohibition.[43] This is a succinct observation. In the south, however, Buddhist conversion discouraged meat consumption, perhaps because animal meat was not as important in the traditional diet as in the north. In 521, Emperor Wu (aka Xiao Yan, 464–549) of the Southern

---

[42] Wang Lihua, *Zhonggu huabei yinshi wenhuade bianqian* (Changes in food and drink culture of North China during the middle imperial period) (Beijing: Zhongguo shehui kexue chubanshe, 2001), 278

[43] Yao Weijun, "*Fojiao yu Zhongguo yinshi wenhua*" (Buddhism and the food and drink culture in China), *Minzhu* (Democracy monthly), 9 (1997), 32–33.

Liang dynasty (502–557) issued the first decree prohibiting meat. Known for his devotion to Buddhism, which earned him the sobriquet of "the Buddhist Monarch" in history, Emperor Wu practiced asceticism and stayed away from meat in his diet. He only ate one meal a day, which consisted merely of coarse rice and bean stew without alcohol or meat.[44]

Several Tang rulers were also known as Buddhist followers but by and large meat consumption was not prohibited in the Empire (the south included), possibly due to the Li family's nomadic ancestry from the northwest regions. In a paper on the Central Asian influence on the northwestern Chinese diet, E. N. Anderson finds that "the northwestern cuisine shares a fondness for meat, especially lamb, a flesh otherwise little used in China."[45] This is not surprising. In his *Essential Techniques for the Peasantry*, Jia Sixie, who spent most of his life in the north before the Tang, already details methods of raising animals, goat and sheep in particular, for consumption. Wang Lihua, a Chinese food scholar, also observes that from the fifth century, lamb gradually became the more preferred meat among the Chinese. Drawing on a number of historical sources, Wang argues that during the Tang period, lamb had already replaced pork to become the more consumed meat in North China. The Tang government, he notes, often rewarded its outstanding officials with lamb meat, but seldom with other animal flesh. As a result, lamb was also mentioned most frequently in Tang historical texts.[46] In brief, meat consumption rose in Tang China as compared with that in the earlier periods.

Of course, it remains perhaps an issue for debate whether the phenomenon of increased meat consumption in Tang society can help explain the majority of metal utensils excavated from that period. People's taste in things could have been influenced by practical needs as well as by tradition, custom and belief. But it is also obvious that metal is more hard-wearing than wood and bamboo and that cooked meat remains tougher than fish and vegetables – the latter tend to dissolve after heat is applied. Koreans' preference for metal utensils, which is somewhat unique in the chopsticks cultural sphere, might support the speculation, for meat figures more centrally in Korean cuisines than in any other Asian cuisines. Korean

---

[44] Yao Silian, *Liangshu* (History of the Southern Liang dynasty) – "Wudi benji" (Biography of Emperor Wu), HDWZK, 63–94.

[45] E. N. Anderson, "Northwest Chinese Cuisine and the Central Asian Connection," *Di 6 jie Zhongguo yinshi wenhua xueshu yantaohui lunwenji* (Proceedings of the 6th academic symposium on Chinese food and drink culture) (Taipei: Zhongguo yinshi wenhua jijinhui, 1999), 173.

[46] Wang, *Zhonggu huabei yinshi wenhua de bianqian*, 112–116.

chopsticks were traditionally made of brass and bronze but nowadays are made more of stainless steel. Sharing the Chinese belief that silver can detect poison, wealthy Koreans also prefer silver chopsticks, then and now. By contrast, meat had been generally excluded from Japanese cookery for many centuries until the modern era. The Japanese have overwhelmingly favored wooden chopsticks; the metal variety seems to have had no appeal for them. (Other reasons for the Japanese to choose wooden chopsticks will be discussed in the next chapter.)

Eating more meat and meat-based dishes often turns people to the knife and fork. But in Tang China, the most common utensils remained *bizhu*, or spoon and chopsticks, as in the earlier periods. Following the culinary tradition of the Han and pre-Han periods, the Chinese continued to prepare meat in bite-size morsels before cooking. As a result, chopsticks remained the ideal tool for conveying food. Moreover, besides boiling and stewing, a new cooking method, stir-frying, gained ground beginning in the post-Han period; its popularity reinforced and ensured the continual prevalence of chopsticks in this role. Stir-frying requires that one first heat the cooking oil in a pan or a wok before putting in the ingredients, which are already cut into small pieces for easy frying and better mixing. One important advantage of stir-frying is its energy efficiency – cooking food rapidly on the flame instead of heating it for a long time, as in baking and roasting.[47] Extending the culinary tradition of cutting meat and other foodstuffs in small portions, stir-frying not only shortens the cooking time but also brings out the blended taste of all the components in the dish. Historical texts show that as milling became widely adopted to process grain food during the Han era, the Chinese also ground other plants such as sesame seeds and rapeseeds to make cooking oil. For instance, in his *Essential Techniques for the Peasantry*, Jia Sixie discusses ways to plant and grow sesame. He also offers recipes for cooking dishes with sesame oil. One recipe in his book is for cooking scrambled eggs. What is intriguing is that Jia's method, except for recommending using sesame oil, is exactly the same as how people cook scrambled eggs today.[48] From the Tang period, thanks to the use of high-quality charcoal, stir-frying became a more popular and more mature cooking method. Indeed, scholars have regarded this cooking method as one of the important breakthroughs in the Chinese culinary

[47] Roberts, *China to Chinatown*, 21–22.
[48] Jia, *Qimin yaoshu*, http://zh.wikisource.org/zh/齊民要術, *juan* 6, "Yangji" (raising chickens).

tradition.[49] As the food items are small in a stir-fried dish, chopsticks become an effective tool for picking them up. Indeed, some may even use the utensil to stir-fry the dish – to turn, arrange and mix the ingredients for a better result.

Despite the strong evidence that chopsticks gained more appeal in Tang society, the spoon retained its original function in conveying *fan*, grain starch, which remained for many a more important component in a meal. Of course, what constituted *fan* in the Tang reflected regional differences as before. Due to the continued southern/northern divide in Chinese food culture, rice had to be the daily staple for the people living around the Yangzi River regions, as it had been for the previous centuries. Unfortunately, most literary sources from the period are from North China, where the Tang central government was located. And in the north and northwest, millet remained the leading grain. Besides its toughness in resisting drought and flood, millet also has another advantage: it is immune to insects, which turned it into the best reserve grain for famine relief. The Tang document records that the government stored millet in granaries. But interestingly, the same source also reveals that wheat had become a reserve grain too in the Tang granaries.[50]

In other words, due to the continual attraction of floured wheat foods, the daily grain food consumed by the northern Chinese became more diversified – millet's dominance was undermined by wheat.[51] "Wherever a Tang text talks about food," finds Wang Saishi, another scholar of Tang food culture, "it uses ubiquitously the term '*bing*' [doughy food]." He also notes that compared with the Han period, the variety of *bing* multiplied notably in this period. *Hubing*, the *naan* bread of which many Chinese in the Han had become enamored, remained popular. Yet its popularity was now challenged by the *zhengbing* (steamed bread/bun) and the *jianbing* (pan-fried bread/cake), the latter cooked with heated oil. There were also more varieties of *tangbing* (noodles) in the Tang. For instance, the Tang people ate both hot and cold noodles; the latter resembles the way *soba*

---

[49] Liu, *Zhongguo zhu wenhuashi*, 205. Zhao Rongguang states that stir-frying began in the post-Han period, made more strides during the Tang and eventually became a mature and widely adopted cooking method in the post-Tang periods. *Zhongguo yinshi wenhua gailun*, 173–174. K. C. Chang deemed stir-frying to be one of the revolutions in Chinese culinary history, "Zhongguo yinshishi shangde jici tupo" (Several revolutions in the Chinese food history), *Di 4 jie Zhogguo yinshi wenhua xueshu yantaohui lunwenji* (Proceedings of the 4th academic symposium of Chinese food and drink culture) (Taipei: Zhongguo yinshi wenhua jijinhui, 1996), 1–109.

[50] See Bray, *Science and Civilization in China*, vol. 6, pt. 2, 420.

[51] Wang, *Zhonggu huabei yinshi wenhuade bianqian*, 69.

(buckwheat noodle) is consumed in Japan today. Tang texts also showed that, as is common in North China today, a noodle dish became a food for guests in Tang society.[52]

Yet besides wheat doughy foods, *fan* to the northern Chinese still meant boiled or steamed grains, usually millet (both the broomcorn and foxtail varieties) and wheat, which were continued to be boiled whole in making porridge and gruel.[53] Thus in a Tang text, *fan* usually denoted a mushy form of cooked grain food. In their poems and essays, Tang writers described how they applied a spoon in scooping *fan*. Xue Lingzhi (683–?), a once high-ranking official dismissed by Emperor Xuanzong (r. 712–756), masks his discontent in a poem, in which he complains how he was unappreciated by the Emperor, just as someone uses the wrong utensil to eat a meal: "when cereal (*fan*) is sticky, it is hard to use a spoon whereas if a stew (*geng*) is thin, then chopsticks need to be rounder."[54] Xue's poem helps confirm that the people then used spoons for eating *fan* and chopsticks for *cai*. Xue also says that *fan* should not be cooked viscously (like cooked rice?), for it is hard for the spoon to transport it. In a letter to a friend, Han Yu (768–824), another Tang scholar-official, also writes that he used the spoon to convey *fan*, particularly if it was mushy when cooked. As he was aging and had loose teeth, Han tells his friend, he preferred the *fan* cooked rather soft and soggy so it could be scooped easily with a spoon. He would then slowly and repeatedly chew on it like a cow regurgitating its cud.[55]

One can imagine that since it was so mushy, the *fan* Han Yu preferred might have been more like *zhou* (porridge) in texture. Yet the distinction between *zhou* and *fan* never seems so definitive, but porous and fluid. Some *zhou* can be quite consistent, or thick like gruel, whereas some *fan* can contain much liquid, and hence be rather mushy. From the post-Han period through the late nineteenth century, in addition to *zhou* and *fan*, the Chinese coined and employed such terms as *shuifan* (lit. watered cereal) and *tangfan* (lit. cereal in hot water), which bordered as well as bridged the

[52] Wang Saishi, *Tangdai yinshi* (Food and drink culture in the Tang) (Ji'nan: Qilu shushe, 2003), 1–17; quote on 2.

[53] Ibid., 18–24. A search in the Tang texts in ZJGK shows that *maifan* appeared a total of fifty times, compared with *shufan* (broomcorn millet) which appeared eighty times and *sufan* (foxtail millet) fifty-five times.

[54] Xue Lingzhi's poem is in Wang Dingbao, *Tang zhiyan* (Anecdotes of Tang literati), *juan* 15, ZJGK, 90.

[55] Han Yu, "Zeng Liu Shifu" (To Liu Shifu), *Changli xiansheng wenji* (Essays of Han Yu), *juan* 5, ZJGK, 38.

zhou–fan distinction. And from the Ming dynasty (1368–1644) a new term *xifan* (lit. thinned or diluted cereal) gained currency. Interchangeable with *zhou*, *xifan* remains in use in modern Chinese. Both terms refer to a kind of grain cereal cooked in a liquid form, though the ways they are made may be slightly different.[56] Both *zhou* and *xifan* are best eaten with a spoon.

Tang literary writers and poets, like Han Yu, often called the spoon for scooping *fan liuchi*. Combining the character *liu* (flowing and floating) and *chi* (spoon), the term connotes, figuratively, that when put into use, the utensil enables its user to dig swiftly into the *fan* and scoop it up effortlessly. That is, *liuchi* was a type of spoon that would not allow extra grains to adhere to it. To stress its effectiveness, Tang poets often used the verb "slide/ glide" (*hua*) to describe how *liuchi* worked in eating *fan*. In a short poem about a lavish dinner, Bai Juyi (772–846), a Tang poet contemporaneous with Han Yu, exclaimed, and exaggerated: "The fish is so delicious whose fat dropped on the flame below making flickers; the cereal granules are so refined and smooth that they slide on the spoon [down to my mouth]."[57]

In order to achieve such an effect – moving a spoon smoothly into the *fan* and scooping it freely as one desires – it seems that two conditions must be met. One is that the spoon must have a smooth surface and the other is that the cooked grain food must contain a certain amount of water to make it less gluey. The first condition seems to be there as most utensils in Tang China were made of metal, silver or brass, which tends to have a smoother surface than the wooden ones. The second condition is hard to prove with material evidence, but the frequent usage of *liuchi* – its combination with the verb *hua* – in Tang literature seems to indicate that the *fan* consumed by the people during that period could have bordered between *fan* and *zhou* as they do in modern days. It had to contain enough liquid for people to scoop it up swiftly without extra grains sticking to their spoons.[58] Scholars

---

[56] *Shuifan* is first mentioned in Ge Hong, *Zhouhou beijifang* (Convenient prescriptions for emergencies), ZJGK, 74, and *Xifan* is first found in Feng Menglong, *Jin'gu qiguan* (Curious spectacles of past and present), *juan* 32, 410. A search in ZJGK shows that *xifan* was not used until the Ming, whereas *zhou* has been in use since antiquity. In some regions, *zhou* is made by boiling the grain whereas *xifan* is made by adding water to the already cooked grain, or *fan*, to make it watery.

[57] Bai Juyi, *Baishi changqing ji* (Collected works of Bai Juyi), ZJGK, 604.

[58] It must be noted that in literary writings, it was a cliché for poets and essayists to describe how they ate *fan* with the *liuchi* spoon effortlessly. That is, whenever *liuchi* was used, they used the verb *hua* to go with it, even after, as we now believe, the spoon was no longer in use for transporting grain food. A search in ZJGK finds that the phrase appeared a total of 143 times (*hualiuchi* ninety-five times and *liuchihua* forty-eight times) in the texts from the Tang to the Qing.

have also pointed out that porridge was popular during the Tang period because many believed that it had a medicinal effect, ideal for a patient.[59] Archaeological excavations have provided confirmation: two types of spoons have appeared in Tang tombs, one has a shallower – almost flat – bowl and shorter handle and the other a deeper and larger bowl and a longer handle. The former is believed to be used for grain food whereas the latter is for drinking soup.[60] By contrast, the dagger-like *bi* with a sharp edge, ubiquitously seen in the Neolithic Age, had by and large disappeared. But the term *bi* remained in use, still referring to a spoon, for several centuries.[61]

In addition, Tang texts reveal that the decline of millet as the most important grain cereal was due as much to the growing appeal of wheat as to the spread of rice across China. Wheat and wheat-based foods entered Tang poetry quite frequently. Yet a number of Tang poems also describe rice farming in areas of North China where rice is rarely grown nowadays. Ennin, the Japanese monk, mentioned that rice porridge was typically provided at Buddhist temples as he crisscrossed Tang China.[62] Thus during the Tang, while wheat consumption increased significantly, the government also encouraged rice farming in North China, especially in the Guanzhong region where the Tang capital Chang'an was located.[63] Rice was then grown in Guanzhong, it seems, not only because the region was relatively moist, ideal for growing rice, but also because there was a great demand for it from the people working for the Tang government. As mentioned before, for the northern Chinese, eating rice had been tantamount to leading a good, even luxurious, life in China since the age of Confucius. Ennin's diary recorded that the price of rice was still higher than that of millet in Tang China.[64] One could imagine that officials

---

[59] Liu Pubing, *TangSong yinshi wenhua bijiao yanjiu* (A comparative study of food and drinking cultures in the Tang and Song periods) (Beijing: Zhongguo shehui kexue chubanshe, 2010), 119–121.

[60] Liu, *Zhongguo zhu wenhuashi*, 219–221.

[61] In his study of the food culture in Han China, H. T. Huang has also noticed the shift from dagger-shaped spoons to lacquered wooden ones. He noted that the latter first appeared in the late Zhou period and "reached the heights of popularity during the Han." Huang, "Han Gastronomy," 148.

[62] *Ennin's Diary*, 31, 56, 66, 73–74, 157, 172. It should be noted that Ennin used the character *zhou*, which usually refers to rice porridge and which was what he often consumed at breakfast in China, though *zhou* could also be made of millet or other grains, which he mentioned on page 190.

[63] Wang, *Zhonggu huabei yinshi wenhuade bianqian*, 74–80; and Liu, *TangSong yinshi wenhua bijiao yanjiu*, 57–58.

[64] *Ennin's Diary*, 190.

working in the Tang capital, many of whom had succeeded in the civil service examination instituted by the government, might be interested in eating rice to show their success in climbing up the social ladder.[65] Du Fu (712–770), a famous poet, might not be the best example, for his official career in the Tang government did not go very far. Yet he left a poem about eating rice at a dinner near the Tang capital Chang'an. As a northerner, Du was very impressed by the quality of rice; he compared rice grains to the white stones (*yunzi*; lit. small cloud) in the Go game (*weiqi*), a popular chess game in China and East Asia. In his later life, Du spent several years in Chengdu, Sichuan, a rice-growing region in the upper reaches of the Yangzi River. But to stick to the tradition, Du scooped rice with a spoon, according to his poem.[66]

In his study of the Tang food system, Wang Lihua has argued that since North China was a political center during the period, "rice should have occupied a much higher ratio of all grain production than it does today." During the Tang, he explains, irrigation was developed to an unprecedented level to nourish rice paddies. But court records from the period also contained a number of legal disputes over the irrigated water because some used it instead to drive the waterwheel to power the flourmill.[67] The competition for water usage, states Wang, reflected the growing interest in rice farming as opposed to wheat milling. Edward H. Shafer also recognizes that rice was grown more than before in North China. But he maintains that "even through rice was grown in the north in Tang times, it could not rival wheat and millet there."[68] So in North China, the *fan* in the Tang remained mostly made of millet and wheat, instead of rice. And because of the draw of tradition, even if people ate rice, they might continue employing a spoon. Xue Lingzhi's case is quite telling. Having grown up in Fujian where rice was the staple grain, he would have known that he could use chopsticks to move rice as effectively as the spoon. But he says in his poem that he used a spoon in eating *fan*.

---

[65] Using examinations to recruit government officials was first attempted during the Sui dynasty in the sixth century. But it was during the Tang period that the system became fully institutionalized. Tang records show a dramatic increase in rice (from 200,000 *shi* to over three million *shi*) being transported from the south to the north from the early Tang to the late Tang. See Li Hu, ed. *Han Tang yinshi wenhuashi* (A cultural history of the food culture in Han and Tang China) (Beijing: Beijing shifan daxue chubanshe, 1998), 13.

[66] Yang Lun, *Dushi jingquan* (Annotated poems of Du Fu), *juan* 2, ZJGK, 39.

[67] Wang, *Zhonggu huabei yinshi wenhuade bianqian*, 75.

[68] Edward H. Shafer, "T'ang," *Food in Chinese Culture*, 89.

In sum, from Han to Tang China, several notable changes took place in agriculture and food culture, which impacted utensil use. Early in the period, using spoons and chopsticks, rather than one's hands, to eat a meal, became a well-established dining habit in Chinese society. Throughout the period, the spoon was a primary eating implement, for millet more or less retained its importance as a grain cereal and required the spoon to transport it for convenience as well as for modishness (as it was recommended by ancient Confucian rituals). But thanks to the broad appeal and increasing variety of floured wheat foods, especially the popularity of noodles, people all across China seemed to realize the usefulness of chopsticks and apparently began to use the instrument more than before in conveying both grain and nongrain foods. As a result, chopsticks gained significant inroads in undermining the spoon's primacy as a utensil. Little wonder that in both stone carvings and mural paintings of the Han and the Tang, chopsticks were often depicted as the main – sometimes the only – utensil in many eating scenes (Plate 10). Thanks to the widespread influence of Tang culture in Asia, the growing popularity of chopsticks also became extended beyond the Tang territorial border, into such regions as the Mongolian pastureland in the north, the Korean Peninsula and the Japanese islands in the northeast and east, and the Indochina Peninsula in the south. A chopsticks cultural sphere thus began to take shape, albeit with discernible variations in time and place.

4

Forming a chopsticks cultural sphere: Vietnam, Japan, Korea and beyond

> The harmony between Oriental food and chopsticks cannot be merely functional, instrumental; the foodstuffs are cut up so they can be grasped by the sticks, but also the chopsticks exist because the foodstuffs are cut into small pieces; one and the same movement, one and the same form transcends the substance and its utensil: division.
>
> Roland Barthes, *Empire of Signs*

In 1996 Samuel P. Huntington (1927–2008), then professor of government at Harvard University, published *The Clash of Civilizations and the Remaking of World Order*, a *New York Times* bestseller that year. Huntington argued that three major civilizations had been formed in the world: the Western Judeo-Christian civilization, the East Asian Confucian civilization and the Middle Eastern Islamic civilization. Interestingly, if this tripartite partition could indeed map out the world, then these civilizations are distinguished from one another not only in terms of religious traditions, cultural ideals and political institutions (factors Huntington considers most seriously) but they also differ in culinary practices and dining customs, which are little noted in Huntington's book. As mentioned in the Introduction, from the 1970s, food historians in Japan, such as Isshiki Hachirō, and American historian Lynn White in the 1980s had already observed that three dining customs, or food cultural spheres, existed in the world: (1) eating with hand(s); (2) eating with forks, knives and spoons; and (3) eating with chopsticks. Isshiki detailed that the first sphere, constituting about forty percent of the world's population, consists of peoples living in South and Southeast Asia, the Middle and Near East, and Africa. The second sphere, about thirty percent of the population, is composed of the peoples of Europe and North and South America. And the third, or the chopsticks cultural sphere, constituting another thirty percent of the world population, includes the Chinese, the Japanese, Koreans and the Vietnamese. These marked differences in dining customs, Isshiki further explained, reflect and extend the differences in food intake (e.g. whether one eats meat or not and whether the grain staple is a plant or a root tuber), food preparation, and eating etiquette and table manners.[1] Geographically and demographically speaking, Isshiki's, White's and Huntington's divisions of the world are identical.

Yet these overarching generalizations tend to overlook subtle differences within a particular sphere. While using chopsticks to carry food is a distinct dietary custom, their users have, at times, also employed other implements to assist the transportation. An observant visitor to the chopsticks cultural sphere may see visible differences in what kinds of chopsticks people use and how they use them, whether or not they also use a spoon, and when and how. For instance, although chopsticks are made of various materials, wooden chopsticks seem most popular, preferred particularly by the Japanese. In an up-market restaurant in Japan, customers are usually given a pair of whitewood chopsticks, possibly of willow tree wood, whereas on the same occasion in China, its customers more likely find on the table a colorful porcelain spoon and a pair of chopsticks that have either a gold-plated top or a top decorated with exquisite engravings. In Korea, employing both a spoon and a pair of chopsticks is seen everywhere, and the implements are usually made of metal, such as stainless steel. Beginning in ancient China, besides wood, the Chinese used bamboo to make chopsticks, and both remain popular today. Bamboo chopsticks are widely used in Vietnam too, since the plant is common. Yet Vietnam is also well known for exporting high-quality rosewood chopsticks to the rest of Asia. While the Vietnamese use bamboo chopsticks whereas the Japanese wooden ones, they do share one thing in common: compared with other chopsticks users, both the Vietnamese and the Japanese tend to take chopsticks as the only utensil in dining, without the spoon. How do these differences occur? Have they changed over time? This chapter will address these questions while covering and discussing the history and the characteristics of the chopsticks cultural sphere.

In describing the formation of the chopsticks cultural sphere, it seems logical to begin with Vietnam, for among all of China's neighbors the Vietnamese could be the earliest in adopting the dining custom of utensil

---

[1] Isshiki, *Hashi no Bunkashi*, 36–39.

use, and chopsticks use in particular, from China. In his survey of Vietnamese history and culture, Nguyen Van Huyen (1908–1975), an eminent historian in Vietnam, describes the dietary custom in his country as follows:

At meals, the dishes are placed on a wooden or copper tray which is displayed in the middle of the bed. The participants eat while sitting around with crossed legs. Each has his bowl and his pair of chopsticks. The dishes are common for all, one uses one's chopsticks to take foodstuffs which are prepared and cut into small pieces.[2]

This description, without question, can be readily applied to characterizing the cooking and dining practices in China. This is understandable because since antiquity, the Vietnamese foodway, or that of mainland Southeast Asia in general, has shared resounding similarities with that of South China. Meanwhile, Vietnam was distinguished from its Southeast Asian neighbors in history: from approximately the third century BCE to about the tenth century, various Chinese governments exercised their control over the land, especially in the north, making Vietnam much more receptive to Chinese influences.

As in South China, or the Yangzi River or Pearl River regions, rice has been the dominant grain crop in Vietnam. Although the earliest rice remains have so far been found in the Yangzi River Delta, it is believed that rice had been grown in Vietnam no later than in South China, in the Neolithic Age. Vietnam indeed was one of the origin places of Asian rice. "Wet-rice cultivation," writes Francesca Bray, "established in the Red River Delta by the mid-third millennium BC, or perhaps earlier."[3] The Red River Delta produces rice as its main crop because the region, especially the Mekong River Delta, is crisscrossed by a maze of rivers and lakes. Fish thus also became the main produce in Vietnam. When characterizing the food culture of South China, Sima Qian, the Han historian, states that "rice was the chief grain and fish stew the main dish." This statement could readily apply to the food culture in Vietnam, just as Nguyen Van Huyen's description of Vietnamese dining customs could be applied to the Chinese's.

Like the Chinese living in the reaches of the Yangzi River, the Vietnamese take rice as their daily food and fish-based dishes as their main nongrain food. In the Vietnamese language, a plethora of proverbs describe the centrality of rice and fish. "Nothing is [better than] rice with

[2] Nguyen Van Huyen, *The Ancient Civilization of Vietnam* (Hanoi: The Gioi Publishers, 1995), 212.
[3] Francesca Bray, *The Rice Economies: Technology and Development in Asian Societies* (Berkeley: University of California Press, 1994), 9–10.

fish," one maxim goes, "Nothing is [better than] a mother with a child." And "If you have rice," goes another, "you've all. You are short of rice, short of all." For the Vietnamese, to treat a guest is to treat them with rice and fish. "When you go out," they tell the visitor, "you can eat fish; when you come in, you can consume [glutinous] rice." Many varieties of rice are thus cultivated in Vietnam. Some are planted on the dry upland as in the lowland paddies. A Vietnamese aphorism states, "If you have upland rice, you can sleep peacefully; if you have lowland rice, you can sleep up your fill." More interestingly, an adage in *muòng* Deng, a rice-producing region, suggests that stew, too, is a well-liked dish: "If you want to eat rice, go to *muòng* Deng; if you want to eat *keng* [geng], go to *muòng* Ha."[4] That is, as in South China, fish stew may well be the most common dish for the locals.

Many of the rice-eating customs among the Vietnamese and the southern Chinese are also comparable. For example, they both cultivate glutinous rice (*nuo* in Chinese) and regard it as a festive and ritual food. In Vietnamese, the glutinous rice is *gao nep*, while the ordinary type is *gao te*. In celebrating the New Year in China and Vietnam, which occurs on the first day of the first month of the lunar calendar in both countries, steamed glutinous rice cakes are indispensable. These rice cakes take various forms in China, whereas in Vietnam one kind of rice cake, or *banh Tet*, is particularly reserved for the New Year celebration. Nir Avieli, an anthropologist at the University of Pittsburgh, has called *banh Tet* an "iconic festive dish," essential to the Vietnamese national identity. In preparing the *banh Tet*, the Vietnamese usually first soak the glutinous rice in water overnight and then mix it with pork and green beans before wrapping and tying it up with bamboo leaves and splinters. It is then cooked for many hours in water before serving.[5] The way to prepare and cook the rice cake is identical to how the southern Chinese make *zongzi*, a ritual food now most consumed during the Dragon Boat Festival across South China and Taiwan. The *zongzi* is for commemorating the death of Qu Yuan (339–278 BCE), an official-cum-poet in the State of Chu, one of the Warring States in China. But in the southern part of Zhejiang, which

---

[4] Quotes from Nir Avieli, "Eating Lunch and Recreating the Universe: Food and Cosmology in Hoi An, Vietnam," *Everyday Life in Southeast Asia*, eds. Kathleen M. Adams & Kathleen A. Gillogly (Bloomington: Indiana University Press, 2011), 222; and Nguyen Xuan Hien, "Rice in the Life of the Vietnamese Thay and Their Folk Literature," trans. Tran Thi Giang Lien & Hoang Luong, *Anthropos*, Bd. 99 H. 1 (2004), 111–141.

[5] Nir Avieli, "Vietnamese New Year Rice Cakes: Iconic Festive Dishes and Contested National Identity," *Ethnology*, 44:2 (Spring 2005), 167–188.

bordered Nanyue (*Nam Viet* in Vietnamese), an early Chinese kingdom in Vietnam, there has also been a time-honored custom to eat *zongzi* during the New Year season.

Rice cakes can also be made with rice flour. While the people in North China grind wheat grain into flour and make doughy food, the southern Chinese and the Vietnamese powder rice, their grain staple. Powdered rice, especially the glutinous variety, is used to make either salted or sugared cakes as principal food offerings at cultural and religious ceremonies. They are not wrapped in leaves but often colored with some leaf extract. Since these cakes are mostly steamed, chopsticks might be the ideal tool to pick them up in the steamer when hot. As celebratory food, however, these cakes are often eaten after the ceremony. In other words, they are not eaten hot, so one can hold them in one's hands. Rice cakes are a common food not only in South China and Vietnam, but also across Southeast Asia, where rice is grown and where rice cakes are more customarily eaten with fingers.

With rice flour, one can also make rice noodles. Rice noodles are transported with chopsticks in China, Vietnam and even elsewhere in Southeast Asia. In recent decades, *pho* (rice vermicelli), a noodle soup often served with thinly sliced beef, Asian basil, mint leaves, lime and bean sprouts, has become arguably the most famous Vietnamese food outside Vietnam. But in fact, rice noodle soups, served with different ingredients, are a staple dish across South and Southwest China and many other places in Southeast Asia. Rice noodles can be served with a broth, as in the case of *pho*, but they can also be stir-fried over high heat, as in the case of *char kway teow*, a common noodle dish in Singapore, Taiwan, Malaysia and Indonesia. *Char kway teow* is usually cooked with beansprouts, whole prawns, Chinese chives, and soy and chili sauces. Both *pho* and *char kway teow* registered culinary influences from China; the word *pho* is derived from *fun*, or "rice noodle" in Cantonese, and *char kway teow* comes from *chhá-kóe-tiâu* in Hokkien, a language spoken by the Chinese in southern Fujian. It is likely that emigrant Chinese communities initially brought these noodle dishes to Southeast Asia.[6]

Migration, whether forced or voluntary, was an important means of intercultural exchange.[7] In early imperial China, after a successful

---

[6] See entries on *pho* and *char kway teow* on Wikipedia. As for the origin of *pho*, the entry says that the term might be derived from the French word *pot-au-feu* (beef stew).

[7] Jack Goody notes how immigration caused the spread of foods around the modern world, which, it seems to me, was also true in ancient ages. *Food and Love: A Cultural History of East and West* (London: Verso, 1998), 161–171.

campaign the Qin and Han dynasties often created garrison forces, which later became emigrant communities, on the newly conquered borderland regions for the purposes of defense and colonization. In historical texts from the period, such as the work by Sima Qian, the areas that encompassed the whole littoral zone of Southeast China, extending from the modern Zhejiang and Fujian Provinces to the Red River Valley in northern Vietnam, are referred to under an umbrella term *Yue*. In the Warring States period, the State of Yue, centering in Zhejiang, was once a strong power.[8] *Yue* is written as *Viet* in Vietnamese and Vietnam is called *Yuenan* in Chinese, which literally means "south of *Yue*." After Qinshihuang, the founding emperor of the Qin dynasty (221–206 BCE), unified China proper, or North China, he immediately sent five armies to conquer the Yue lands. Zhao Tuo (*c.* 230–137 BCE; Trieu Da in Vietnamese) commanded one of them, and succeeded in establishing military rule in northern Vietnam. But the quick dissolution of the Qin dynasty meant that Zhao was left in full control of the Qin soldiers in Vietnam. By severing his ties with China, or the newly established Han dynasty, and by expanding deeper into southern Vietnam, Zhao subsequently founded an independent kingdom – Nanyue (*Nam Viet* in Vietnamese), which again means "south of *Yue*."

In order to defend his kingdom and consolidate his power, it was said that Zhao Tuo "sealed the mountain passes leading north and eliminated all officials not personally loyal to him." But in his later years, Zhao resumed his relations with China by acknowledging Han suzerainty over his kingdom. Several decades after Zhao's death in 111 BCE, the Kingdom of Nanyue (or the Trieu dynasty in Vietnamese history) came to an end. On its demise, the Han government divided the old land of Nanyue into seven prefectures – two of them were located in modern Vietnam. The passes leading to the north, now placed under the jurisdiction of provinces to the north, were reopened, ensuring the Chinese influence would flow more freely into Vietnam.[9] This situation remained more or less unchanged for the following millennium. During the period, there appeared some autonomous Vietnamese governments. All of them were short-lived, until Ngô Quyèn (897–944) established his independent dynasty in 938. Of all the lands in the chopsticks cultural sphere, Vietnam thus received most Chinese influence. While studying culinary cultures in mainland

---

[8] Keith Weller Taylor, *The Birth of Vietnam* (Berkeley: University of California Press, 1983), 42.

[9] Ibid., 27–30.

Southeast Asia, Penny Van Esterik comments that "As the most Sinicized country in the region, Vietnam adapted principles of Chinese cuisine and today is the only country in Southeast Asia to rely primarily on chopsticks for all meals." She also points out that in areas outside Vietnam in Southeast Asia, chopsticks use is limited to Chinese meals and noodle dishes.[10]

In their study of the chopsticks cultural sphere, Mukai Yukiko and Hashimoto Keiko acknowledge that the Chinese cultural influence was a crucial element in the Vietnamese adoption of chopsticks as a dining tool necessary for conveying meals; from what is discussed above, this eating custom might have taken root in Vietnam when it first came under Chinese rule. Not only have bamboo chopsticks been the most common variety in both countries, the Chinese and Vietnamese chopsticks also share similar designs and characteristics. More specifically, the chopsticks are usually round at the bottom but square on top, a design which reflects and extends, maintain Mukai and Hashimoto, the cosmological belief of "squared earth and round heaven" from ancient China. And the lengths of the chopsticks in Vietnam and China are also comparable; averaging 25 cm long (if not longer), they are lengthier than, for instance, the ones preferred by the Japanese and Koreans. And as in China, wealthy Vietnamese also desire ivory chopsticks. By comparison, such preference never took root in Japan, Mukai's and Hashimoto's home country.[11] Of course, geography plays a role in this case – elephants existed – and still exist – in areas of Southeast and South Asia, as well as across China in earlier times, whereas they were never found in Japan.

Despite the above differences, the foodway in the Japanese archipelago is rather similar to that of South China and Vietnam. Rice and fish also figure centrally in Japanese food, thanks to the abundant water resources and generally mild climate in Japan's main islands (Hokkaido is an exception). As mentioned above, the Vietnamese and Japanese could be called exclusive chopsticks users, for the eating tool is quite sufficient, and efficient, for conveying their daily meals, which consist usually of boiled rice and fish-based dishes. Isshiki Hachirō has argued that it is due to the Japanese fondness for rice and fish that from early on, they turned to chopsticks as their eating impliment and turned their back on forks and knives. For not only can chopsticks transport rice from the bowl to the mouth, he explains, they are also convenient and effective for separating

[10] Van Esterik, *Food Culture in Southeast Asia*, 5.
[11] Mukai & Hashimoto, *Hashi*, 136–139.

and removing bones from the fish meat, the most common food ingredient in Japanese cookery.[12] Isshiki's explanation, obviously, needs qualification because rice and fish are also central to Southeast Asian cuisines, but the Vietnamese are the only chopstick users in the region. Moreover, although the Japanese are well known for their fondness for rice, some research, such as that by Emiko Ohnuki-Tierney, an anthropology professor at the University of Wisconsin, has found that before the mid-nineteenth century, ordinary Japanese did not, or could not afford to, eat rice on a daily basis. Instead it was quite common for them to mix rice with red beans and other ingredients. In other words, it is a myth that the Japanese have always been committed rice eaters; some may even argue that their rice fondness reflects a longing for the luxury.[13]

If the Vietnamese and Japanese are exclusive chopsticks users today, the latter did not use the utensil until about the seventh century. Information about the early history of Japan is found in Chinese historical texts. Chen Shou's *History of the Three Kingdoms* of the third century is an example, which contains descriptions of certain aspects of the Japanese life of the period. Chen records that the Japanese grew rice and hemp, and that they bred silkworms on mulberry trees to produce silk. As for their food habits, according to Chen, the Japanese used their hands to bring foods from wooden bowls or bamboo baskets to their mouth. If this was the case, then it did not change for several centuries. In the *History of the Sui* (Sui shu), compiled between 621 and 636 by court historians in Tang China, the dietary customs in Japan are described as follows: "The Japanese usually did not have trays and/or plates; holding food instead in leaves, they used their hands to carry them to their mouths." In both accounts, the Japanese are depicted as skilled fishermen who preferred fish and clams to animal meat. Chen Shou's book even points out that large land animals, such as cattle, horse, tiger, leopard and sheep, were nonexistent in Japan.[14]

While accepting the information given by the *History of the Sui*, Mukai Yukiko and Hashimoto Keiko have surmised that beginning in the seventh

---

[12] Isshiki, *Hashi no Bunkashi*, 40.

[13] Emiko Ohnuki-Tierney, *Rice as Self: Japanese Identities through Time* (Princeton: Princeton University Press, 1993); and Penelope Francks, "Consuming Rice: Food, 'Traditional' Products and the History of Consumption in Japan," *Japan Forum*, 19:2 (2007), 151–155.

[14] Chen, *San'guozhi* – "Wei Shu" (History of Wei), HDWZK, 855; and Wei Zheng, *Suishu* (History of the Sui dynasty) – "Dongyi – woguo" (Barbarians in the east – Japan), HDWZK, 1827.

century, some upper-class Japanese were possibly already turning to chopsticks and spoons for eating meals, for the Tang history records that in 607 and 608, Ono no Imoko, a Japanese court official, was twice sent by Empress Suiko as an official envoy (*Kenzuishi*) to meet Emperor Yang of the Sui dynasty in China. Ono no Imoko's trips marked the beginning of a series of missions launched by the Japanese government to learn about Chinese culture. While in China (and taught by the Chinese), Ono no Imoko and his entourage learned for the first time how to use chopsticks and a spoon as a set of eating implements. And on Ono no Imoko's first return trip, Emperor Yang of Sui China also sent his envoy Pei Shiqing (Hai Seisei in Japanese) with twelve staff members to accompany him back to Japan. Both Pei and Ono no Imoko introduced the custom of using utensils for eating food to the Japanese court, a custom that was embraced with great enthusiasm.[15]

In 618 the Sui dynasty was replaced by the Tang in China. But the Japanese enthusiasm for importing Chinese culture did not wane; rather, it intensified. As a result, Chinese influences – *tairikufū* (lit. mainland wind) or *tōfū* (lit. Tang wind) in Japanese – swept over the Japanese islands and continued unabated until the later part of the ninth century. As Prince Shōtoku (572–622) took a strong interest in Tang political institutions and legal code, his effort inspired others to emulate and import other aspects of Chinese culture into Japan. The official missions sent by the Japanese court to China were now called *Kentōshi*, reflecting the Sui and Tang dynastic transition. After a total of thirteen missions, the last *Kentōshi* mission went to China in 893. Mahayana Buddhism, which had reached Japan via Korea previously, developed a stronger presence in Japan through those envoys as well as through the Chinese missionaries who managed to cross the sea and land in Japan. In addition, Japanese Buddhist converts, such as Ennin, made trips to visit China. While the Japanese court and aristocrats became enthralled by Chinese culture, the ordinary Japanese still used their hands to convey food in the period. Verses in the *Collection of Ten Thousand Leaves* (Manyōshū), compiled in the mid-eighth century, described how the Japanese placed foods in baskets woven from bamboo peelings at home and used tree leaves to hold them while away from home. This description echoed the record in the *History of the Sui* quoted above.

Archaeology shows that chopsticks began to appear in seventh-century Japan, as compared to only spoons in previous ages. Excavations of Yayoi cultural remains (*c.* third century BCE) in Toro, Shizuoka and in Karako,

[15] Mukai & Hashimoto, *Hashi*, 44–45; and Isshiki, *Hashi no Bunkashi*, 54.

Nara, for example, yielded only wooden spoons or ladles, which might be serving utensils. (Several wooden sticks were found in Toro. They were 35 cm in length and 0.2–0.6 cm in diameter; it is believed that they were not eating utensils.) Yet in 646, or several decades after Ono no Imoko's mission to China, Japan produced what scholars believe to be the earliest example of chopsticks, suggesting a connection between chopsticks use and Chinese cultural influence. These chopsticks were found in the remains of the Itabuki Palace of the Asuka City in Nara, an imperial capital between 592 and 693. Made of cypress wood (*hinoki* in Japanese), a common evergreen tree in Japan, these chopsticks were thicker in the middle with either one pointed end or both ends tapering off in shape. Their length was between 30 and 33 cm and the diameter of their pointed ends was between 0.3 and 1.0 cm. Another group of chopsticks surfaced in the remains of the Fujiwara Palace of the Fujiwara City, which was Japan's capital between 694 and 710. These chopsticks were also made of *hinoki* wood, the same material used in constructing the Palace. Their shapes, with two pointed ends, also resembled the ones found in the Itabuki Palace. But their length was much shorter (between 15 and 23 cm) and their thickness at the bottom was between 0.4 and 0.7 cm. These differences have led Mukai and Hashimoto to speculate that these two groups of chopsticks had been made for different purposes. Those found at the Itabuki Palace were longer serving utensils in ritual ceremonies whereas the ones in Fujiwara Palace were more likely used for meals and thrown away by the workers who constructed the Palace.[16]

In 710 the imperial court moved again, from Fujiwara to Heijō, located in today's Nara Prefecture. And in Heijō, which served as the capital city between 710 and 784, a total of fifty-four *hinoki* chopsticks were discovered in the ditches and wells around the Heijō Palace where the imperial kitchen was located. All of them had a similar shape: thicker in the middle with one or two tapered-off ends. Their lengths varied from 13 cm to 21 cm and their diameter was about 0.5 cm. In 1988 an even greater discovery was made in Heijō: in the vicinity of Tōdaiji, one of the oldest and biggest Buddhist temples built in the Nara Period, no fewer than 200 *hinoki* chopsticks were found, with designs similar to the ones unearthed earlier. They were about 25 cm long. Their pointed lower end was 0.5 cm and their thicker and rounder top was 1.5 cm in diameter. Mukai and Hashimoto again believe that the chopsticks found in both the Heijō Palace and Tōdaiji were likely abandoned by the workers after being used as eating utensils.

---

[16] Mukai & Hashimoto, *Hashi*, 21–22.

Archaeologists also uncovered wooden chopsticks in Iba, Shizuoka, the remains of a cultural site of the late eighth century. Of the same *hinoki* cypress wood, these chopsticks were between 22 and 26 cm long, with a diameter of 0.6 cm. Carefully polished, they were thicker in the middle – polyhedral in shape – with two slightly sharpened ends. This finding suggested that by the eighth century, chopsticks use perhaps was no longer simply a lavish and exotic custom for the royal family and Buddhist converts.[17]

The characteristics of all the chopsticks found from early Japan were similar to those uncovered in Sui and Tang China: they were rounder in the middle with either one pointed lower end or with two tapered-off ends. The Tang chopsticks also varied in length, between 18 and 33 cm. Averaging 24 cm, they were longer than their counterparts from earlier periods in China.[18] Thus the discovery of wooden chopsticks in Japan is significant for studying the history of chopsticks in East Asia generally. First, from the same period, or Sui–Tang China, few wooden chopsticks have been unearthed in China; wooden chopsticks mostly appear in Tang literature, in addition to those made of gold, jade, rhinoceros horn and aromatic wood.[19] Second, whether wood or metal, many of the chopsticks found in Japan and China from the period share the same design: a round body and two tapered-off ends. While being copied and retained in Japan (for reasons to be discussed below and in later chapters), however, this design seems prevalent only in Sui–Tang China, and not in later periods. The other shape, with only one tapered-off end at the bottom, became more common in China. Their other end, or the sticks' top, became four-sided, possibly to prevent chopsticks rolling off the table. This type of chopsticks has also been quite popular in Vietnam, as mentioned before. And third, if some of the Japanese wooden chopsticks were indeed being thrown away by construction workers working on the site, then those might well be the earliest disposable chopsticks in the world.

Beginning in the eighth century, chopsticks also appeared in Japanese texts. The *Records of Ancient Matters* (Kojiki) and the *Chronicles of Japan* (Nihon shoki), two of the earliest histories from the early part of the century, both contain stories featuring chopsticks. The utensil is also mentioned in other texts. In their account book, for example, the Buddhist monks in Tōdaiji record that the Temple received tortoiseshell chopsticks as a donation. In addition, the record shows that a special pair

---

[17] Ibid., 22–24.   [18] Liu, *Zhongguo zhu wenhuashi*, 222–223.   [19] Ibid., 221–222.

of wooden chopsticks, made of ziricote wood (a tree that supposedly is native to South America) was kept in its stores. Ironically, these two unusual pairs have not survived today, while the much more mundane *hinoki* chopsticks, discarded perhaps by the workers or monks after use, were later unearthed around the Temple, as mentioned above.[20]

The records at this Buddhist Temple do suggest that in the period, the Japanese continued to bring back chopsticks from outside Japan, or *hakurai no hashi* (lit. overseas chopsticks). And these imported chopsticks were made of various materials, including silver and various types of alloyed copper. *The Procedures of the Engi Era* (Engishiki), a ninth-century compendium of rituals and laws compiled by imperial fiat in Japan, shows that like their counterparts in China and also in Korea, the Japanese upper class also favored metal chopsticks, such as those of silver and cupronickel. Since the metal chopsticks might be imports, *The Procedures of the Engi Era* specifies that these were reserved only for Japanese royalty and the top noble class. Anyone below rank six was only supposed to use the bamboo variety. Yet the bamboo chopsticks might also have been imports, for no bamboo chopsticks have hitherto surfaced in archaeological sites of early Japan.[21] Bamboo does grow in Japan. But bamboo chopsticks have not been as common in Japan as in China and Vietnam (a subject deserving some explanation below).

When Ono no Imoko first brought chopsticks from China to Japan, he demonstrated their use together with the spoon, for this was how he learned to use them back in China.[22] During the following two or three centuries, or from Nara (710–794) to Heian Japan (794–1185), Japanese royalty and aristocrats continually followed this time-honored Chinese custom. The *Tale of the Hollow Tree* (Utsubo Monogatari), a literary text describing the noble life in Japan written in 970, records an instance where after a nobleman's wife gave birth to her child, the family received a variety of gifts – cooked dishes and food vessels and utensils. Both silver chopsticks and spoons were included in the utensils. In *The Pillow Book* (Makura no soshi), another literary text from the tenth and early eleventh centuries, the author, a court lady, says that as she was writing, she heard clanking noises from the next room where some others were using both metal spoons and chopsticks to dine.[23] Over time, however, the Chinese influence waned in Japan. Metal utensils became less common, as did the custom of using both a spoon and chopsticks as a set in dining. According

---

[20] Mukai & Hashimoto, *Hashi*, 26.   [21] Ibid., 31, 49.
[22] Isshiki, *Hashi no Bunkashi*, 54–55.   [23] Mukai & Hashimoto, *Hashi*, 47.

to the *Assorted Records of Kitchen Matters* (Chūji ruiki), a recipe book from the thirteenth century, silver chopsticks were only for eating appetizers whereas the wooden variety was for transferring rice, the main grain food. And the two varieties also differed in length: the silver was longer and the wooden shorter.[24]

The decline of Chinese influence after Heian Japan might have caused a decreased interest, or disinterest, among the Japanese in making bamboo chopsticks. The Japanese had used bamboo to make household items. The *History of the Sui* and the *Collection of Ten Thousand Leaves* both record that the Japanese made bamboo baskets to hold food, a tradition that still can be seen in some parts of Japan today. Bamboo is portrayed positively in Japanese literature and folklore. The *Tale of the Bamboo Cutter* (Taketori monogatari), the oldest extant *monogatari*, a special literary genre in Japan, contains a well-known bamboo cutter story. One day in the bamboo forest, the bamboo cutter discovered a beautiful girl inside the stalk of a bamboo plant and he brought her home. While raising her with his wife as their daughter, he always found gold in the stalks of bamboo plants whenever he went to cut them. When the girl came of age, her beauty attracted many suitors, including even the reigning emperor. But she rejected all of them and explained that, as a goddess from the moon, she had to leave the earth and return there. And she did exactly that to end the story.

Since stories about a bamboo cutter also appear in the poems of the *Collection of Ten Thousand Leaves*, this folktale could have had a Japanese origin. Meanwhile, the unfolding of the story might have also registered Chinese influences. Japanese researchers have lately pointed out that the bamboo girl's revelation as a moon goddess and her departure from the earth could have been adapted from Chinese folktales. The famous Chang'e legend, describing a young woman growing up on earth with aspirations to live on the moon – she eventually became the goddess there – was proverbial in China since antiquity. According to the Chinese fairytale, there was a woodcutter named Wu Gang living on the moon. In Sichuan, China, where bamboo is particularly common, there were also stories about a girl growing up in a bamboo stalk.[25]

Bamboo chopsticks appeared in the *Records of Ancient Matters* and the *Chronicles of Japan*. When Empress Jingū decided to invade Korea,

---

[24] Ibid., 49.

[25] Cf. Itō Seiji, *Kaguya-hime no tanjō: Kodai setsuwa no kigen* (The birth of the bamboo girl: origins of ancient legends) (Tokyo: Kōdansha, 1973).

she sought the gods' blessings for her campaign. The Empress ordered her soldiers to burn a *hinoki* tree into ashes and throw them, together with plates made of *kashiwa* tree leaves (*kashiwa* is another evergreen cypress tree in Japan) and bamboo chopsticks, into the sea as offerings to the sea and mountain gods. These items, especially the bamboo chopsticks, floated in the sea, accompanying her fleet to the Korean Peninsula. All this worked; the Empress succeeded in her invasion and consequently ruled Korea in the early third century.[26] Besides the legend, there is evidence that some chopsticks were made of bamboo in Japan. The *manabashi*, a kind of cooking chopsticks for preparing fish-based dishes, are a well-known example. The *manabashi*, which nowadays are more likely to be made of wood or even metal, are usually longer than the wooden chopsticks the Japanese use to eat food.

However, Empress Jingū's use of bamboo chopsticks is the only mention in the two early histories. In all the other mentions in the *Records of Ancient Matters* and the *Chronicles of Japan*, the chopsticks were made of wood. One story that is recorded in both texts says when Susanō no Mikoto, a *kami* (deity in Japanese) was sent down from Heaven and walking along a river, he saw chopsticks flowing down in the stream. This sighting led him to believe that there must have been people living in the upper part of the river. He went upstream and did find a family. This story shows that by this time (or by the eighth century) when the two historical texts were compiled, the Japanese took it for granted that humans used chopsticks to eat food. Were those chopsticks floating in the river being used in pairs? One poem in the *Collection of Ten Thousand Leaves* offers an answer. It describes the sadness of a man over the loss of his brother. "Our parents raised both of us like a pair of chopsticks facing each other," the man deplores, "how come my brother's life was as ephemeral as the morning dew?"[27]

As Japan is a country boasting a high percentage of forestation of its land, wood is readily available throughout the Japanese archipelago. Thus, wooden chopsticks are most common in Japan. Cypress and pine trees are widely available; of the former, the Japanese favor *hinoki* and *sugi* cypresses. As evergreens, these trees have come to symbolize the vitality of life in Japanese culture. There is a tradition among the Japanese of worshiping old trees by referring to them as *shinboku* (or divine trees), which often draw flocks of pilgrims. As such, chopsticks made of cypress wood receive high status, as opposed to those of other materials, bamboo included.

---

[26] Isshiki, *Hashi no Bunkashi*, 8–9. [27] Mukai & Hashimoto, *Hashi*, 45–46.

Isshiki Hachirō in his book discusses the *hashisugi shinkō*, or a worship of the chopsticks made of *sugi* cypress wood, practiced among many Japanese throughout the centuries.[28] Besides *sugi*, other varieties of wood – for example, *hinoki* cypress and willow trees – are also commonly used in making celebratory chopsticks.

Tree worship is a Shinto belief, and thus the Japanese fondness for wooden objects, and wooden chopsticks in particular, extends the influence of Shintoism. According to Shintoism, trees (along with rocks, rivers, mountains, etc.) were one of the "natural forces" that carried the spirit of nature in the "land of the *kami*," as Japan was referred to by Shinto believers. Trees have their own spirits, or *kodama*. To be close to and pay homage to the *kodama*, the Japanese only use undressed lumber to construct Shinto shrines. Inside the shrine, furniture and utensils are also mostly made of bare wood, without paint or lacquer, even though Japan was first known to the West as a country of lacquer paint and lacquerware. Occasionally, one can find bamboo objects at Shinto shrines, such as the ladles provided for the visitors for washing their hands before entering the shrine, but wooden objects are far more common.

Shintoism has influenced Japanese chopsticks culture in many ways, including how chopsticks are made and how they are used. To prolong the life of wooden chopsticks, for instance, one can paint them with lacquer, a practice seen in both China and Japan. Lacquered chopsticks are known in Japanese as *nuribashi*, which has a number of varieties, depending on where they are made and what types of paint (lacquer being just one kind) are used in glossing them. But like the use of undressed wood at Shinto shrines, the unpainted and slightly polished whitewood chopsticks, or *shirakibashi*, are regarded as being of the highest status by the Japanese, perhaps because without paint, these whitewood chopsticks allow their users to have unimpeded communication with nature, or the tree spirit. As such, whitewood chopsticks, made of willow or cypress wood, have traditionally been used at religious ceremonies in shrines and temples. The idea is that as *kami* and people form a connected living in the world, they also share their foods together – using whitewood chopsticks maximizes this connection. Hence these whitewood chopsticks are generally referred to as *ohashi* (honored chopsticks), but depending on their use, they can also be called *shinhashi* (divine chopsticks) or *reibashi* (spiritual chopsticks). Since the emperor in Japan is believed to be a Shinto deity, Japanese royalty also use whitewood chopsticks.

---

[28] Isshiki, *Hashi no Bunkashi*, 11–15.

Buddhism also shaped the chopstick culture in Japan – their preference for whitewood chopsticks included – in important ways. Buddhist tenets shun worldly attachments, including meat and other lavish food, hence in Buddhist temples across Asia, monks and nuns eat simple meals, consisting mostly of porridge and vegetables. *Ennin's Diary* mentions how the Japanese Buddhist was treated as such when he took lodging in Buddhist temples in Tang China. This emphasis on simple meals extends to simple utensils. Indeed, if chopsticks were to become the exclusive tool in conveying meals, it is quite likely that Buddhist monks piloted this practice before anyone else. And the most common chopsticks used by Buddhist monks are made of wood or other inexpensive materials.

In the mid-eighth century, or about a century before Ennin went to China, Jianzhen (688–763), a Chinese Buddhist missionary, landed in Japan after several failed attempts, not long after chopsticks had been introduced to Japanese royalty and nobility. Lan Xiang, a private collector of chopsticks in China, speculates that as the Chinese monks dined with chopsticks, this exemplary dining style influenced the Japanese, causing a broad conversion. As Ono no Imoko taught the Japanese court to eat with utensils, Lan argues the Chinese Buddhist monks possibly helped spread the dining custom among the ordinary Japanese. Since a number of wooden chopsticks were unearthed at Tōdaiji, where Jianzhen had presided after arriving in Japan, Lan's speculation becomes plausible. Buddhist influence was also registered in Japanese culinary tradition. The famed *kaiseki-ryōri* (*kaiseki* cuisine, a multi-course dinner) had originated in Buddhist temples. While the *kaiseki-ryōri* has now become both exquisite and expensive, the utensil required for eating the meal remains a pair of plain whitewood chopsticks. Incidentally, Japanese chopsticks etiquette – placing chopsticks horizontally on the table and raising them politely with both hands before eating – has also been found in Buddhist temples elsewhere.[29]

The chopsticks used to eat *kaiseki-ryōri* are also called *rikyūbashi*, because Sen no Rikyū (1522–1591), a Zen Buddhist monk and tea master, gave the formal meal its name. The *rikyūbashi*, or "*rikyū* chopsticks," are thicker in the middle and thinner at both ends, resembling the design of the chopsticks uncovered from early Japan, as well as that of their counterparts in Tang China. With two tapered-off ends, this style of chopsticks is

---

[29] Lan Xiang, *Kuaizi, buzhishi kuaizi* (Chopsticks, not only chopsticks) (Taipei: Maitian, 2011), 271–274. Lan Xiang also points out that in Buddhist temples in China, monks place their chopsticks horizontally on the table and raise them with both hands before eating, 159.

also known as *ryōkuchibashi* (lit. two-ended chopsticks), as opposed to *katakuchibashi* (lit. one-ended chopsticks) – chopsticks with only pointed bottoms. One reason for using *rikyūbashi*, or *ryōkuchibashi*, to eat the *kaiseki-ryōri*, as one believes today, is that since the meal consists of several courses, one can use the chopsticks' different ends to convey different food contents, and relish each dish in its purity. But the chopsticks, usually plain wood, are also required on other formal occasions, religious or celebratory, which will be discussed in later chapters.

The idea of using different chopsticks to convey different food items did not start with *kaiseki-ryōri* in Japan. The *Assorted Records of Kitchen Matters*, cited before, has already suggested that silver chopsticks be used for appetizers but the wooden pair for rice. In later years, people used *manabashi*, or fish chopsticks, to convey seafood dishes and *saibashi* (lit. vegetable chopsticks) for vegetables. Both chopsticks are tapered off at one end, making them *katakuchibashi*; only *manabashi* is longer than *saibashi*. During the Muromachi period (1337–1573), Japanese culinary practice reached a level of sophistication, marked by the creation of *honzen ryōri*, a multi-course meal, even though the term literally means "main-course meal." To eat a *honzen ryōri*, one initially also employed both *manabashi* and *saibashi*; the former separated bones from fish or mined out meat in a clam whereas the latter gripped vegetables. But toward the late sixteenth century, states Xu Jingbo, author of a history of Japanese food culture, most Japanese began to use only one pair of chopsticks to eat the meal. This pair tended to have sharply pointed ends for the convenience of eating seafood, as did *manabashi*, but were short in length like *saibashi*. This design remains popular in Japan today, distinguishing Japanese chopsticks from their counterparts in Asia (Plate 16).[30]

In the Korean Peninsula, chopsticks use possibly has a longer history than it does in Japan. Chopsticks were not the first eating tool used by Koreans; archaeological evidence indicates that the spoon was the first eating implement used by people in the Korean Peninsula. The earliest spoon found in Korea was made of bone. It was located in the Rajin Remains of the Hamgyong Province in today's North Korea dated 700–600 BCE. In another archaeological site, in the Rakrang Prefecture near Pyongyang, lacquered wooden spoons were discovered, which were dated between 108

---

[30] Xu Jingbo, *Riben yinshi wenhua: lishi yu xianshi* (Food culture in Japan: past and present) (Shanghai: Shanghai renmin chubanshe, 2009), 87, 127. Also Isshiki, *Hashi no Bunkashi*, 130–131.

and 313 BCE.[31] The earliest example of chopsticks, made of bronze, was dated in the early sixth century, or during Korea's Three Kingdoms period (53–668), and was found in a royal tomb of a Baekje King, who ruled during 501–523 CE. Baekje was one of the three kingdoms; the other two were Goguryeo and Silla. These chopsticks were uncovered together with some bronze spoons in the tomb, suggesting that the Korean court might have employed both of them for their meals. As evidence that this was an extension of the Chinese custom, these chopsticks were comparable in design to the Chinese chopsticks of the period. They were thicker and rounder in the middle with two slightly pointed ends – the top was 0.5 cm in diameter and the bottom was 0.3 cm in diameter. And they were approximately 21 cm long, within the range of the chopsticks found contemporaneously in China and Japan.

Prior to the Three Kingdoms period, around the second century BCE, Han China had established four military commanderies in the northern part of the Korean Peninsula, which were more or less in existence for approximately four centuries. Little evidence, however, suggests that these Chinese military presences in Korea had influenced the locals' dining habits. In fact, since the Goguryeo Kingdom arose in the same area as early as the first century BCE, one may surmise that these Han commanderies were in constant battle against Koreans throughout their existence. But the Baekje Kingdom, located in the southwest of the Peninsula, kept in contact with the Chinese regimes through the sea route during the post-Han periods, and to a lesser degree so did Silla. After the Tang dynasty rose to power in China, Tang rulers allied with Silla and put down both Baekje and Goguryeo, ending the Three Kingdoms period in Korea. As such, Tang historians described Goguryeo, Silla and Baekje, not only their contact with the dynasty but also their geography, culture and history. Yet the Chinese texts from the period make no comment on whether Koreans then used eating tools, except to say that they "liked to squat on the floor and eat food on short-legged tables."[32]

Since the Baekje Kingdom made regular contact with the Chinese government, sending tributes to the latter, could the chopsticks and spoons found in its king's tomb be a return gift from a Chinese ruler? This likelihood certainly exists, for there is no corroborating textual evidence that Koreans had applied eating utensils for meals. The history of the Three Kingdoms is also covered in the Korean historical texts – Kim Pu-sik's

---

[31] Mukai & Hashimoto, *Hashi*, 14–20.
[32] Li, *Beishi* – "Gaogeli" (Goguryeo), HDWZK, 3116; and Wei, *Suishu* – "Dongyi-Gaoli" (Eastern barbarians – Goryeo), HDWZK, 1814.

Historical Records of the Three Kingdoms (Samguk sagi) and Iryōn's *Memorabilia of the Three Kingdoms* (Samguk yusa), appearing respectively in the early twelfth and early thirteenth centuries. But neither mentions that chopsticks had been used in the Three Kingdoms either. But toward the late Three Kingdoms period, Chinese influence had a stronger presence in the Peninsula. Confucianism, Daoism and Buddhism all exerted their impact on shaping the fabric of Korean society, with a varying degree of regional characteristics. Moreover, in ending the Kingdom, the Tang army invaded and occupied part of the former Goguryeo territory. One could thus imagine that ordinary Koreans became exposed to Chinese dietary customs. In a word, most Koreans could have begun using eating tools around the sixth century.

In the wake of the Tang dynasty's fall, the Korean Peninsula saw the rise of a new dynasty – the Goryeo dynasty (918–1392), unifying the land in 936. Goryeo Korea was an important time in Korean history – the term "Korea" even stems from it. Many examples of chopsticks from this period have been discovered across the Peninsula. All these excavated chopsticks were made of silver, brass or other alloyed copper. Their shape took on that of the earlier examples, having a round or polyhedral body and two thinner ends. And wherever the chopsticks were found, there were always accompanying spoons for them; and the latter were usually made of the same material. All this suggests that the custom of utensil use became widely practiced among Koreans. And like the Chinese in Tang China, when transporting food, Koreans at that time used both a spoon and chopsticks, a dining habit that is still recommended in Korean society today.

Perhaps because the Korean Peninsula lies approximately on the same latitude as North China, the foodways in these two regions were/are similar. While failing to describe how Koreans in early days ate their meals, the Tang Chinese historical texts do record, rather consistently, that the Peninsula's agronomy bore notable similarities to China's. For instance, Li Yanshou's *History of the Northern Dynasties* (Beishi), written in the mid-sixth century, describes that in Silla, "the land is fertile and crops are planted in both wet and dry fields. Silla's five cereal grains, fruits and vegetables, birds and animals, and other produces are more or less the same as those in China." Other Tang texts reiterate Li's description verbatim.[33] However, like other ancient writers, Li and others fail to specify what

---

[33] Li, *Beishi* – "Xinluo" (Silla), HDWZK, 3123; and Wei, *Suishu* – "Dongyi-Xinluo" (Eastern barbarians – Silla), HDWZK, 1821.

the five grains were. Since Li mentions that Koreans grew crops in both wet and dry fields, rice might be one of them. But like in North China, rice seems not to be the leading grain, for it only appears twice in Kim Pu-sik's *Historical Records of the Three Kingdoms*, while millet appears nineteen times and wheat eleven times. Interestingly, while mentioning wheat a number of times, Kim Pu-sik often describes it in contexts such as how the crop was damaged by drought or frost. In a nutshell, millet had to be the grain crop more favored by Koreans, as it was resistant to both drought and flood.[34]

About the same time that Kim Pu-sik's *Historical Records of the Three Kingdoms* was written, Xu Jing (1091–1163), a Chinese envoy sent by Emperor Huizong of the Northern Song dynasty (960–1127), visited Korea in 1123 and wrote a comprehensive travelogue – *An Illustrated Record of the Chinese Embassy to the Goryeo Court during the Xuanhe Era* (Xuanhe fengshi Gaoli tujing). It offers a comprehensive description of the Korean Peninsula. Besides wheat, barley and rice, Xu notes that several varieties of millet were grown in Korea. He also points out that the price of wheat was quite high because it was planted only in certain regions. With respect to rice, Xu observes that only the *geng* (*sinica/japonica*) rice variety was planted in Korea, not the *xian* (*indica*) or the *nuo* (sticky/sweet) varieties.[35] In other words, like wheat, rice was rare, hardly a grain staple for Koreans at the time. When Xu notices that Koreans only grew *sinica/japonica* rice, he is possibly making a comparison with the situation in China, for this was in the age when *indica* rice, especially the Champa variety, began to be introduced into South China. This introduction made rice more available to the Chinese (a topic to be treated in the next chapter). All in all, Xu Jing's account demonstrates that before the twelfth century, the foodway in the Korean Peninsula was comparable to those of North China before and during the Tang period.

Like the earlier texts, Xu Jing's account fails to mention whether or not Koreans by that time used spoon and/or chopsticks for meals. But he gives detailed information on other utensils in Korean life, such as the bowls, plates, basins, bottles, jars and other kitchen objects that were made of

---

[34] Kim Pu-sik, *Samguk sagi*, annotated by Sun Wenfan (Changchun: Jilin wenshi chubanshe, 2003). About how wheat was damaged by the inclement weather, see 41, 133, 212, 282, 289 and 312.

[35] Xu Jing, *Xuanhe fengshi Gaoli tujing* (Illustrated record of the Chinese embassy to the Goryeo court during the Xuanhe era), in *Shi Chaoxian lu* (Records of Chinese embassies to Korea), eds. Yin Mengxia & Yu Hao (Beijing: Beijing tushuguan chubanshe, 2003), vol. 1, 180, 186 and 262.

brass, ceramic and wood (often painted with lacquer). Xu is particularly impressed by the quality of metalcraft in Korea and the way Koreans plated the metal objects with gold or silver, as the latter were more precious. He also praises the color and texture of the celadon-ware produced in Korea at that time.[36] Since Xu Jing does not mention that Koreans used dining tools, one easy conclusion might be that these had not been adopted in Korean society. But from another perspective, one might say that Koreans already did because Xu was quite watchful and observant on his trip. Had Koreans not already used spoons and chopsticks, he would most likely have pointed it out in his account.

In the late Goryeo Period, rice seems to have increased its appeal, though slowly. In the *History of the Goryeo Dynasty* (Goryeosa), a multi-volume work compiled during the mid-fifteenth century, rice is mentioned more frequently than in earlier texts; it had also become a reserve grain stored in government granaries for famine relief. Moreover, the royal court rewarded loyal and model officials with rice. These instances show that rice had become more available, if also rare and valuable. But the text also mentions millet the most, far more frequently than all other cereals in popularity. This indicates that for most Koreans, millet remained their staple starchy food. As such, perhaps, it was understandable for them to continue the dining custom of Tang China and use both a spoon and chopsticks together in eating a meal. Both were present in the excavations from the Goryeo dynasty and the following Joseon dynasty (1392–1897). Already discussed in Chapter 2, millet is best cooked into gruel and porridge, making the spoon a better eating tool than chopsticks.

When in Korea, Xu Jing was quite struck by the high quality of metalwork. Did the advanced technology in metallurgy that he saw help account for the phenomenon that, in contrast to Japan, to date the overwhelming majority of the utensils that have been unearthed from early Korea are made of metal instead of wood? It is certainly a possibility because without question, whether made of silver or brass, metal utensils are much more durable, and thus preferred by many users. Of course, for ordinary Koreans, it is hard to imagine that they could all afford the metal variety, let alone those made of silver. But even the less wealthy families might still desire metal utensils for their durability, such as those fashioned from brass and cupronickel. Perhaps a more important reason is that the Korean Peninsula, and especially the northern part, is rich with gold, iron and

[36] Ibid., 191, 275.

copper, making it relatively easy for Koreans to make everyday utensils from metal. By contrast, bamboo is not as common in the Peninsula as in China and Vietnam. One could even add that Koreans' fondness for metal, especially gold, is shown in their family names – as of today, about twenty-five percent of Koreans are named Kim, which means "gold." And in East Asian culture, gold often stands for all metals. Last but not least, one might consider Tang China's lasting influence. Although the dynasty fell in early tenth-century China as an important power in East Asia, Tang culture and customs retained an exemplary and enduring influence in China and its neighboring regions for many centuries. Koreans' preference for metal utensils might be an example of this influence, since metal chopsticks and spoons also constitute the majority of the food utensils excavated from the Tang period.

During the late Goryeo Period, the rise of the Mongols and their subsequent invasion of the Korean Peninsula occasioned a significant change in Korean food and culinary culture. For the Mongols, it was by no means easy to conquer Korea. Having battled Koreans for several decades, they eventually prevailed in the 1270s and turned Korea into a province in the massive Mongolian empire. The coming of the Mongols meant that unlike in the previous periods, when meat had been absent from the Korean cuisine due to Buddhist influences, meat now returned to the Korean diet and, over time, became quite a fixture in Korean cookery, at least for those who could afford it. The Mongolian culinary practices, such as barbecuing and boiling (blanching) thinly sliced meat in a hot pot, were also introduced to Koreans.[37] Chinese travel accounts, again, offer interesting and valuable information about how Koreans resumed meat consumption from the thirteenth century onward. In his *Illustrated Record of the Chinese Embassy to the Goryeo Court during the Xuanhe Era*, Xu Jing observed that per Buddhist teaching, Koreans seldom ate lamb, pork or other animal meat in the twelfth century.[38] But when Dong Yue (1430–1502), an envoy from Ming China to Korea in 1488, wrote his *Miscellaneous Records of Korea* (Chaoxian zalu), he describes instead how Koreans consumed beef, lamb, pork and goose, and that of the four, lamb

---

[37] Yi Sông-u, "Chōsen hantō no shoku no bunka" (Food culture on the Korean Peninsula), in *Higashi Ajia no shoku no bunka* (Food cultures in East Asia), eds. Ishige Naomichi et al. (Tokyo: Heibonsha, 1981), 129–153; and Kim Ch'on-ho (Jin Tianhao), "Han, Meng zhijian de roushi wenhua bijiao" (A comparative study of meat consumption cultures between the Koreans and the Mongols), trans. Zhao Rongguang & Jiang Chenghua, *Shangye jingji yu guanli* (Commercial economy and management), 4 (2000), 39–44.

[38] Xu, *Xuanhe fengshi Gaoli tujing*, 176, 188.

was most popular.[39] Needless to say, this marked change in food interest registered the Mongolian influence in Korea. In other words, it was not coincidental that metal utensils had an enduring appeal among Koreans, which has lasted to this day. As perhaps in Tang China, where metal utensils also seemed prevalent, the requirements associated with consuming meat-based dishes had turned people to more durable and strong eating tools. And in both cases, there were identifiable nomadic culinary and cultural influences, including the increased consumption of lamb and mutton and other animal meats in general.

Traditionally, metal utensils have been most favored among the Asian nomads, including the Mongols, Tibetans and Manchus and their ancestors (e.g. Xiongnu). In contrast to their agronomic neighbors (the Chinese, Japanese, Vietnamese as well as Koreans) who used knives and forks mostly for cooking rather than for eating, these nomads had adopted knives and forks, especially the former, as eating implements over many centuries. The knife was more essential because once meat was cut into smaller portions, one could eat them by hand. This habit of using hands to convey food, or *shoushi* 手食 (feeding with fingers), became a standard expression for the Chinese to describe their neighbors' dining habit; the term appeared in a number of Chinese texts from the third century onward, especially during and after the Tang dynasty when the Chinese made more contact with other ethnic groups.[40]

But coming into contact with the Chinese, some nomads also learned to make and use chopsticks and spoons to cook and convey food. The beginning of the chapter mentioned that the Chinese influence moved into Vietnam because of the Qin conquest of the land during the third century BCE. Around the same time that he sent Zhao Tuo to the south, Qinshihuang, the Qin ruler, also commanded Meng Tian (?–210 BCE), another of his generals, to lead an army of 300,000 to fight against the Xiongnu, a powerful nomadic group in control of the northern steppe regions. After the campaign was over, Meng's soldiers were deployed in the Ordos Desert, encircled by the Great Bend of the Yellow River, and became a garrison force on the

---

[39] Dong Yue, *Chaoxian zalu*, in *Shi Chaoxian lu*, vol. 3, 807–808.
[40] An early mention of the Central and South Asians who used hands to transport foods was entered by Xuanzang in his *Da Tang xiyuji* (Great Tang records of western regions), *juan* 2, ZJGK, 19. Also, *Jiu Tangshu* – "Xirong liezhuan" (Biographies of western barbarians), ZJGK, 2657; *Xin Tangshu* – "Xiyu" (Western regions), ZJGK, 2057; and "Nanman" (Southern barbarians), ZJGK, 2101. A similar custom was found in Zhuawa, or today's Indonesia, by Fang Hui (1227-1307) in his *Tongjiang xuji* (Sequel to the Tongjiang collections), *juan* 26, ZJGK, 301.

border. In addition, Qinshihuang sent a number of forced laborers there to construct a defensive wall in the region, which became an early part of the Great Wall known in modern times. After the Qin's fall, Han rulers continued the effort to push the Xiongnu back into the steppe and had intermittent success. Beneath the veneer of military conflict, however, cultural exchanges also took place. A recent archaeological excavation has uncovered that the Xiongnu, like the Chinese in the Han, used *zeng* to steam grain food. The Xiongnu also made and used bone chopsticks in transporting food.[41] This might be an isolated example; but it nevertheless shows that cultural exchanges were hardly unidirectional. As Central Asian influences entered Han China through contact with the nomads, Chinese culinary practices and dining customs also extended into regions beyond China proper.

After the fall of the Tang, chaos erupted in China for several decades. In its wake, Zhao Kuangyin (927–976), a military man, rose to power and founded the Northern Song dynasty in China proper. But the Song territory was considerably smaller than the Tang's because it had no control of the pastureland, mountain ranges and desert areas in the north and northwest. That is, the Song shared their control of the Asian mainland with other ethnic groups, such as the Kitans, the Jurchens and the Mongols. Song historians often commented on the social behavior and cultural customs of these nomadic groups. The *Collection of Documents of the Song Diplomatic Relations with the Northern Regimes* (Sanchao beimeng huibian), a historical text by Xu Mengxin (1126–1207), points out that the inhabitants in Manchuria were finger feeders – no utensils were employed by them to transport food.[42] This observation is supported by archaeology. In the 1970s Chinese archaeologists discovered a Kitan tomb – the Kitans had founded the Liao dynasty (907–1125) centered in Manchuria. Of the kitchen items that surfaced there were pitchers, jars, pots, basins, bowls and knives, but no chopsticks. One of the wall paintings in the tomb depicted a man (chef?) using a knife to cut a leg of an animal, suggesting that once the meat was cut, it would be placed on a plate – plates were found in larger quantities than bowls in Kitan and Mongol tombs of the period – for people to transfer it to their mouths with their hands.[43]

[41] He, *Tianshan jiayan*, 145–146.   [42] Xu, *Sanchao beimeng huibian, juan* 3, ZJGK, 15.

[43] Xiang Chunsong, "Liaoning Zhaowuda diqu faxian de Liaomu huihua ziliao" (Paintings discovered in a Kitan tomb of the Zhaowuda area, Liaoning), *Wenwu* (Cultural relics), 6 (1979), 22–32.

But archaeological evidence reveals that over time, Asian nomads began using chopsticks to convey grains, meat and vegetables. Compared with the Mongols and the Jurchens, the Kitans were more receptive to Han Chinese influences. Archaeological digs of a Kitan tomb in today's Inner Mongolia yielded several household items made of brass, silver and porcelain, including pots, jars, vases, bowls, plates, cups and mirrors. A pair of brass chopsticks was found among them. They were 23 cm long with lightly carved lines decorating their top.[44] And this was not an isolated case, nor did the Kitans use only metal chopsticks. Many lacquered wooden chopsticks have surfaced in Kitan tombs of the twelfth century or later throughout North and Northeast China. Bone, brass and wooden chopsticks have been found in Jurchen tombs too, showing that chopsticks gradually became accepted among the Jurchens.[45] At a later time, the Mongols turned to chopsticks use too. Excavations in Chifeng, Inner Mongolia, seem quite telling. From the 1970s to the late 1980s, mural paintings were uncovered in two tombs that belonged to either a Kitan or a Mongol noble (the area was first controlled by the Kitans and later by the Mongols). One painting portrays an eating scene: on a short-legged rectangle table metal bowls, plates, spoons and chopsticks are placed.[46] The mural painting found in another Chifeng tomb offers better evidence that chopsticks were used in handling food. It depicts an eating scene with a maid serving her master; she holds a big bowl in her left hand and a pair of chopsticks in her right hand, as though preparing to stir the food in the bowl with the chopsticks for serving the master.[47] The latter tomb dates back to the fourteenth century, hence it was more likely a Mongol tomb. The excavations prove that after their conquest of China in the late thirteenth century, the Mongols gradually adopted the dining custom of chopsticks use. The court protocol of the Yuan dynasty (1271–1368), founded by the Mongols in China, offers corroborating evidence; it specifies that a proper court burial should contain one set of eating utensils – including bowls,

---

[44] Xiang Chunsong, "Neimenggu jiefangyingzi Liao mu fajue jianbao" (Concise report on the dig of the Liao-dynasty tomb in Jiefangyingzi, Inner Mongolia), *Kaogu* (Archaeology), 4 (1979), 330–334.

[45] Liu, *Zhongguo zhu wenhuashi*, 280–285.

[46] Xiang Chunsong & Wang Jianguo, "Neimeng Zhaomeng Chifeng Sanyanjing Yuandai bihuamu" (Wall paintings in the Yuan tomb in Sanyanjing, Chifeng, Zhaomeng District, Inner Mongolia), *Wenwu*, 1 (1982), 54–58.

[47] Liu Bing, "Neimenggu Chifeng Shazishan Yuandai bihuamu" (Wall paintings in the Yuan tomb in Shazishan, Chifeng, Inner Mongolia), *Wenwu*, 2 (1992), 24–27.

plates and chopsticks – for the deceased, demonstrating that the Mongols considered chopsticks an essential eating utensil.[48]

In sum, multiple sources have shown that by the fourteenth century the chopsticks cultural sphere had not only become well established in today's China, Vietnam, Korean and Japan but also penetrated successfully into the areas of the Mongolian steppe, Manchuria and into the Gobi and Taklamakan Deserts in North and Northwest China. This expansion, however, did not cause the Mongols, the Kitans and the other inhabitants of those regions to completely forsake their more traditional utensils, such as knives and forks. Instead, they tended to combine them with chopsticks and used them together, though the combination could vary – chopsticks could be grouped together with a spoon and a knife, a knife and a fork, or a spoon and a fork.[49] The utensils used by the Manchu court are an example, consisting of a knife, a fork and a pair of chopsticks (Plate 9). A nomadic group from Manchuria, the Manchus, established the Qing dynasty (1644–1911) in the wake of the Ming dynasty's fall. But despite their rule in China, Manchu royalty combined the use of chopsticks with knives and forks.

---

[48] Song Lian, *Yuanshi* (History of the Yuan dynasty) – "Guosu jiuli" (Old rituals of our country's customs), HDWZK, 1925.

[49] More examples of how the Mongols, the Manchus and their (nomadic) neighbors on the Mongolian steppes use both knives and chopsticks are found in Lan, *Kuaizi, buzhishi kuaizi*, 129–135.

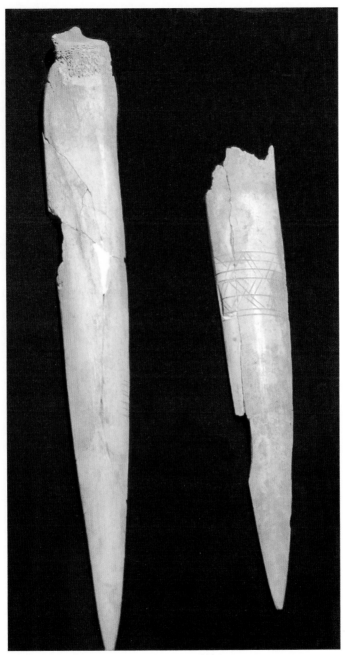

PLATE 1. Bone spoons unearthed at a Neolithic cultural site in Sichuan, China.
(Courtesy of Ai Zhike, the Sanxia Museum, Chongqing, China)

PLATE 2. Neolithic bone chopsticks found in Longqiuzhuang, a Neolithic cultural site in Jiansu, China.
(Courtesy of the Yangzhou Museum, China)

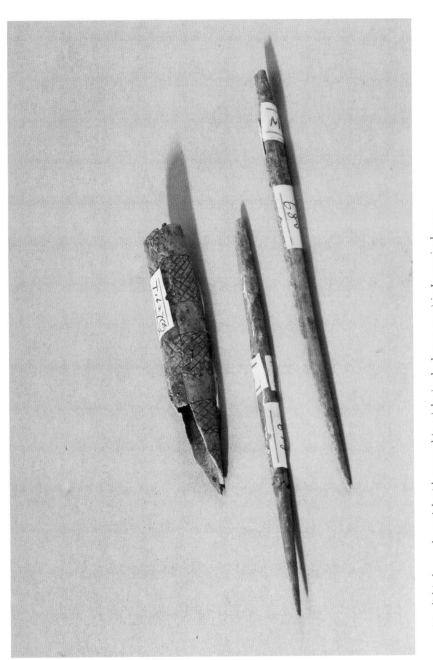

PLATE 3. Neolithic bone chopsticks (the two thin sticks in the lower part) in Longqiuzhuang. (*Courtesy of the Yangzhou Museum, China*)

PLATE 4. This brick carving shows how chopsticks were used in early China, *c.* first century CE.
(Zhongguo huaxiangzhuan quanji [Complete collections of Chinese brick carvings], ed. Yu Weichao, Chengdu: Sichuan meishu chubanshe, 2006, p. 59)

PLATE 5. Eating customs in early China – sitting on the floor with foods placed on short-legged tables, shown on a brick carving, first to third centuries CE.
(Zhongguo lidai yishu: huihua bian [Chinese art in different dynasties: painting], Beijing: Renmin Meishu Chubanshe, 1994, part 1, p. 72)

PLATE 6. Brick painting from the Fresco Tombs of the Wei and Jin Dynasty showing chopsticks used as utensils for cooking in early China, *c.* third–fifth centuries CE.
(Painting from the Fresco Tombs of the Wei and Jin Dynasty located in the Northwestern Gobi desert 20 km from Jiayuguan city. Mural paintings in Jiayuguan, Jiuquan tombs of the Wei and Jin periods, ed. Zhang Baoxun [Lanzhou: Gansu renmin chubanshe, 2001], p. 261

PLATE 7. A food tray with wooden bowls and a pair of bamboo chopsticks found in the Mawangdui Tombs, Han China, *c.* second century BCE.
(Changsha Mawangdui yihao hanmu [Mawangdui # 1 Han tomb in Changsha] (Beijing: Wenwu chubanshe, 1973), II. p. 151.)

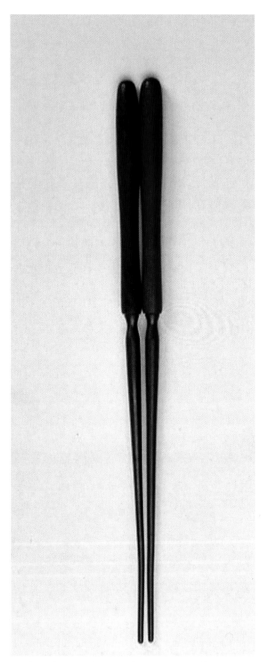

PLATE 8. "Fire sticks" from Edo-period Japan – used to arrange charcoals and stoke flames – are another example of how chopsticks could be used other than as an eating utensil.
(Courtesy of the Edo-Tokyo Museum, Japan)

PLATE 9. The Manchus usually combined the use of chopsticks with knives and forks. *(Manchurian implements, c. 17th–19th centuries. Courtesy of Lan Xiang, a private collector of chopsticks in Shanghai)*

PLATE 10. Eating and drinking in a tent tavern portrayed in a fresco in Dunhuang, a famous Buddhist grotto of Tang China, eighth–ninth centuries.
(*Dunhuang shiku quanji* [*Complete collections of Dunhuang Grotto murals*], ed. *Dunhuang yanjiuyuan, Shanghai: Shanghai renmin chubanshe, 2001, vol. 25, p. 45*)

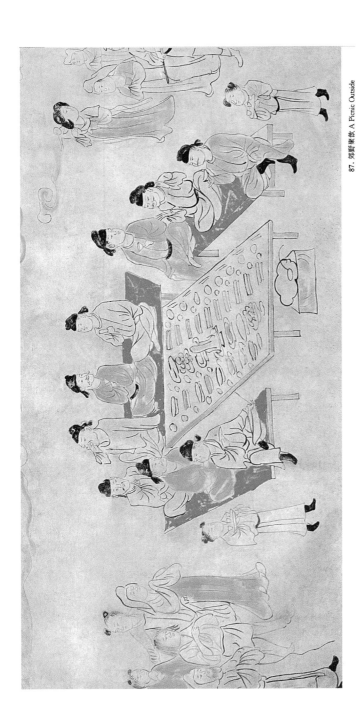

PLATE 11. "A Picnic Outside" – a mural painting of the Tang Dynasty showing that chopsticks were used to convey foods and that diners sat on benches instead of the floor, c. eighth century.
(DaTang bihua [Mural paintings of the great Tang dynasty], eds. Tang Changdong & Li Guozhen, Xi'an: Shanxi lüyou chubanshe, 1996, p. 127)

87. 郊野聚饮 A Picnic Outside

PLATE 12. "Literary Gathering", Zhao Ji (1082–1135). Handscroll, ink and colors on silk, 184.4 × 123.9 cm.
(Courtesy of the National Palace Museum, Taipei)

PLATE 13. "Han Xizai's Night Banquet," or "The Night Revels of Han Xizai" (detail), c. 970, by Gu Hongzhong, showing that the Chinese sat on chairs to eat individually rather than communally as in later periods. Handscroll, ink and color on silk, 28.7 cm high, 335.5 cm wide.
(Courtesy of the Palace Museum, Beijing)

PLATE 14. A mural found in a tomb from Song China (960–1127) portraying a couple, or the Zhaos, eating together at a table on high chairs, suggesting communal eating had begun in the family after the tenth century in China. *(Zhongguo mush bihua quanji: Song, Liao, Jin, Yuan [Complete collections of Chinese tomb murals: Song, Liao, Jin and Yuan dynasties], Shijiazhuang: Hebei Jiaoyu chubanshe, 2011, p. 86)*

PLATE 15. A family eating together at one sitting during the Jurchen period (*c.* thirteenth century), suggesting the spread of a communal eating style in Asia. *(Zhongguo mush bihua quanji: Song, Liao, Jin, Yuan [Complete collections of Chinese tomb murals: Song, Liao, Jin and Yuan dynasties], Shijiazhuang: Hebei Jiaoyu chubanshe, 2011, p. 114)*

PLATE 16. "*Women 22*" by Utagawa Kuniyoshi (1797–1862). The Japanese have been accustomed to chopsticks since approximately the seventh century, as shown in this Ukiyo-e painting, a popular genre in Edo Japan. ("*Women 22*" by Utagawa Kuniyoshi [1797–1862], *Public Domain*)

PLATE 17. "A Group of Trackers," drawing by a European visitor to eighteenth-century China depicting how the Chinese ate with chopsticks.
(From Views of Eighteenth Century China: Costumes, History, Customs, by William Alexander & George Henry Mason, © London, Studio editions, 1988, p. 25)

PLATE 18. Portrait of Li-Lieu Ying, Empress Tzu-Hsi's Great Eunuch, late nineteenth century.
(Chinese School, nineteenth century, Private Collection / Bridgeman Images)

PLATE 19. "The Latest Craze of American Society, New Yorkers Dining in a Chinese Restaurant," Leslie Hunter (fl. 1910), Illustration from *The Graphic* Magazine, 1911.
(Private Collection / The Stapleton Collection / Bridgeman Images)

PLATE 20. Pairs of chopsticks to be packed into bentō boxes in Japan.
(Author's photograph)

PLATE 21. Japanese "husband–wife chopsticks," which are often painted with lacquer. The pair for the husband are slightly longer and less colourful than the pair for the wife.
(Author's photograph)

PLATE 22. Japanese festive chopsticks, shaped with two tapered ends and a round body, reflecting the belief in humans and deities sharing food together at one meal on holidays and at festivals. (*Author's photograph*)

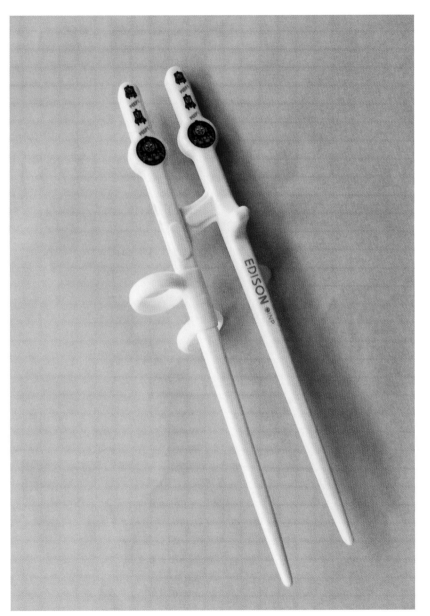

PLATE 23. Training chopsticks, a Japanese invention, ensure that a young child can easily put the tool on his/her fingers and pick up food. (*Author's photograph*)

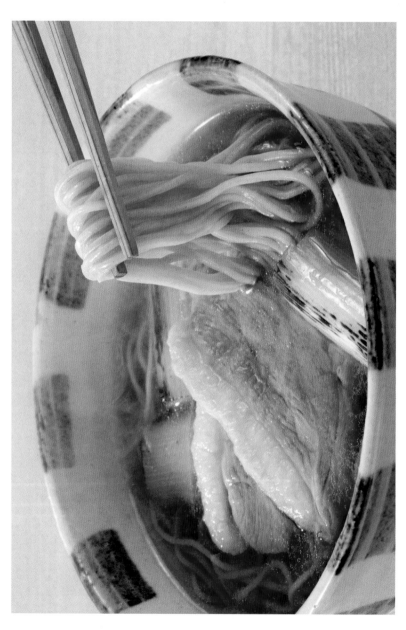

PLATE 24. Using Japanese chopsticks to eat soba noodles and duck meat.
(© TOHRU MINOWA/a.collectionRF/ amana images inc. / Alamy)

PLATE 25. The fact that rice can be transported in clumps using chopsticks has led
to chopsticks becoming the main utensil used in Asia.
(© Keller & Keller Photography / Bon Appetit / Alamy)

PLATE 26. Chinese chopsticks, chopstick rests, porcelain spoons and bowls at a market stall, Stanley Market, Stanley, Hong Kong, China.
(© Steve Vidler/ SuperStock / Alamy)

PLATE 27. Decorative chopsticks sold in Japanese stores, which are more of a gift than an eating implement.
(Author's photograph)

PLATE 28. Eating Chinese takeout with disposable chopsticks.
(© Kablonk RM/ Golden Pixels LLC / Alamy)

PLATE 29. Couples dressed according to Han dynasty customs eating together in a group wedding ceremony in Xi'an, China. (© *Corbis*)

5

Using chopsticks: customs, manners and etiquette

Another function of the two chopsticks together, that of pinching the fragment of food; to *pinch*, moreover, is too strong a word, too aggressive; for the foodstuff never undergoes a pressure greater than is precisely necessary to raise and carry it; in the gesture of chopsticks, further softened by their substance – wood or lacquer – there is something maternal, the same precisely measured care taken in moving a child: a force no longer a pulsion; here we have a whole demeanor with regard to food ... the instrument never pierces, cuts, or slits, never wounds but only selects, turns, shifts.

Roland Barthes, Empire of Signs, 16.

Der Mensch ist was es isst (a man is what he eats).

German proverb

In ancient times, people used both spoons and chopsticks to eat food, as recorded in histories and biographies. Korea also followed this custom. However, when the Central Plain [China] was in chaos, hundreds and thousands of military officers left and went east [to Korea]. When eating food, regardless of how it was cooked, they only used chopsticks, never a spoon. I don't know when this way of eating began. It is said that Ming Emperor Taizu [Zhu Yuanzhang] once vowed that before he defeated Chen Youliang, he would not dare to use a spoon to eat and drink. He wanted to demonstrate his resolve. From then on, eating without a spoon gradually became adopted as a custom. However, I do not know whether this story is believable.

Yun Kuk-Hyong (1543–1611), a Korean envoy to the Ming dynasty (1368–1644), makes this observation in his *Random Records of 1604* (Capchin Mallok), a journal chronicling his trip to China in the early seventeenth century.[1] By the time Yun went to China, it had become an established practice for the Joseon dynasty (1392–1897) in Korea to send cultural and diplomatic missions, biannually or annually, to Ming China and pay tributes to the Chinese dynasty, for the Korean rulers shared the belief with the Chinese that Confucianism was an ideal guide in government. Schooled in Confucian learning when young, those Korean envoys left a number of travelogues, offering valuable information on various aspects of Ming culture and society – its food culture and dining habits included. Yun Kuk-Hyong's account is one of them. When he landed in China, where Confucianism originated, Yun was surprised to see that the Chinese did not follow the dining etiquette recommended by such Confucian texts as the *Classic of Rites*, in which he himself was possibly quite versed. He was taken aback that the Chinese he met only used chopsticks, but not together with a spoon to eat. Yun did not quite understand this (new) dining method, nor did he accept credulously the Chinese explanation for his query.

Using chopsticks to transport both grain and nongrain foods, however, was nothing new in seventeenth-century China. More than a century earlier, Ch'oe Pu (1454–1504), a Korean Confucian scholar, had already observed in his journal that chopsticks had become the only tool for the Chinese to consume meals. After arriving in South China in the sixteenth century, European travellers and missionaries made the same observation.[2] As speculated previously, since rice has long been the staple in South China and rice can be moved in globs like sliced meat and vegetables, the southern Chinese possibly had used, perhaps for the sake of convenience and economy, only chopsticks for meals from antiquity. But in their trips, Ch'oe Pu and Yun Kuk-Hyong went to North China. When did the northern Chinese experiment with this dining method, shedding the spoon in consuming their daily meals? In other words, when did chopsticks become the exclusive eating tool for the Chinese throughout China, as seen today? This becomes an intriguing question because, as stated in Chapter 3, until the Tang dynasty, despite the expanded chopsticks use in Chinese society, the spoon had remained

---

[1] Yun Kuk-Hyong, *Capchin Mallok*, available at http://db.itkc.or.kr/itkcdb/mainIndexI frame.jsp.

[2] Ch'oe Pu, *Ch'oe Pu's Diary: A Record of Drifting across the Sea*, trans. John Meskill (Tucson: University of Arizona Press, 1965), 93, 135–136, 144, 147, 157. The European observations were in the writings of Galeote Pereira, Gaspar da Cruz and Martin De Rada in *South China in the Sixteenth Century*, ed. C. R. Boxer (London: Hakluyt Society, 1953), 14, 141, 287.

the primary implement for carrying *fan* (cooked grain) for the Chinese. Instances where spoons and chopsticks were used in unison are duly recorded in Tang literature, since the term *bizhu* or *chizhu* (spoon and chopsticks) always appears. What happened in the periods after the Tang's fall in the tenth century, causing this conversion to occur throughout China?

Actually, not only did something happen but it was also recorded in writing. The demise of the Tang had given rise to several regimes vying for control of China for several decades, until the victory of the Northern Song dynasty in 960. But the Song dynasty was ineffective in defending its northern borders. In 1127, the dynasty suffered a huge defeat in confronting the Jurchen, a nomadic power from Manchuria, and subsequently lost Kaifeng, its capital. In his memoir, Meng Yuanlao (*c.* 1090–1150), a Kaifeng native who retreated to the south, reminisces about the prosperous life the city had had, with many detailed descriptions. He mentions that while eating out in inns and restaurants, the diners "all used chopsticks today, instead of spoons as in older days." As Kaifeng is located in North China, Meng's statement suggests that chopsticks had become the only eating tool among the northern Chinese, if only for eating outside home, as early as the twelfth century.[3] This was a stark contrast to dietary practices during the Tang. The *Old Tang History* (JiuTang shu), compiled a few decades after the Tang in the mid-tenth century, records that Gao Chongwen, a Tang general known for his strictness in disciplining his army, gave the specific order that his soldiers must use both spoons and chopsticks at local lodges. Gao would punish, according to the record, anyone who disobeyed the order by a death penalty.[4]

Since people's choice of utensil often results from the type of food they eat, we need to see if, after the Tang, the northern Chinese discarded the spoon and only used chopsticks because they ate different foods. Meng Yuanlao recalled that in the city of Kaifeng everyone eating at a restaurant had all switched to chopsticks as their eating tool; however, he did not specify what types of food were served at those eateries. But it seems that at least they were not eating millet, for Lu You (1126–1200), a contemporary poet and a petty official in South China, professed that when he ate the grain, he used a spoon. In one of his poems,

---

[3] Meng Yuanlao et al., *Dongjing menghualu, Ducheng jisheng, Xihu laoren fanshenglu, Mengliang lu, Wulin jiushi* (Beijing: Zhongguo shangye chubanshe, 1982), 29.
[4] Liu Xu, *JiuTangshu* (Old Tang history) – "Gao Chongwen zi Chengjian" (Biographies of Gao Chongwen and his son Gao Chengjian), HDWZK, 4052.

Lu describes vividly how he slid his spoon smoothly into cooked millet and scooped it up. Born and raised in Shaoxing, a city in the Yangzi River Delta, Lu You had to be more accustomed to eating rice than millet. Yet on occasions when millet was the grain food, Lu turned to the spoon, following the traditional etiquette recommended by ancient sages. This shows that even in the late twelfth century, cooked millet was likely eaten with a spoon among the Chinese literati.[5]

Perhaps due to their own consumption of rice, Japanese scholars have all agreed that the Chinese turned more to chopsticks use in the post-Tang periods because they ate more rice. Back in the 1950s, Aoki Masaru (1887–1964), a sinologist, had already argued that the primary reason for the northern Chinese to discard the spoon and only employ chopsticks for meals was that rice had spread to North China. In particular, Aoki pointed out, it was the variety of *sinica/japonica* rice, which he called the *nenshitsumai* (lit. glutinous rice), that grew across China. In other words, as the rice variety is viscous (not to be confused with the sticky rice used for making holiday food), the *sinica/japonica* rice is more integrated after cooking, enabling one to move it easily in clumps with chopsticks. Citing Aoki in their work, Mukai and Hashimoto have supported Aoki's argument with new evidence that the above conversion occurred around the fifteenth century. Shū Tassei, another Japanese scholar, also states that in North China, the custom for the Chinese to turn to chopsticks as their exclusive eating tool began in the Ming period, or after the fourteenth century.[6] It is possible that Japanese scholars have drawn on their own dining experience in Japan, for *sinica/japonica* rice is the most consumed rice variety among the Japanese. It has also been a long-practiced dietary custom for the Japanese to use chopsticks exclusively for their daily meals. However, if rice consumption did encourage exclusive chopsticks use, the rice did not have to be the *sinica/japonica* variety. Like the Japanese, the Vietnamese also mostly use chopsticks as their only eating tool for daily meals. But in Southeast Asia, due to geographical and climatic similarity, the *indica* rice is quite common, especially in Thailand but in Vietnam too. But regardless of the variety, the Vietnamese can move cooked rice with only chopsticks.

---

[5] Lu You, *Jiannan shigao* (Complete collections of Lu You's poems), *juan* 60, ZJGK, 756. Another possibility is that since he was writing a poem, Lu might have just preferred an archaic usage, a common practice among Chinese poets. Millet, after all, might not have even been his daily staple in real life.

[6] Mukai & Hashimoto, *Hashi*, 41–44; Shū, *Chūgoku no Shokubunka*, 125.

Without question, rice gained a much more important status as a grain food in China after the Tang. During the Song period, observes E. N. Anderson, "rice became far more important, at last gaining its modern status as China's chief grain." Indeed, Anderson summarizes, "rice was the miracle crop of Sung (Song)."[7] The advantage of rice is that when climate permits, rice fields have a higher yield than that of other crops. "On the basis of mean grain yield," states Te-tzu Chang when writing for *The Cambridge World History of Food*, "rice crops produce more food energy and protein supply per hectare than wheat and maize. Hence, rice can support more people per unit of land than the two other staples."[8] Rice also has a number of varieties. The *indica* variety mentioned above, for example, generally takes less time to ripen than does the *sinica/japonica* variety. Since the sixth century, many varieties of *indica* rice had been grown extensively in Southeast Asia, of which the Champa rice, cultivated in today's central and southern Vietnam, was especially well known for its early ripening quality. The Vietnamese called it "hasty rice" because it could be harvested two or three times a year in semi-tropical climate zones.[9] In 1012, by the decree of Emperor Zhenzong, the Song dynasty official introduced Champa rice to Chinese farmers in the southeastern littoral regions. Known in Chinese as the *xian* rice, Champa rice (and its variations) became widely farmed in the Yangzi River and Pearl River regions, even though other varieties of *indica* rice had grown in the same regions since antiquity. In a word, from the Song dynasty as rice became more consumed in China than before, the Chinese turned to more rice varieties than only the *sinica/japonica* type suggested by Aoki Masaru.

In Song China, besides the increase in consumption of rice, chopsticks use expanded also because Chinese cookery entered a new phase of development. Indeed, argues Michael Freeman, it was during the Song period that cooking in China became a cuisine, characterized by the adoption of new ingredients and new cooking techniques.[10] In his account of city life in Kaifeng, Meng Yuanlao describes these new culinary developments in detail. In fact, of all the businesses in the city recorded by Meng, over half of them were public eateries, including low-priced noodle shops, noisy teahouses, lively inns and famous restaurants, in addition to a number of food stands and vendors in the city's boisterous night

---

[7] Liu, *TangSong yinshi wenhuade bijiao yanjiu*, 58. Anderson, *Food of China*, 65.
[8] Chang, "Rice," *Cambridge World History of Food*, vol. 1, 132.
[9] Nguyen, *Ancient Civilization of Vietnam*, 224.
[10] Freeman, "Sung," *Food in Chinese Culture*, 143–151.

markets. The foods offered at those places were cooked in a great variety of ways, ranging from various kinds of stews, prepared traditionally but with new ingredients, to new, innovative stir-fried dishes, displaying the marked improvement of this relatively new cooking technique. One could well imagine that to eat all these foods, plus noodles and dumplings, people naturally turned to chopsticks as the eating utensil, for it was economical and convenient; they were likely to be provided by the eateries.[11]

Apparently, Kaifeng was not the only city in Song China that had such an animated and exciting life. When the Song dynasty retreated to the south, it made Lin'an, or today's Hangzhou, its capital. The city Lin'an, according to a contemporaneous account, quickly became a hub of a great variety of restaurants at which many schools of cuisines competed to attract customers.[12] That is, the improvement and diversification of Chinese food culture continued and expanded, despite the regime change. Not only were southern crops like rice grown in parts of North China; expanding on the effort already begun in the Tang, northern crops such as wheat were also planted widely in the south, partly to meet the demand of the northern Chinese who migrated to the south following the Song regime. Their dining habits also influenced the southern residents: from then on, if not earlier, wheat flour foods (e.g. noodles and wonton) became daily staples for the people in the south, if mostly only for breakfast and snacks.

After the Mongols established the Yuan dynasty (1271–1368) in China, such mixing and mingling of culinary traditions persisted. A famous example is the introduction of "mutton hot pot" (*shuanyangrou*) into China proper. The dish had a Mongolian origin but also appealed to the Chinese, especially those in the north (a topic we will turn to below). The Yuan dynasty was overthrown by Zhu Yuanzhang (1328–1398), who founded the Ming dynasty in its ruins in 1368. In his early reign, Zhu migrated peasants from the south and northwest to the north, in hope of reviving the agricultural economy in those war-wrecked regions. He also issued policies to restore and maintain good irrigation systems, which benefited the growth of all grain crops in general, and rice in particular. These measures caused southern foods and cuisines to either spread or take deeper root in the north. After Zhu's death, his son Zhu Di, or Emperor Yongle (1360–1424), made Beijing the new capital, which further strengthened the economic and cultural link between the north and the

---

[11] Meng, *Dongjing menghualu*.
[12] Ibid., especially *Mengliangu* and *Xihu laoren fanshenglu*.

south. Toward the late Ming, as the government was staffed more and more by officials from Jiangnan (lit. south of Yangzi, or Yangzi Valley), it designed policies to cultivate rice in the suburbs of Beijing and other regions in North China, in addition to transporting it in large quantities from the south through the Grand Canal.[13] When Song Yingxing (1587–1666) wrote his *Exploitations of the Works of Nature* (Tiangong kaiwu), he estimated that "Nowadays seventy per cent of the people's staple food is rice, while wheat and various kinds of millet constitute thirty per cent."[14] Concurring with Song, E. N. Anderson states that during the Ming, "rice became even more important, reaching its modern level of significance as China's great staple. At the same time, wheat was spreading in the south, the flour was becoming an important food."[15] European missionaries who went to South China during the Ming confirmed that while "the principal food of all Chinos [sic] is rice ... there is also much and very good wheat, whereof they make very good bread."[16]

Ming China, spanning nearly three centuries, was a prosperous era; its prosperity is reflected in the many novels appearing in the age. These novels provide unequivocal evidence that the Ming Chinese only used chopsticks for their meals, as observed by Yun Kuk-Hyong at the beginning of the chapter. The novels by Feng Menglong (1574–1646), a prolific writer of the time, recorded multiple and useful examples. Feng was interested in portraying the life of the common people, or the townspeople living in urban areas in coastal China. His *Stories to Awaken the World* (Xingshi hengyan), for instance, depicts an occasion at which Qin Chong, a candidate en route to the imperial examination, was received warmly by a local family. Qin was offered rice and wine, together with a pair of chopsticks and a wine cup – the only two utensils given to him. He used the chopsticks to eat the rice, which was described as "snow white," and took a little sip of the wine in the cup. Another character in the novel, Wu Ya'nei, or Young Master Wu, was a big eater. On one occasion, as the story depicts, Wu was only given two bowls of rice. "Holding his chopsticks," Feng writes, "he quickly shoveled them down,

---

[13] Yin Yongwen, *MingQing yinshi yanjiu* (Studies of food and drink in the Ming and Qing dynasties) (Taipei: Hongye wenhua shiye youxian gongsi, 1997), 5–6.

[14] Song Yingxing (Sung Ying-hsing), *T'ien-kung k'ai-wu: Chinese Technology in the Seventeenth Century*, trans. E-tu Zen Sun and Shiou-chuan Sun (University Park: Pennsylvania State University Press, 1966), 4.

[15] Anderson, *Food of China*, 80.

[16] See the writings of Martin de Rada and Gaspar da Cruz in Boxer, *South China in the Sixteenth Century*, 287, 131.

with only two or three scoops," still appearing quite unsatisfied.[17] A native of Suzhou, a major city in Jiangnan where rice was the grain staple, Feng proved that it had been customary for the people to transfer rice from bowls to their mouths with a pair of chopsticks.

Ming novels also show that rice was consumed quite commonly in North China. *The Plum in the Golden Vase* (Jinpingmei), a well-known erotic novel written anonymously in the late sixteenth century, is a prime example. The story depicted in the novel was supposed to have taken place in Shandong, North China. The novel hence illustrated how food habits and dietary customs had changed among the northern Chinese in the period. The protagonists of *The Plum in the Golden Vase* are a rich merchant named Ximen Qing and his concubines and lovers. Li Ping'er was one of Ximen's concubines who, suffered an untimely death. Upon her departure, Ximen Qing went to Li Ping'er's quarter. Saddened and sobbing, Li's servants served Ximen with several dishes on the dining table. To console them, Ximen "raised his chopsticks from the table and said: 'Please eat some rice,' as though Li were still alive. But his consolation gesture only made them cry more."[18] Clearly, not only did the northern Chinese like Ximen Qing eat rice, they also used chopsticks to convey the grain.

As rice was grown and consumed in North China, a new term, *damifan* (lit. big rice), appeared in Ming texts. As a result, cooked millet became called *xiaomifan* (lit. small rice); both are still in popular parlance among the northern Chinese today because they still consume them as daily grains. These neologisms appeared because in terms of grain size, rice is undoubtedly larger than millet, even its *huangliang* variety. *The Plum in the Golden Vase* frequently mentions how people cooked rice *fan*, and quotes such aphorisms as "[whoever] put in the rice (*mi* – uncooked rice) first, would eat the *fan* first too."[19] Yet interestingly, the *fan* described in the novel was often called *tangfan*, literarily meaning "rice in hot water or soup." This term reveals that in cooking rice, the northern Chinese perhaps still liked to make it a gruel or porridge, just as they would if it were millet. Besides rice, the people in *The Plum in the Golden Vase* also ate other grains. To cultivate his love affairs, Ximen Qing threw many parties, at which a variety of foods was served. Among those made of grain

---

[17] Feng Menglong, *Xingshi hengyan*, *juan* 3 and *juan* 28, ZJGK, 35, 414.
[18] Xiaoxiaosheng, *Jinpingmei*, *juan* 13, ZJGK, 515.
[19] "*Xian xiami, xian chifan*," which appears four times in *Jinpingmei* in *juan* 4, *juan* 15, *juan* 18, ZJGK, 135, 664, 725, 729.

cereals were buns, pancakes, noodles and rice, demonstrating a more diverse food system than that in Jiangnan. But regardless of the variety and whether the food appeared solid or soft, Ximen and his friends only used chopsticks, in addition to a cup for drinking either wine or tea, without the presence of a spoon. In fact, the eating scenes described in the novel suggest that by this time this combination (a pair of chopsticks and a tea/wine cup) of eating tools had replaced the earlier spoon and chopsticks combination.[20] Gaspar da Cruz, a Jesuit missionary who visited the Ming, also wrote that a "small porcelain cup" was provided for the diners to hold wine, without mentioning the spoon.[21]

By using chopsticks to eat, again shown in these Ming novels, people sat around a dining table and placed cooked dishes on it for everyone to share. In his journal, Ch'oe Pu, the Korean mandarin, also recalls that when he crisscrossed China, he saw the Chinese use only chopsticks to eat foods at a common table.[22] The Europeans who went to China in the period made a similar observation:

The Chinas [Chinese] are great eaters and they use many dishes. They eat at one table fish and flesh, and the base people dress it sometimes all together. The dishes which are to be eaten at one table, are set all together on the board [table?], that every one may eat which he liketh best.[23]

This has become a typical eating scene in China and beyond in the chopsticks cultural sphere. But it marked a contrast to the dietary custom of the earlier periods, such as that of Han and Tang China. For Han stone carvings and mural paintings show that the Chinese dined on the floor, not on a chair nor at a table, and the food was either placed on a mat or on a short-legged tray (the tray was called *shi'an*, appearing first in a Han text) (Plate 5).[24] In modern Chinese, "banquet" is still referred to as *yanxi*, or "dining on the mat," indicating the residual influence of the ancient custom. This dietary tradition seems to have continued more or less through the Tang. Meanwhile, some Tang paintings show that people had begun to sit on a bench and eat food on a table. But it seems that they still had food served to them in their individual bowls and plates (Plate 11).

---

[20] See *Jinpingmei, juan* 12, ZJGK, 443. There were more eating occasions described throughout the novel where wine cups and chopsticks were provided instead of spoons.

[21] Boxer, *South China in the Sixteenth Century*, 142.   [22] *Ch'oe Pu's Diary*, 157.

[23] da Cruz, Boxer, *South China in the Sixteenth Century*, 141.

[24] Huan Kuan, *Yantie lun* (Debates on salt and iron), *juan* 5, ZJGK, 31.

However, during the post-Tang periods, together with the ascent of chopsticks as an eating tool, a new dining habit emerged in China; diners began sitting on chairs around a table, on which food dishes were placed for everyone to sample. Chinese food scholars call this new dining style *heshizhi* (communal eating style), as opposed to the *fenshizhi* (individual eating style) of the earlier periods (Plate 12). Had the emergence of the communal eating style also encouraged the Chinese to turn to increased chopsticks use rather than to the spoon? Liu Yun believes it did, and cites the evidence that the chopsticks from the Ming period tended to be a bit longer – averaging over 25 cm – than their earlier counterparts. The increased length, observes Liu, was for diners to pinch and pick up the food contents at the middle of the table.[25] (It is worth mentioning here that in Chongqing, where hot pot is the local delicacy, restaurants that serve hot pot provide their customers with longer chopsticks, in order to facilitate the food sharing.) By comparison, as communal eating is uncommon in Japan, Japanese chopsticks are shorter (18–20 cm), a point that lends support to Liu's observation. The Japanese prefer eating in the so-called *meimeizen* (lit. one meal per person) style, with food items pre-served to their individual plates and bowls.

It was practical for the Japanese, as well as the early Chinese, to eat their meals individually, rather than communally, because they dined on the floor (e.g. sitting on the tatami as the Japanese customarily did). It made sense for food to be served to them – it would be too awkward and cumbersome for anyone to crawl on the floor to get the food for themselves. The development of the communal eating style, therefore, was predicated on the use of chairs and tables, especially the former. Chairs were not found in ancient China; they were introduced to China by the nomads, or the *huren*, in the Han dynasty. When Emperor Ling of the Han demanded that everything be *hu*, *huchuang*, or "*hu* seat," was included. The seat was possibly made of animal skins and supported by wooden legs. It was light and foldable, resembling an outdoor chair today. It might have evolved from the saddle used by the nomads in horse riding. In the post-Han period, according to a fourth-century text, the *hu* seat came to be adopted by the Chinese, especially among the rich.[26] As it became more accepted, *huchuang* changed to *jiaochuang*, dropping the *hu* prefix; *jiaochuang* instead described how the sitter crossed their legs in the seat. The

[25] Liu, *Zhongguo zhu wenhuashi*, 327.
[26] Gan Bao, *Soushenji* (In search of the supernatural), *juan* 7, ZJGK, 30.

word *chuang*, however, still suggests that it was less a chair than a bench, without the back. And benches are indeed shown in Tang paintings.[27]

Once the stool height was raised and a back attached, then the bench became a chair. The Chinese equivalent of the chair is *yizi*, which first appeared in the Tang.[28] The famous *Night Revels of Han Xizai* (Han Xizai yeyantu; Plate 13), a painting from the tenth century, not long after the Tang's fall, offers a glimpse of what chairs were like in Tang and post-Tang China. The seat was high enough for a sitter to extend his legs straight down and, with a back, the sitter could also rest his body. That is, the chair had become like a chair one uses today. When Han Xizai (902–970), a respected scholar-official at the time who refused to serve in government, entertained his guests, as the painting depicts, he gave them several dishes on the rectangular table in front of them, which was not much higher than the chair on which he and his guests were sitting. It looked more like a coffee table in modern times. While chopsticks and wine cups were on the table, the painting shows that Han and his friends were eating together, but *not* eating communally as in the later periods.

But communal eating did begin to take place, first among family members, in the following periods. A mural painting (Plate 14) found in a Song tomb in Hebei, near Beijing, shows a middle-aged couple sitting across from each other, with foods, chopsticks and wine cups on a table, apparently having a family dinner together. The square-shaped table in the painting is considerably higher than the one in the *Night Revels of Han Xizai*.[29] Food scholars in China believe that communal eating started as early as the Song period, or from the twelfth century onward, as a result of the marked culinary advances of the period. "Communal eating began to be widely adopted in Song society," Zhao Rongguang states, "because food dishes on the table became multiplied and diversified. People desired to sample and share these dishes together at a meal, making communal dining a logical choice. The individual eating style became obsolete."[30] That people in the Song had shared food together at one sitting is also described in novels, such as in the famous *Water Margin*

---

[27] Wu Jing, *Zhen'guan zhengyao* (Essentials about politics in the Zhen'guan reign), *juan* 16, ZJGK, 156.

[28] See www.baike.com/wiki/椅子 which cites a Tang record that used *yizi*. The next appearance of *yizi* is in Yuchi Wo's *Zhongchao gushi* (Stories of the Tang dynasty), written in the tenth century, ZJGK, 6.

[29] Tomb mural of Mr. Zhao and his wife eating at a table, served by their daughter and servants, *c.* 1099. Tomb no. 1, Yuxian, Henan Province.

[30] Zhao Rongguang, *Zhongguo yinshi wenhua gailun*, 219.

(Shuihu zhuan). Song Jiang, the hero in the novel who organized a revolt against the Song dynasty in the twelfth century, is depicted often having meals and drinks with his friends while sitting together at a big table.[31] But the novel was written in the fourteenth century, or in the early Ming; it thus might have projected the Ming dining style into the earlier Song period.

The adoption of communal eating had to be a gradual process in Chinese society. But apparently by the Ming it had become rather common. As the Ming exercised some control in Vietnam, it was likely that the Vietnamese also adopted communal dining during the period.[32] To facilitate the need for sharing of dishes, the table size, too, became bigger from the Ming onward. The dining tables mentioned in such Ming novels as *The Plum in the Golden Vase* were of two types – *kangzhuo*, or "bed-stove table," and *baxianzhuo*, or "eight-immortal table." Both terms only began to appear in Ming texts, not earlier. (Square tables, or *fangzhuo*, had appeared in the Song, but they were not mainly used for dining.[33]) The bed-stove table, as its name suggests, is a table for putting on a platform bed, also called a bed-stove. Built with bricks or fired clay, the bed-stove – *kang* in Chinese and *nahan* in Manchu – channels the heat of the cooking fire into the bedroom to keep it warm in the winter. Occupying usually two thirds of a room, the platform (approximately 2 × 1.8 m) is not only for sleeping at night but also for other activities, such as dining, during the day. In other words, the bed-stove table, which is usually square-shaped but could also be rectangular, is placed at the center of the platform in the daytime for the family to eat their daily meals or entertain their guests; it is then moved to the side and leaned against the wall at night when the family goes to sleep. The platform bed and the table remain in use among the Chinese, Koreans and Manchus living in the north today. For several diners to eat at the bed-stove table, most of them have to sit around it and the rest on the benches next to the bed (Plate 15). This was exactly how Ximen Qing and his women did it, according to *The Plum in the Golden Vase*.[34]

---

[31] In his *TangSong yinshi wenhuade bijiao yanjiu*, Liu Pubing argues that communal eating began in Song China, though he cites *Water Margin* as evidence, which was a Ming novel. 313–322.

[32] As quoted in Chapter 4, Nguyen describes his country's eating customs as follows: "The dishes are common for all, one uses one's chopsticks to take foodstuffs which are prepared and cut into small pieces." *Ancient Civilization of Vietnam*, 212.

[33] Chen Kui, *NanSong guangelu* (Records of Southern Song archives and history-offices), ZJGK, 27.

[34] *Kangzhuo* appears in *Jinpingmei* in *juan* 4, 135, *juan* 5, 181, *juan* 6, 223, *juan* 15, 604, *juan* 18, 717, and *juan* 18, 751; all pages are in ZJGK.

In the Ming novel, Ximen Qing also used eight-immortal tables to entertain his guests, especially when he was hosting a big party.[35] As its name indicates, the eight-immortal table is larger than the bed-stove table. Approximately 1.2 × 1.2 m, it is big enough for eight people to sit rather comfortably around it and have a meal together. And the table seems more common in South China, where the platform bed was absent, than it was in the north. Feng Menglong's *Stories to Awaken the World*, for instance, never mentions the bed-stove table. When he describes how Qin Chong was welcomed with a meal, as cited above, Feng points out that the foods, fruits and confections were presented to Qin on an eight-immortal table for him to savor and enjoy. Indeed, whenever eating is described in the novel, the eight-immortal table is always used, suggesting its broad acceptance in South China.[36]

Wang Mingsheng (1722–1797), a scholar of the Qing dynasty (1644–1911), traced the evolution of dining tables in China, and the origin of the eight-immortal table in particular, as follows:

The table used today had the same origin as *huchuang* [*hu* seat]. Ancient people sat on the floor, behind a mat. So they did not use a chair. If they used a table, or *ji* 几, it was rather small, as described in the *Classic of History* and the *Classic of Odes*. By contrast, the table we use today is quite big. In common parlance, it is called the table of eight immortals, for it could have eight people eating together at a sitting. Though similar in use, today's table is quite different from the table of ancient times.[37]

Wang's remarks showed that during his time, the eight-immortal table was the most common dining table. The table has actually retained its popularity more or less to this day in many parts of China. A major reason for its persistent attraction seems to be its big size, enabling more to sit around it and more food dishes to be presented. Beginning in the Ming but continuing through the Qing, the population in China experienced a steady growth, rising roughly from less than 100 million in the fifteenth century to over 300 million in the mid-eighteenth century. In 1712 when Emperor Kangxi (1654–1722) removed the poll tax, it undoubtedly helped to increase the family size, making the table almost indispensable for many enlarged households. But the increase had already begun in the Ming, partly because of the introduction of the "New World crops" (maize,

---

[35] *Baxianzhuo* appears six times in *Jinpingmei*.
[36] Feng, *Xingshi hengyan, juan* 3, ZJGK, 35.
[37] Wang Mingsheng, *Shiqishi shangque* (Critiques of seventeen histories) (Shanghai: Shanghai shudian chubanshe, 2005), *juan* 24, 171–172.

sweet potatoes, potatoes, etc.) from the Americas to China, which helped reduce mortality among the poor. As more cheap labor became available while the gap between the rich and poor remained, the rich Chinese pursued luxury, including haute cuisine and other "superfluous things." The enlarged body of literature of connoisseurship of the period documented the development of this "luxury culture." The popularity of the eight-immortal table was material evidence, confirming the extent of such a culture in Chinese society.[38]

The adoption of tables and chairs, therefore, was correlated to the propagation of communal dining among the Chinese; the latter enabled diners to taste and try several dishes at one sitting. The flexibility of chopsticks enhances such a process, especially if the dishes are stir-fried or stewed because the food items have been cut into small pieces. Yet people could also share several food contents in one dish. "Mutton hot pot" (*shuanyangrou*), a popular hot pot mentioned above, is a typical example. Eating mutton hot pot has made chopsticks indispensable, for it requires one to cook the food items in the simmering pot at the center of the table. The nimbleness of chopsticks allows one to choose the thinly sliced meat and chopped vegetables in a desired portion and load them in the pot. Once the meat is ready – having swished it in the hot broth – it is lifted up by the chopsticks and dipped first into the sauces before being finally delivered to one's mouth. In brief, chopsticks are essential in eating a hot pot. By contrast, it is hard to use a spoon for the above tasks, for the food items can slip off and fall from it.

Chinese legend attributes the invention of mutton hot pot to Kublai Khan (1215–1294), the grandson of Genghis Khan and founder of the Yuan dynasty in China. It is said that while campaigning in China, Kublai once had a craving for mutton stew, common in Mongolian cookery. As the chef was making it, his army came under attack. To save time, the chef sliced the mutton into thin pieces and threw the slices in the boiling water for fast cooking. He then spread salt and condiments on them. Kublai quickly gobbled them all up and praised the taste. To many Chinese, mutton hot pot might be the quintessential hot pot. But the hot pot also

---

[38] "Luxury culture" in the Ming is identified by Jack Goody in his "The Origin of Chinese Food Culture," *Di 6 jie Zhongguo yinshi wenhua xueshu yantaohui lunwenji* (Proceedings of the 6th symposium of Chinese food and drink culture) (Taipei: Zhongguo yinshi wenhua jijinhui, 2003), 2–4. Also Craig Clunas, *Superfluous Things: Material Culture and Social Status in Early Modern China* (Urbana: University of Illinois Press, 1991); and Timothy Brook, *The Confusions of Pleasure: Commerce and Culture in Ming China* (Berkeley: University of California Press, 1998).

resembles a stew, which has been a common dish throughout Asia for centuries. In a recipe book written by Lin Hong in the twelfth century, for example, the author recalls that once he went to Mt. Wuyi, located in Southeast China, to visit a recluse on a snowy day. He was treated with rabbit meat, which, according to his description, was cooked the same way mutton hot pot was made: the meat was first sliced thinly then loaded into a boiling broth. Lin also records that he, along with other guests, was asked to use chopsticks to load the meat into the broth. After cooking the meat in the broth for a little while, they used chopsticks to pick up the meat and dipped it in sauces before delivering it to their mouths. This too is the way mutton hot pot is usually eaten nowadays. In fact, Lin points out that besides rabbit, people also cooked pork and mutton the same way – the cold weather at the top of the mountains might have helped them to prepare the meat this way. He also mentions that several years later, he saw restaurants in Lin'an (Hangzhou) adopting the same cooking method, though he did not specify what meat was used.[39]

The way mutton hot pot, or any hot pot in general, is cooked and its main food ingredient (lamb and mutton) is prepared suggests that it must have been more popular among the nomadic peoples. Compared with the people in the south, people in the north, the nomads in particular, consumed more animal meat, be it lamb, pork or beef. They also preferred to eat food hot, which is essentially how a hot pot is usually eaten; the diners pick the food from the hot broth right after it is cooked and deliver it to their mouths. One essential step in cooking the hot pot is to first freeze the meat so that it can be sliced very thinly. After being loaded into the pot, the cold meat will then hiss in the boiling broth and quickly roll up. Before the invention of refrigerators, it would have been hard to freeze the meat in the temperate and subtropical south. After founding the Qing dynasty, it was the Manchus who made mutton hot pot a more popular dish in North China. Although they themselves preferred pork to lamb, the Manchu court turned to the dish on occasion. Over time, mutton hot pot also found acceptance among city residents in Beijing and other neighboring regions.

Besides promoting mutton hot pot, the Manchus were also credited with creating their own hot pot, which used sliced pork – their favorite meat – and Chinese cabbage, among other things. Koreans are also fond of hot pot dishes, or *sinseollo* and *jjigae*. The former is more similar to a

---

[39] Lin Hong, *Shanjia qinggong* (Simple foods at mountains) (Beijing: Zhongguo shangye chubanshe, 1985), 48.

Chinese hot pot in that the broth is boiled in the middle of the table, whereas the latter resembles more a thick soup, often cooked beforehand. Hot pot, or *nabemono* (lit. foodstuffs [cooked] in a pot), is also popular among the Japanese. There are two kinds as well. One is *shabu shabu*, or "swish swish," which is cooked similarly to mutton hot pot and other hot pots from the Asian mainland. The other is *sukiyaki*, which seems more Japanese but may have some Portuguese or European influences. As the chief ingredient of these two particular varieties of hot pot is sliced beef or other meat, both the *shabu shabu* and *sukiyaki* register modern influences in Japanese cuisine, as the Japanese consumed little animal meat before the nineteenth century. But cooking foods (fish, kelp, vegetables, mushrooms, tofu, etc.) in a pot to make a stew or a hearty soup (as *nabemono*) must have had a long history in Japan, as boiling is a common cooking method there and around the world.

After chopsticks gained their advantage over the spoon in eating communal meals, and hot pots in particular, their position on the table was also adjusted. As shown in Tang mural paintings, the Chinese placed their chopsticks horizontally on the table. But in Ming paintings, chopsticks were already positioned vertically, pointing in the direction of the food dishes at the middle of the table, as if to ready them for transportation (Plate 18). This placement has become most common nowadays in China, Korea and Vietnam, where communal eating has been adopted to a varying degree. By comparison, having retained the custom of eating meals individually, the Japanese have continued to place their chopsticks horizontally on the table, such as in a bento box. When they use the utensil to lift and deliver the food in front of them to their mouths, this movement is mostly horizontal, moving from right to left as tradition demands one use one's right hand to hold chopsticks. But interestingly, when eating *shabu shabu* and/or *sukiyaki*, the Japanese sometimes also put and leave chopsticks vertically, so they face the ingredients at the center of the table.

If the Chinese in the Ming began to place chopsticks vertically on the table, this might also be because their emperor demanded it. A Ming historical text records that after Zhu Yuanzhang founded the Ming, he invited some noted literati to a banquet at his court. After the banquet, one of them, named Tang Su, raised his chopsticks with both of his hands, thanking the Emperor. Surprised by his gesture, Zhu asked him what kind of table manners this was. Tang answered that this was what he had learned as a child in his hometown. Instead of appreciating Tang's politeness, Zhu scolded, "How could you treat me, the Son of Heaven, with vulgar village manners!" Tang was dismissed and exiled as punishment.[40] In hindsight, Tang was perhaps not at fault, for what he did might have drawn on a recommended dining tradition in China before that time. (Chapter 4 has mentioned that this gesture might have originated in Buddhist temples and the Japanese still do it today, though they tend to do it before a meal, rather than after.) However, the Ming Emperor was annoyed by it, perhaps because he had grown up as a poor peasant child and was too embarrassed to admit that he was ignorant of older traditions.

This episode indicates that as communal eating came to be widely practiced in Chinese society, chopsticks etiquette and table manners also changed as a result. But outside China, some of the traditional customs remained, and hence are preserved well to this day. The fact that by social norms modern-day Koreans still use both spoons and chopsticks as an inseparable set to convey meals is a good example. In Korea today, it is common for the two utensils to be sold together at a store, which could well surprise other Asians in the chopsticks cultural sphere. That is, just as Ch'oe Pu, Yun Kuk-Hyong and other Koreans who went to Ming China were shocked that the Chinese no longer used a spoon in convey-ing grain food, a Chinese person visiting Korea today might be equally surprised by the fact that s/he cannot purchase a pair of chopsticks without also buying a spoon! The Korean case is a unique one in the chopsticks cultural sphere.

That the Japanese have generally continued the *meimeizen* (one meal per person) style in eating is another example. To some degree, the bento box meal, ubiquitous in Japanese society today, especially at lunch time, is emblematic of how successfully the Japanese have upheld the dietary custom of olden days. In ancient China, foods in a tray were called *shan* (*zen* in Japanese), so the word *shan/zen* refers to a meal. Thus, *meimeizen* means that everyone has one's own food tray. Along with the use of individual food trays come individualized utensils; in Japanese, a pair of chopsticks is most commonly called *ichizen* 一膳, suggesting that one pair of chopsticks goes in one meal tray. Over time, the food tray became the food box, or bento box, for portability. The making of a bento box meal reflects Japanese culinary influences. For instance, as items are placed into various compartments in the box, the bento box meal pays attention to the visual presentation of the food, a tradition in Japanese cuisine. Since the meal is meant to be portable, the bento box is small enough to be held in one hand, which means that the chopsticks placed in the box are also short, another

---

[40] Cited in Lan, *Kuaizi, buzhishi kuaizi*, 82.

Japanese characteristic since most chopsticks used in Japan are shorter than their counterparts elsewhere (Plate 20).[41] Last but not least, continuing the *meimeizen* tradition, the bento box meal is individually packaged. From the fourteenth century, this dining style has become distinctly Japanese, for the Chinese, the Vietnamese and Koreans all have more or less adopted communal eating. By comparison, many Japanese families still serve cooked dishes on individual plates or bowls; it is frowned upon for anyone to dig and pick up foodstuffs with their chopsticks from a common dish before serving. Called *jikabashi* (lit. direct chopsticks), using chopsticks this way is unacceptable for many Japanese, particularly if they are dining with guests at a public restaurant. Instead, the Japanese are expected to use *toribashi*, or serving/community chopsticks, to transfer the food contents from common dishes to their own plates or bowls.

Communal eating seems also connected to the communal use of chopsticks. Outside Japan, it is normal to see a family sharing the use of utensils; before a meal, each member randomly picks up a pair of chopsticks or a spoon in a container or in a drawer. But in Japan, this is more a practice for eating at a restaurant (where one finds a bunch of chopsticks in a receptacle on the dining table) than in a household. Members of a Japanese family tend to have their own chopsticks and other utensils (spoons and bowls, etc.) for daily meals. And the shape, quality and length of chopsticks can differ markedly among members of a family, reflecting the position and gender of their users in the family. For instance, the chopsticks used by adults tend to be of better quality than those used by children, based on the assumption that children are not as careful with the utensil. There is also a gender difference: the utensils for a female member of the family tend to be shorter and smaller, since women's hands are generally smaller. But these could be more colorful and more highly decorated than those for a male family member, as shown by the characteristics of *miotobashi* – "husband–wife chopsticks" (Plate 21). To a varying degree, all these practices, too, exist in societies

---

[41] Mukai & Hashimoto, *Hashi*, 205–208; and Harada Nobuo, *Riben liaoli de shehuishi: heshi yu Riben wenhua* (A social history of Japanese cuisine: on Japanese food and Japanese culture), trans. Liu Yang (Hong Kong: Sanlian shudian, 2011), 63–68. Also, Xu, *Riben yinshi wenhua*, 85–88. Several Chinese scholars have also pointed out that the Japanese use shorter chopsticks because of their individual dining custom. See Lü Lin, "ZhongRi kuaizhu lishi yu wenhua zhi tantao" (Explorations of the chopsticks' history and culture in China and Japan), *Keji xinxi* (Science and technology information), 10 (2008), 115–117; Li Qingxiang, "Riben de zhu yu wenhua: jianyu Zhongguo kuaizi wenhua bijiao" (Chopsticks and chopsticks culture in Japan: a comparison with Chinese chopsticks culture), *Jiefangjun waiguoyu xueyuan xuebao* (Journal of PLA University of Foreign Languages), 32:5 (Spring 2009), 94–97.

outside Japan – it is likely that a senior member in a family will have his/her special utensil, chopsticks or otherwise, in China, Korea and Vietnam. But it is uncommon, or less common, for each and every member of the family to have their individual eating tools.

Although invented in Japan, serving chopsticks, or *toribashi*, have also become increasingly popular with to Koreans, the Chinese and, more recently, the Vietnamese, on social and formal occasions rather than in a family situation. But even if employing a pair of serving chopsticks is not as common as in Japan, it is often observed among the Chinese and the Vietnamese that when a host wants to serve foodstuffs to a guest's plate to show their hospitality, they will reverse their chopsticks and use the end not touched by their mouth to complete the task. Indeed, as discussed in Chapter 2, how to carry food neatly without affecting others' appetite was a constant concern, already receiving ample attention in ancient China, as demonstrated by many detailed instructions given by the *Classic of Rites*. In the chopsticks cultural sphere, as the utensil gained increasing importance in conveying food, there developed several unwritten yet generally accepted rules of etiquette, including but not limited to the following:

(1) Chopsticks are not used to make a noise (especially in the mouth), to draw attention, or to gesticulate. Playing with chopsticks is considered bad mannered, even vulgar.

(2) Chopsticks should not be used to dig around or mine for food in the dishes, looking for a particular morsel.

(3) Chopsticks are not used to move bowls or plates.

(4) Chopsticks are not used to toy with one's food or with communal dishes.

(5) Chopsticks are not used to impale food, save in rare instances. Exceptions include tearing large food items asunder, such as fish, vegetables and kimchi. In informal use, small, difficult-to-pick-up items such as cherry tomatoes or fishballs may be speared, but this use might be frowned upon.

(6) Chopsticks should not be left standing vertically in a bowl of rice or other food. Any pair of stick-like objects pointing upward resembles the incense sticks that some Asians use as offerings to deceased family members; certain funerary rites designate offerings of food to the dead using standing chopsticks.[42]

---

[42] These guidelines are provided, with some revision, by the "chopsticks" entry on Wikipedia (English), accessed on August 15, 2012. I cite these guidelines because they are, presumably, most accessed among peoples around the world today.

This not-to-do list addresses concerns in three categories. First and foremost is to prevent any messy and unpleasant dining behavior, as it spoils the appetite as well as the food of others. These rules are cross-cultural, comparable to the utensil etiquette in other cultures outside Asia. The second are directions specific to chopsticks use; namely, how to employ the instrument properly in transporting food, not disturbing and offending others. This could be at times challenging when one shares food with others at a table, using either chopsticks or a spoon or both, hence deserving more discussion below. And the third are relevant cultural and religious issues and meanings involved in using the utensil, a topic to be treated in the next chapter.

Specifically, some terms in the Japanese language describe several common taboos in chopsticks use, frowned upon by most users across Asia, in spite of the noted differences in their dietary practices and traditions. For instance, it is a *faux pas* for anyone to hold chopsticks stuck with rice grains or other food remains, or to use chopsticks to lift food that have either droped or driped onto the table. The latter is called *namidahashi* or "tearing chopsticks," in Japanese. In addition, there are such descriptions as *saguribashi* – probing chopsticks, *mayoibashi* – lost chopsticks, and *utsuribashi* – transporting chopsticks. *Saguribashi* refers to the act of using one's chopsticks to dig or mine for food, rather than grasping a particular morsel swiftly and decisively. *Mayoibashi* describes how one points one's chopsticks at different dishes as though one cannot decide which to eat, whereas *utsuribashi* refers to transporting food items from one pair of chopsticks to another, without first putting them down in a bowl or plate. The Japanese also frown upon those who keep chopsticks in the mouth for a long time and make a noise. Such behavior is called *neburibashi* – licking chopsticks. With minor variations, these characterizations also exist in the Chinese language.[43]

To ensure that one avoids all these impolite acts while using chopsticks, it is generally required that one first learn to hold the utensil correctly and properly. Over the centuries, chopsticks users have indeed come up with one effective way of using the implement, accepted and practiced almost universally across the chopsticks cultural sphere. A brief description of this method is already given in the Introduction. Since nowadays children often fail to learn the correct method at home when growing up, some elementary schools in South Korea have gone as far as to offer drill lessons to teach the children how to apply the utensil in

---

[43] Li, "Riben de zhu yu wenhua: jianyu Zhongguo kuaizi wenhua bijiao."

conveying a meal. In order to encourage chopsticks use among children, an annual chopsticks festival (August 4) was created in Japan in 1980, which was introduced initially by some local governments but now has spread to many parts of the country.[44] The Japanese also designed and made training chopsticks for children, which are connected at the top part with a proper space in-between. The upper chopstick also has rings in which users put their index and middle fingers so that they can hold both sticks correctly for effective use (Plate 23).

Such efforts to continue the traditional method of chopsticks use are made because experience has shown and proven that in order for the two sticks to grasp a food item firmly, it is best that one keep a certain space between them and only use the upper stick to make the pincer movement. This is why, as exemplified by the Japanese training chopsticks, the upper stick has two rings for one to insert the index and middle fingers for making the stick move, whereas the lower stick has none, since it is to be rested securely in the hand. All this is to address the need to clutch and carry a food item swiftly and adroitly, but avoid touching other items as much as possible, nor to let items drop or drip on the table. "All rules of table manners," wrote Emily Post, author of the popular *Etiquette* (1922), "are made to avoid ugliness; to let anyone see what you have in your mouth is repulsive; to make a noise is to suggest an animal; to make a mess is disgusting."[45] That is, table manners were developed, primarily, to create and maintain a neat and pleasant eating environment. This seems a universal concern.

Take the "tearing chopsticks" as an example. This conduct, caused either by sloppiness or by their lack of skill in using the utensil, becomes odious and even offensive in the chopsticks cultural sphere because it looks messy, unclean and unpleasant, ruining the eating environment. Yet the way to prevent it has varied from place to place. In China and Vietnam, diners are either encouraged or required to transfer, using chopsticks as they generally do, food contents from the common dishes first to their own bowls before delivering them to their mouths. In so doing, they can at times lift and move their bowls closer to the dishes from where the foodstuffs are being transferred. As the travel distance is shorter, it decreases the chance of food dropping or dripping from the chopsticks

---

[44] N. A., "Hanguo kaishe kuaizike" (Koreans teaching chopsticks in schools), *Hebei shenji* (Hebei audit), 12 (1995). About the chopsticks festival in Japan, see www.subject-knowl edge.us/Wikipedia-960158-Japanese-chopsticks-Festival.html.

[45] Quoted in Giblin, *From Hand to Mouth*, 64.

into the dishes or onto the table. By comparison, it is frowned upon in Korea to raise the rice bowl from the table. In order to avert "tearing chopsticks," Koreans apply the spoon, instead of chopsticks, in carrying any dripping food. Koreans are taught to use a spoon to transport rice for the same reason. For if the rice bowl is not to be picked up from the table, when one uses chopsticks to transport rice from the table directly to the mouth one tends to drop grains along the way. Thus, it is seen in some Korean families that someone moves rice from the rice bowl first to a soupy dish and then moves the second bowl closer to the mouth, using a spoon to eat both in a mixed form. This practice, which is informal, might suggest that Koreans remain accustomed to eating grain starch in a soupy form, explaining their tendency to use the spoon for its transportation.

Koreans do not raise the rice bowl from the table and hold it in their hands, for such behavior is associated with begging, as beggars tend to do that while asking for food. To prevent rice grains falling in the process of delivery, it is acceptable for Koreans to lower their heads when eating a meal. The idea is to shorten the distance from the bowl or plate to the mouth. But the Chinese tradition is generally against lowering one's head in eating food, for doing so reminds one of pigs eating. Instead, while keeping their backs straight, the Chinese lift the rice bowl from the table and use chopsticks to push rice into the mouth, as do the Vietnamese and Japanese. The idea however is the same – to cut down the distance for which the food item is carried by chopsticks, lest it drop or drip, or make a "tearing chopsticks" scene. Since the Japanese, the Vietnamese and the Chinese tend to only use chopsticks to transport both grain and nongrain foods in their day-to-day life, it is practical for them to lift their bowls to their mouths in order to avoid any dropping incidents and maintain a neat eating style. On occasions when a spoon is also used to eat a food, such as a soup noodle (e.g. *lamian/ramen*), one can use both the spoon and the chopsticks simultaneously. But in Korea, while the two utensils are always paired together, one is only allowed to use one of them at a time. Custom demands that one hold either the spoon or the chopsticks in one hand (usually the right per tradition), but not the two of them in both hands to carry both grain and nongrain foods simultaneously.

"One is what one eats," as a common adage goes. Perhaps one is also *how* one eats. Table manners are created for all diners at one sitting to enjoy the food pleasantly, not being disturbed or disgusted by unusual or unruly behaviors. For an individual, to abide by the accepted dining custom usually means to keep up one's appearance – earning respect for showing politeness or not being looked down upon by others. The Chinese character for "eating" – *chi* – is the word "to beg" plus the mouth radical, which literally means "the mouth that begs." But obviously, few Chinese want to beg for food or eat like a beggar. In the case of raising one's rice bowl to the mouth, the correct way is to open one's palm and use the four fingers to hold the bowl while placing the thumb on its rim. Keeping the thumb on top of the bowl is necessary not only because it helps stabilize the grip, but also because holding the rice bowl in this way distinguishes one from a begger. Presumably to lower themselves while asking for and receiving food, beggars are thought to hold the bowl with all five fingers at the bottom, not leaving any of them on the rim. Tapping the bowl is another taboo, for this is what a beggar might do to attract attention.

One should do one's best to avoid rude eating behavior. Conversely, one could also, in pursuit of sophistocation, make an effort to imitate and adopt a more refined dining style. Koreans' insistence on using both a spoon and chopsticks and their inclination for metal utensils might be good illustrations in this regard. When asked about the origin of these two dining customs, many Koreans would answer that these preferences drew on the dining habit of the *yangban* (noble) class in the Joseon dynasty. As Confucianism was held as the ruling ideology during the period, Korean nobles followed the ancient Confucian rituals and employed chopsticks only to clasp the food contents in dishes, instead of using them to convey grain food. To a *yangban*, using chopsticks to shovel rice into one's mouth was undignified and inelegant, hence unacceptable. Little wonder that Yun Kuk-Hyong was dumbfounded when he saw the Chinese regularly doing it in the Ming, for many Korean literati considered the dynasty the exemplar of cultural excellence. The *yangban* class also used mostly metal utensils, which helped turn them – the silver variety in particular – into a status symbol in Korean society, with a lasting influence still present to this day.

But it is not always up to the upper class to set etiquette standards. The evolution of table manners and dietary customs has indicated mutual influences and exchanges between social classes. The acceptance of the communal dining style could well be a good example, as would the habit of employing chopsticks as the only eating tool for meals. At least in China, these two seem to have followed a bottom-up course of development. For even today, when dining at a formal dinner in an up-market restaurant, not only are both spoon and chopsticks provided on the table, but food is also more likely to be served to one's plates, usually by a waiter; diners are much more careful not to put their utensils into the common dishes. As mentioned at the beginning of the chapter, around the twelfth century when most diners at public eateries had switched to chopsticks as their dining tool, Lu You, a scholar-official, pronounced that he still used a spoon to scoop the cooked millet, just as his counterparts would have done in the previous Tang dynasty. The Introduction also noted that in Korea today, while using both the spoon and chopsticks is the social norm, many Koreans are also inclined to pick up rice with their chopsticks, especially in a family setting. Communal eating is not common in Japan, thus *jikabashi* is unacceptable, as said above. But the fact that the term exists in Japanese suggests that such behavior is not so uncommon as one might think, because some Japanese find it acceptable and also do it in family dining.[46]

Needless to say, sharing food is an effective way to improve human relationships. It is usual that when a person desires to extend or pursue a friendship with another person, they often suggest that they have a meal together. When their friendship reaches a certain level, or when the two become lovers, then sharing food and drink becomes frequent, as part of an act of affection. In other words, intimacy often trumps other concerns, health or otherwise. In many parts of the world today, one still sees that a mother feeds her baby with her spoon or even her mouth, which is unhygienic but not so uncommon. No wonder that communal dining tends to take root first among family members, or in informal circumstances, before extending to other more formal occasions. When inviting a guest to a family meal, many Chinese and Vietnamese families find it odd not to share food with the guest, because the occasion is meant to demonstrate their hospitality and extend their friendship. By the same token, while the Japanese feel more comfortable eating food individually, they also like *shabu shabu* and *sukiyaki* (for which they do share food from a common pot) and find them a useful way to develop relationships.

Nonetheless, communal dining does have its downside: many people are uncomfortable about eating food touched by others, especially by a stranger. Some of the aforementioned rules of chopsticks etiquette illustrate that concern. One instance is the so-called "probing chopsticks," or using one's chopsticks to dig and mine for food in the common dishes. "Licking chopsticks" is another. Both examples are distasteful because

---

[46] There are interesting discussions about *jikabashi* and how acceptable it is in Japanese society today. See http://komachi.yomiuri.co.jp/t/2008/0110/163598.htm. It appears that many do not find it so offensive.

people are, presumably, concerned about anyone passing (excessive) saliva, or germs, onto the dishes intended for all. Germ theory and the notion of food hygiene have, of course, only been developed in recent centuries. As late as the nineteenth century, most Americans, finds Nancy Tomes, were little concerned about "contamination of water and food." "They exchanged combs, hairbrushes, and even toothbrushes, and fed babies from their mouths and spoons, with no sense of hazard." However, while it was mostly unknown that food could be an agent for spreading disease, earlier societies were not entirely unaware that one might get sick from eating certain types of food, or from taking food from those who were sick. Nor were they indifferent to the cleanliness of food. Thus, before the notions of germs and hygiene became well known to the public, table manners and eating etiquette had already been developed in some societies, if only for demonstrating politeness and civility. They ruled against certain types of dining behavior not only because they were messy, but also because such messiness made the food look unclean and uninviting to other diners.[47]

Interestingly, using chopsticks, instead of a spoon, in sharing food balances the desire to be friendly with others and the concern about food contamination. For if used properly and carefully, following the right directions, chopsticks minimize the chance of spoiling food with one's saliva. Compared with the spoon, chopsticks are smaller in size. They are also generally pointed at the bottom, not only for the sake of accurately picking up the food item, but also for avoiding touching other food contents in the common dish. The dining custom in Korea is a case in point. While they use both the spoon and chopsticks for their meals, Koreans are more likely to use chopsticks to partake of side dishes (such as kimchi) on the table, but not the spoon. One presumed reason is that the spoon, once used for eating rice or other grain cereal, often has grain particles stuck on it, and hence looks unclean. And an unclean spoon itself is disapproved of by Koreans.[48] In China where communal dining originated, most Chinese traditionally only employed chopsticks to share food, seldom the spoon. Indeed, it was deemed unacceptable if anyone put a spoon that had been in the mouth into a big bowl of soup intended for all

---

[47] See Nancy Tomes, *The Gospel of Germs: Men, Women, and the Microbe in American Life* (Cambridge: Harvard University Press, 1998), 3.
[48] Pan Lili & Jiang Kun, "Guanyu ZhongHan chuantong yongcan lijie de yanjiu" (Studies of the traditional eating etiquette in China and Korea), *Xiandai qiye jiaoyu* (Modern Enterprise Education), 10 (2008), 158–159.

the others at the table. Such a circumstance usually demanded a serving spoon, or a ladle, for everyone to scoop the soup first into their own bowl.

All in all, when communal eating became a widely practiced dietary custom, chopsticks further proved their usefulness. As a utensil, they were now not only used for transporting nongrain food dishes but also grain food, still the main portion of a meal for most people. As such, chopsticks became the primary eating tool whereas the spoon became secondary. And compared with the spoon, chopsticks are more versatile and flexible; in conveying food, chopsticks enable a diner to take whatever they desire, and in a desirable portion. As chopsticks assumed a more important role in the Ming, Chinese archaeologists have found that the two utensils were no longer buried together in tombs. Instead, more chopsticks than spoons were uncovered in Ming tombs, indicating that their separation had begun. And this trend continued into the following Qing period. Compared with their counterparts in the earlier periods, the chopsticks made in Ming and Qing China became more refined. Whether they were made of wood, bamboo or metal, the chopsticks used in the period often had exquisite decorations and engravings, suggesting their increased importance as a dining utensil.[49]

This reversal between spoon and chopsticks, of course, did not lead to the disappearance of spoons in Asia. It only led to the spoon taking on a new role in assisting the eating of nongrain dishes, soup in particular (Koreans are the known exception, even though some Koreans also drink soup with rice in it, as mentioned above). Eating a hot pot meal might be a good illustration. Chopsticks are indispensable for loading as well as conveying the food items cooking in the broth. But at the end, people often like to drink the broth, as it has absorbed the flavor of all the ingredients. For that purpose, a ladle and also a spoon become necessary, for drinking directly from the pot (which is still hot) is impractical. The changing role of the spoon was also shown in its design. The dagger-shaped *bi* had long fallen into disuse, as mentioned above. During the eighteenth century, a new egg-shaped spoon made of porcelain, known as a "soup spoon" (*tangchi*), became popular in China. Like a modern spoon, it is circular, deep, and designed to hold liquids easily. This spoon later also spread to Japan and earned the name of *chirirenge*, literally meaning "fallen lotus petal". The popularity of this new soup spoon perhaps completed the change in roles of the spoon and chopsticks as dining tools for the Chinese and beyond.

---

[49] Liu, *Zhongguo zhu wenhuashi*, 304–328.

While the design of spoons improved, chopsticks changed their name. In early China, chopsticks were pronounced *zhu* and written with either the bamboo or wood radical. But during the Ming, people in the lower Yangzi River region of Southeast China began to call chopsticks *kuaizi* (lit. quick little boys). Lu Rong's (1436–1494) *Notes in the Legume Garden* (Shuyuan zaiji) explains that the new name was given by the sailors along the Grand Canal because of their superstition. Though the pronunciation *zhu* can mean "help," it also sounds the same as "stop," which is a taboo in sailing. Hence the sailors changed it to *kuaizi*, combining the word *kuai* (fast or quick) with the suffix *zi* or *er* – *kuaier*. In a later period, the bamboo radical was added on top of the *kuai*, indicating the material from which chopsticks were usually made. Like the substitution of chopsticks for the spoon in eating cooked grain, this nomenclatural change took a bottom-up route and became rather slowly accepted by the educated class, as admitted by Li Yuheng, another Ming scholar, in his *Random Notes on the Barges* (Tuipeng wuyu).[50] Thus for a long while, *zhu* and *kuaizi* remained interchangeable. In the famous *Dream of the Red Chamber* (Hongloumeng), a novel written in the late eighteenth century, the author(s) used both *zhu* and *kuaizi* to refer to chopsticks. Through the nineteenth century, *kuaizi* remained a vernacular term as scholars still preferred *zhu* in their writings.[51] But over time, it gradually became more accepted by the modern Chinese whereas the word *zhu*, as of today, has become a historical term. By contrast, the name of chopsticks has not changed elsewhere in the chopsticks cultural sphere. It is *jeotgarak* in Korean, *hashi* in Japanese and *dũa* in Vietnamese, all of which might be considered derivatives of the Chinese word *zhu*.

---

[50] Liu Yun, ed., *Zhongguo zhuwenhua daguan* (A grand view of chopsticks culture in China) (Beijing: Kexue chubanshe, 1996), 52–53.

[51] Lu Rong, *Shuyuan zaji* (Notes in the legume garden) (Beijing: Zhonghua shuju, 1985), 8. *Kuaizi* appears in Luo Guanzhong & Feng Menglong, *Pingyao zhuan* (Subduing the demons), and Xizhou Sheng's *Xingshi yinyuan* (A romance to awaken the world), whereas *zhu* is used in the *Mingshi* (Ming history), compiled by Qing official historians, and in Ji Xiaolan's *Yuewei caotang biji* (Stories by Ji Xiaolan). These texts were all written during the seventeenth and eighteenth centuries, or during the late Ming and early Qing.

6

A pair inseparable: chopsticks as gift, metaphor and symbol

The joy of eating is given great importance in China; and cooking, through the decades, has been dreamed and fussed over, in times of want as well as in times of plenty, until it has ceased to be plain cooking, but has grown and developed into an art. Food has been represented through other mediums of art, especially poetry, literature and folklore; and these tales and food beliefs have been handed down, from generation to generation, with ever-increasing glamour.

Doreen Yen Hung Feng, *The Joy of Chinese Cooking*

> Green when young and yellow old
> They have shared their minds forever.
> Whether bitter or sweet,
> They always taste them together.[1]

Zhuo Wenjun, a woman who lived in Han dynasty China, allegedly wrote this poem to her lover Sima Xiangru (179–127 BCE), when she gave him a pair of chopsticks. In his legendary work, Sima Qian records some details about their love story, making it proverbial throughout Chinese history. Sima Xiangru was an illustrious writer, known for his mastery of rhapsody (*fu*), a prevalent literary genre during the period. (Shu Xi, for instance, wrote a rhapsody on doughy food in the third century, as mentioned in Chapter 3.) As Sima Xiangru's fame grew, he also received several marriage proposals. On one occasion, Zhuo Wangsun, the richest man in the country, invited Sima to a banquet. Sima went reluctantly. At the party, he chanted a rhapsody, receiving many accolades. Attracted by Sima's talent,

---

[1] Fu Yun, "Qutan kuaizi wenhua" (An informal talk on the chopsticks culture), *Luoyang ribao* (Luoyang daily), November 13, 2008.

Zhuo Wenjun, Zhuo Wangsun's newly widowed daughter, fell in love with him. But her father disapproved of it because Sima Xiangru was poor. However, the two managed to elope to Chengdu, Sichuan, eventually forcing the father to give in and accept their marriage.

If Zhao was determined to be with Sima Xiangru, her poem also betrays that she was a bit uncertain whether the love between them would be lasting, thus she presented both the chopsticks and the poem to express her wish and hope. Beautiful as it is, the poem, as well as the chopsticks-giving story, was most likely made up by people of later times (it is not found in Sima Qian's work). However, since chopsticks are always used in pairs, demonstrating their inseparableness, they have long become a favorite gift for newlyweds, as well as a token of love exchanged between couples and lovers in the chopsticks cultural sphere. In Japan, when people go to Shinto shrines to ask for fortunes and blessings, they can also purchase several types of chopsticks. Two kinds of chopsticks are most popular: *enmusubibashi*, or "lover chopsticks," and *miotobashi*, or "husband–wife chopsticks." Like those used in Japanese households, these chopsticks vary in length; the stick for the man tends to be slightly longer than the one for the woman (20–21 cm vs. 20–18 cm).[2] Aside from Shinto shrines, these chopsticks can also be purchased in stores and given as a present to lovers and couples (Plate 21).

Likewise, across China, among the Chinese and minority groups, chopsticks are not only a popular wedding gift but also a popular object at wedding ceremonies. In his book, Lan Xiang describes many wedding customs, many of which involve the use of chopsticks. In Shanxi Province of Northwest China, for instance, when the groom and his entourage go to the bride's home to fetch her, her father often prepares a pair of bottles containing some grain. Using red strings, he ties these bottles together with a pair of chopsticks. These are given by the father to both the bride and the groom, carrying his wish for their inseparableness and lasting love after marriage. Elsewhere in Shanxi, the chopsticks given to newly-weds by the bride's family are first to be used by a boy, usually her brother or nephew, at the wedding banquet after he escorts the bride's dowry to the groom's family. To ensure the couple's inseparableness, the two sticks must be as identical as possible and have a smooth surface, in the hope of the couple's perfect "match" and their "smooth" life together in the future.[3] In other words, the pair of chopsticks is not supposed to be

---

[2] Isshiki, *Hashi no Bunkashi*, 59.   [3] Lan, *Kuaizi, buzhishi kuaizi*, 87–88.

in different colors, designs or lengths like the "husband–wife chopsticks" in Japan.

For their "inseparableness," chopsticks have become a useful tool for proposing marriage and announcing a new relationship – the Japanese *enmusubibashi* is an illustration of the latter. Among the Klau people in Guizhou, China, once the young man finds his love, his mother will carry a pair of chopsticks wrapped in red paper, to the girl's family to propose marriage. She usually need not utter a word because the chopsticks she brings with her have already made clear her purpose.[4] Few know when this began. But instances where chopsticks are used in making wedding proposals were found in traditional China. According to a thirteenth-century text, when a man intends to marry someone, he is to propose marriage to the bride's parents and seek her family's permission. On such an occasion, he will bring myriad gifts to his intended future parents-in-law. Should his proposal be accepted, the future bride's parents will send his family objects such as rolls of silk and jewelry, together with a pair of wine cups, which hold water instead of wine. Most importantly, the bride's family needs to include a pair of chopsticks, two green scallions and four golden fish to show their agreement to the marriage. The pair of chopsticks is called *huiyu zhu* (lit. give-back fish and chopsticks) though the text does not specify what all these objects stand for. Giving them, however, seems essential in completing the engagement process. In order to exhibit their affluence and strong commitment to the proposed marriage, according to the text, some wealthy families opt for gold or silver to make the fish and chopsticks and silk scallions instead of real ones.[5]

It is quite possible that chopsticks were a part of the gifts from the bride's family because they were deemed indispensable in life. That is, chopsticks are a metaphor, or perhaps a metonymy, for life itself. As marriage indicates a new beginning in one's life, many wedding customs in China often involve chopsticks to mark such an occasion. Examples of this abound. In some regions of Northwest China, when the bride leaves her parents' home for her new home, she is to toss a pair of chopsticks on the floor, bidding farewell to the life she had with her parents. In other places, a male family member – either her brother or her father – throws a pair of chopsticks at the moment when the bride leaves home. After she

---

[4] Ibid., 120.

[5] Wu Zimu & Zhou Mi, *Mengliang lu, Wulin jiushi* (Dreaming of Kaifeng in Hangzhou; History of Lin'an) (Ji'nan: Shandong youyi chubanshe, 2001), 281. Meng Yuanlao also mentions chopsticks in his *Dongjing menghualu*, suggesting that the custom might be practiced in both North and South China. Meng, *Dongjing menghualu*, 32–33.

arrives at her new home, the bride then picks up another pair of chopsticks as a symbolic gesture of embracing her new life. Moreover, picking up the new pair of chopsticks also connotes that she, as a wife, is to help shoulder the responsibility for the wellbeing of the new family. There is also a tradition for the groom's family members to hide chopsticks at the couple's new home, asking the bride to seek them out. This is, symbolically, to test the bride's capability; the difficulty she faces in finding these hidden chopsticks comes to serve as a friendly warning about the future challenges she may encounter in her new life.[6]

Among some ethnic minority groups in China, chopsticks tend to figure even more prominently in wedding ceremonies (Plate 29). The She people, residing in the mountainous areas in Southeast China, have a tradition that before leaving home, as the new bride is having her last meal with her siblings, she needs to pass her rice bowl and chopsticks to them, not only to say goodbye to them but also to ask them to take care of her parents on her behalf. At their wedding banquets, the Yao people in Hunan Province have a custom that the Master of Ceremonies first feeds the newlyweds simultaneously with two pairs of chopsticks in both hands, whereas the Daur people in Manchuria have the newlyweds finish a bowl of glutinous rice together, sharing one pair of chopsticks. While the customs are different, the chopsticks are a useful tool in teaching the new couple the importance of cooperation in sharing their lives together; in the latter case, if the chopsticks are a symbol of "inseparableness," the glutinous rice carries the wish for an affectionate – if also "gooey" – relationship between the couple.[7]

Due to the nomenclatural change occurring in Ming China, discussed in the previous chapter, chopsticks came to be known as *kuaizi* instead of *zhu*. Interestingly, when the sailors called chopsticks *kuaizi* for quick sailing, they perhaps did not realize that the word *kuai* could also combine with *le* to mean "happiness," or *kuaile*, in Chinese. As such, chopsticks became more in demand on festive occasions, not merely for enjoying the abundance of food. Though the word "*zi*" is a suffix in *kuaizi*, it could also take on the meaning of "son" or "child." So with a stretch of the imagination, *kuaizi* could be construed as "having a child/son quickly." This new meaning has added considerably to the appeal of chopsticks as a wedding present from the Ming period to this day. In fact, the propitious meanings associated with the name change have rendered chopsticks a must-have item at and for a wedding, either as

---

[6] Lan, *Kuaizi, buzhishi kuaizi*, 88–89, 96–97.   [7] Ibid., 105, 109, 121.

a present or as a charm for the couple, carrying a wish not only for a good, harmonious marriage but also that they will soon be blessed with children.

The chopsticks-tossing gesture at wedding ceremonies has also gained more vigor. In Zhejiang, there is an old tradition where the guests, after the newlyweds enter their bedroom, stick a bunch of chopsticks through the window into the room – the windows then were covered by paper – and let them drop on the floor, representing a wish for the couple to quickly bear a child. Others would perform the act at the wedding banquet, with someone either singing a song or giving a toast while tossing several pairs of chopsticks on the floor. As chopsticks are a good luck charm, many guests would like to pick them up from the floor and take them home. There is also a practice in the regions of Jiangsu Province where the groom gives away chopsticks to the guests, whereas in Henan members from both the bride's and groom's families can even "steal" the chopsticks at wedding ceremonies to partake in the good fortune of the newlyweds. Just as a female guest at a Western wedding ceremony wishes to catch the bouquet of flowers thrown by bride, Chinese guests desire a pair of chopsticks on such an occasion.[8]

Chopsticks also appear frequently in fairytales about love and marriage in other Asian countries, even though there was no name change of the utensil as in China. The "Hundred-Septa Bamboos" story of Vietnam tells that once upon a time, there was a villager who had a beautiful daughter and a loyal and diligent servant. The young servant fell in love with the daughter, hoping to marry her, since the villager had promised that "He would marry his daughter to a hardworking man." However, he later changed his mind and instead intended his daughter to marry the wealthiest man in the village. The young servant then suggested to the father that as bamboo chopsticks were to be used at the wedding banquet, anyone who could find the bamboos whose stems had exactly one hundred septa should marry her. The villager agreed. Thanks to some magic power, the young man found or made the bamboos with exactly one hundred septa and brought them back. As a result, he succeeded in fulfilling his dream of marrying the villager's daughter.[9]

Among the Japanese, chopsticks are hailed as "sticks for one's life," or *seimei no tsue*, literally supporting one's life from the beginning to the end. As such, chopsticks are used as a helpful marker to celebrate an

---

[8] Ibid., 87–99.

[9] Mukai & Hashimoto, *Hashi*, 249–250. This story also in a way confirms that in Vietnam, chopsticks are quite commonly made of bamboo as they are in China.

important day in life. For example, after a child is born, usually on the hundredth day but it could be as early as the seventh or as late as the hundred and twentieth day, a ceremony is held at which an adult would feed the child a bowl of rice with a pair of chopsticks, usually made of unpainted willow tree wood. The chopsticks used at the ceremony are called *okuizomebashi* and the ceremony itself is named *ohashizomeish-iki*.[10] Of course, at such a young age, a child is unable to use chopsticks. The purpose of the ceremony is to introduce the utensil to him/her, since they are the "sticks for life," with the wish that the child lead an easy, or hunger-free, life. What is also common is to present special chopsticks to elders on important birthdays to wish for and celebrate their long life. These chopsticks acquire names like *enmeibashi* (extend-life chopsticks), *enjubashi* (prolong-life chopsticks), *chōjubashi* (long-life chopsticks) and *fukujubashi* (happy-life chopsticks). They are given to an elder often on his/her sixty-first, seventieth, seventy-seventh, eighty-eighth or ninety-ninth birthday.[11]

Everyone celebrates the New Year in Japan, which makes the month of January, or *shōgatsu* 正月, the most important holiday season. Before the Meiji Restoration of 1868, the Japanese used a lunar calendar so the *shōgatsu* fell between late January and early February. Now that the Western calendar has been adopted in Japan, the New Year occurs at the same time as in the Western world. However, the customs in celebrating the New Year retain elements from the past. For instance, new chopsticks are required to eat the meals on New Year's day, customarily made of unpainted willow tree wood. Called *oiwaibashi* (celebratory or festive chopsticks), these chopsticks take the shape of *ryōkuchibashi* (lit. two-ended chopsticks), with a thicker, or rounder, body and two slimmer and pointed ends (Plate 22). The two-ended chopsticks are required because they enable the Japanese to share food with *kami* around them – one end of the chopsticks is for the people to eat and the other for *kami*.[12] This *shinjin kyōshoku* (*kami* and people sharing food together) extends a Shinto belief. That the Japanese use *toribashi*, or serving/community chopsticks, to distribute food also originated at Shinto ceremonies. After offering foods to *kami*, the priest usually employs a pair of serving chopsticks to serve the foods to the participants.[13]

Oiwaibashi are mostly made of unpainted whitewood because of Shinto and Buddhist influences. While Shintoism prizes direct communication

---

[10] Isshiki, *Hashi no Bunkashi*, 58–59.   [11] Ibid., 60.   [12] Ibid., 57–61.
[13] Ibid., 134–135.

between the human world and the natural world, the Buddhist tenets emphasize simplicity in life. Also, most of the *oiwaibashi* are made of willow tree wood, for if one follows the lunar calendar, the New Year begins in early spring; by then willow trees have already budded, usually earlier than other trees. Using their wood thus celebrates the vitality of life.[14] The round body of the *ryōkuchibashi* chopsticks carries a special meaning for one's wish for the New Year: it portends, as well as promises, the arrival of a lush, fertile and abundant year.[15] As celebratory chopsticks, *oiwaibashi* are also used on other holidays, such as the Coming of Age Day and Children's Day. As such, celebratory chopsticks are also called "ceremonial chopsticks," or *harenohashi*, as opposed to "daily chopsticks," or *kenohashi*. Made of naked wood, celebratory or ceremonial chopsticks are usually purchased anew for the occasion and discarded afterwards because, according to Shinto belief, once placed in the mouth, these unpainted wooden chopsticks carry one's spirit, which cannot be washed off; throwing them away forges a certain communication between human and *kami*.[16] By contrast, daily chopsticks are painted with lacquer for durability and, with one pointed end, are not used to share food with *kami*. And nowadays, most daily chopsticks are made of plastic, a material that has no sacred status in Shintoism.[17]

Pronounced *hashi*, the Japanese word for chopsticks is a homonym of "bridge." On life's important junctures, chopsticks have indeed played such a role for the Japanese, enabling them to establish spiritual connections between one and another, between the realm of humans and the realm of *kami*, between the living and the dead and between this world and the netherworld. When someone travels away from home, such as when a soldier leaves for a war, for instance, other family members would still prepare and serve food for the traveler when they eat a meal, together with the person's chopsticks. Termed *kagezen*, this meal expresses their wish for the traveler's safety and wellbeing. As explained above, since the traveler's chopsticks retain his/her spirit, the family believes that their wishes can be transmitted to the traveler by this "bridge." In a different way, this belief that after use one's chopsticks contain one's spirit also led to the Japanese fondness for disposable chopsticks, a subject to be discussed in the next chapter.

---

[14] Mukai & Hashimoto, *Hashi*, 193.   [15] Isshiki, *Hashi no Bunkashi*, 60–61.

[16] Wilson, *Consider the Fork*, 200. In olden times when the Japanese used chopsticks to eat meals outside, once finished, they would break the chopsticks in half before throwing them away, lest their spirit be attached to the chopsticks. Also see Isshiki, *Hashi no Bunkashi*, 11–15.

[17] Isshiki, *Hashi no Bunkashi*, 67–68.

The action of forming some communication between this world and the netherworld is referred to in Japanese as *hashiwatashi* (lit. bridge-crossing). Thus, a pair of chopsticks is an important must-have object at a funeral, completing its last mission to send the person to the other world. Just like the ceremony where a newborn is fed by an adult with a pair of chopsticks, a dying person, too, is offered a meal, with rice in his/her favorite bowl and a pair of chopsticks standing in it. Since the meal is placed next to the person's pillow, it is called the "pillow meal" (*makur-ameshi*) and the chopsticks are *tatebashi*, as they stand vertically in the bowl. After serving the last meal to the deceased, chopsticks have one more role to play in the traditional Japanese funeral, which is the act of *hashiwatashi* mentioned above. Given the Buddhist influence, it has been a well-established practice for the Japanese to cremate the dead. After the cremation, family members would each hold a pair of chopsticks to pick up a bone from the ashes and pass it from one to another. This act was intended to build a spiritual tie between them and the deceased, or between the living and the underworld. Indeed, for the Japanese, as the aphorism goes, "one's life begins with [the use of] chopsticks, it also ends with chopsticks."[18]

The ways chopsticks are used on those occasions also influenced chopsticks etiquette in Japan. In performing *hashiwatashi*, one holds an item with one's chopsticks and passes it on to another pair of chopsticks. But to do the same at a dining table would be frowned upon. As mentioned in the previous chapter, this act is called *utsuribashi*, one of the chopsticks-use taboos for the Japanese. As one eats, food items should be delivered either to a plate or directly to the mouth, never to another pair of chopsticks in Japan. Also mentioned in the previous chapter, to leave a pair of chopsticks standing vertically in a rice bowl is universally forbidden across the chopsticks cultural sphere. For the Japanese, one only does this when offering the grain to the dying or dead person. Similarly, many Chinese communities dislike having chopsticks stand vertically in bowls because it resembles incense-burning, a Buddhist ritual to mourn the dead.

In the Korean Peninsula, instead of chopsticks, spoons appear more frequently in folklore, reflecting dining preferences. For example, a fable called "Mysterious Snake" describes a nice girl from a wealthy (merchant?) family who fed food to a snake with a spoon. The snake was later killed, but her kindness and her gesture to an animal perceived as malicious was well rewarded – she was later married to a *yangban* and the

---

[18] Ibid., 61–65.

couple lived happily ever after.[19] Interestingly, however, if push comes to shove, Koreans also think that chopsticks are more basic than the spoon for eating. A folk legend from Baekje, Korea, known as "The Set of Three Utensils," is illustrative. The tale goes that after their father's death, the elder brother took all the inheritance, forcing his younger brother to leave home. The younger brother received three basic utensils from a Buddhist monk, which consisted of an eating mat, a bowl made of a dried gourd and a pair of chopsticks. After hiking down the mountain, it turned dark and the young man found no shelter or food. So he unfolded the mat. All of a sudden, a palace with many luxurious rooms appeared. Next he scooped the gourd bowl, and all kinds of delicious foods poured out. He lastly tapped the pair of chopsticks and several beautiful women came to him. In other words, these three items – a mat, a bowl and a pair of chopsticks – are the daily necessities for a Korean in Baekje.[20]

In Vietnam where chopsticks had been adopted as an eating tool earlier than they were in Baekje, Korea, the folklore tradition also depicts the utensil's importance in life. A folktale called "Real Son vs. Adopted Son" is one, which was also about a family dispute over inheritance. A man named Ch'ep, meaning "carp fish," had both an adopted son and a biological son. After he died, his wife complained that the adopted son, who was older, took all the family money, leaving nothing for his younger brother. When a judge was assigned to handle the dispute, he observed how the brothers ate their meals. While chopsticks were given to both of them, the biological son used them properly whereas the adopted son did not use them – he instead used his fingers to put food in his mouth. At dinner, the judge gave them rice and a carp fish dish. The adopted son ate the fish and the rice whereas the biological son did not touch the fish. When asked why, he answered: "Since my father's name means carp fish, I don't feel like eating it [out of my respect for my father]." The two brothers' different behaviors, especially their divergent dining manners, helped the judge to see that the biological son was indeed wronged by his brother, or the adopted son.[21] In a word, using chopsticks to eat food became a way for the Vietnamese to see whether or not one had a proper upbringing.

Since chopsticks use assumes such significance in life, the utensil has become associated with myriad meanings on different occasions. Like

---

[19] Mukai & Hashimoto, *Hashi*, 247. According to the Confucian social order, merchants were ranked lowest in the four-class social structure, below the literati, or the *yangban* in the Korean case, peasants and artisans. So for a girl from a rich merchant family to marry a *yangban* was considered good fortune for her at the time.
[20] Ibid., 246.   [21] Ibid., 248–249.

the Japanese, for example, the Zhuang people in China celebrate a child's birthday with chopsticks, such as when s/he is one year old. Longer than the usual kind, the utensil is used by the child's parents to feed a bowl of long noodles to the birthday child. The long noodles and the long chopsticks extend their wish for the child's long life in the years to come.[22] Using longer chopsticks to deliver birthday food is particular to this case. But eating noodles on a birthday is fairly common, practiced almost everywhere in China and beyond. It also has a long history, and was already quite common during the Tang dynasty.[23] A long life means good fortune. Some fortune-tellers in traditional China thus used chopsticks as a tool for prediction. Beginning as early as the tenth century, this practice continued to gain popularity, fueling the belief in chopsticks' magic and mystic power. By the late nineteenth century, it had become a religious cult for some Chinese as they regularly worshipped and prayed to the "chopsticks spirit" or "chopsticks god" – *kuaizi shen* – for good fortune.[24]

It is unknown if chopsticks, too, were used in fortune-telling in Japan. But there is a well-known legend about why festive chopsticks need to take the shape of *ryōkuchibashi* with thicker, rounder bodies and two tapered ends. It involves the death of a short-lived shogun named Ashikaga Yoshikatsu (1434–1443). Ashikaga Yoshikatsu became the shogun at a young age in 1441, after his father, Ashikaga Yoshinori (1394–1441), was murdered by one of his lieutenants. Several months later, either in the first month or the fifth month of the lunar calendar, the young shogun entertained his ministers with a banquet. When he was eating a pancake, his chopsticks suddenly broke in half. Then in the fall, he unexpectedly fell from his horse on an excursion and died ten days later. Ashikaga Yoshikatsu was succeeded by his brother Ashikaga Yoshimasa (1435–1490) who, in order to prevent the same misfortune from befalling anyone else, made chopsticks that had thicker, stronger bodies so they would not break easily.[25]

In the history of China, no similar cases are found where broken chopsticks portended an untimely death. But there are instances in which one breaks a pair of chopsticks in order to manifest one's determination. According to a Tang history, Emperor Xuanzong (r. 847–859) once ordered his daughter, Princess Yongfu, to marry someone. But the Princess was utterly unhappy with the order. While eating with the Emperor, she broke

[22] Liu, *Zhongguo zhu wenhuashi*, 289.   [23] Wang, *Tangdai yinshi*, 6.
[24] Liu, *Zhongguo zhu wenhuashi*, 230.
[25] Mukai & Hashimoto, *Hashi*, 193; Isshiki, *Hashi no Bunkashi*, 18.

her chopsticks and spoon to protest. Her act, which implied that she would kill herself if forced, changed her father's mind. The Emperor later married off another of his daughters in place of Princess Yongfu.[26] To what extent chopsticks represent, symbolically and spiritually, life itself certainly varies from people to people. But by and large, across Asia it is regarded as ominous if an accident happens to the utensil. Indeed, even if someone fails to hold chopsticks properly or carefully, causing them to drop on the floor, it could also be considered inauspicious. To some, this might bode ill for the person's future, especially if this occurs at an important juncture in life. In imperial China, if a candidate en route to the civil service examination, for instance, accidentally dropped a pair of chopsticks while eating his food, it would be seen as unlucky, causing him, as well as others, to think that he would fail the upcoming examination.[27]

If dropping chopsticks was an omen for failing exams, raising chopsticks had the opposite meaning. In Tang China, poetry writing was particularly popular among members of the literati. Seeing an old friend whom he had known since he was a child, who was en route to the imperial examination, Liu Yuxi (772–842), a famous Tang poet, wrote a poem in which he sang:

> At your birth when they first hung out the bow,
> I was the most honored guest at the birthday feast.
> Wielding my chopsticks I ate boiled noodles,
> And composed a congratulatory poem on a heavenly unicorn.[28]

Here Liu wished that by raising his chopsticks, he could help the young man to launch, through passing the examination, a high-flying career, like the Heavenly Unicorn. Few had the luck to be blessed by Liu Yuxi in a poem. But raising chopsticks at a dining table has been commonly practiced among chopsticks users as a good gesture. It is usually seen when a host invites the guests to eat the food. Among the Japanese, it is polite for anyone, before eating his/her food, to first say to the others, be they family members or friends and guests, "*itadakimasu*," which literarily means "I now accept it," or "I shall start eating." When saying it, one usually

---

[26] Ouyang Xiu, *Xin Tangshu* (New Tang history) – "Yu Zhining, Xiu Lie, Ao Zong, Pang Yan" (Biographies of Yu Zhining, Xiu Lie, Ao Zong and Bang Yan), HDWZK, 4010.

[27] One reason that such an incident (dropping chopsticks on the floor) is taken as bad luck is that "to fall on the floor" (*luodi* 落地) is the homonym of "to fail the examination" (*luodi* 落第) in Chinese; the second characters in the two phrases are pronounced exactly the same.

[28] Translation is from David R. Knechtges, "A Literary Feast: Food in Early Chinese Literature," *Journal of the American Oriental Society*, 106:1, 61.

also raises one's chopsticks horizontally with both hands and bows slightly. Although the gesture perhaps started in Buddhist temples (mentioned in Chapter 4), the sentence seems more Shintoistic (Buddhism and Shintoism did blend and coalesce in their practices). Since in traditional Shinto beliefs *kami* is omnipresent, the sentence denotes that the eater receives, or accepts, food from *kami* – s/he is asking permission from the deity to begin eating the food.

While offering food to ancestors and spirits is common among the Chinese, they do not traditionally partake in, nor practice, the idea that humans share food simultaneously with supernatural beings. But in offering the food to the spirits, utensils are always provided, on the assumption that the spirits also need them to eat. This notion was/is commonly practiced among various peoples in China. For example, when offering food and drinks to spirits and ancestors, the Manchus always placed a pair of chopsticks and a spoon either on top of or next to the bowls. And this custom had begun before the Manchus entered China proper in the mid-seventeenth century, or before their extensive exposure to Han Chinese customs.[29] After the offering, eating began – there was no such custom that one needed to express acceptance of the food from deities among various peoples in China.

However, the Chinese have attached certain meanings to the act of wielding chopsticks, or *juzhu*. While seemingly a natural act – one has to first lift chopsticks from the table before moving them to the dishes to clasp food – it could at times become an important gesture with both intended and unintended consequences. Examples of this abound, past and present, shown in historical texts and literary tropes. While he writes in his poem that he wielded his chopsticks to send his best wishes to his friend, Liu Yuxi was not the first to coin the phrase. An earlier usage of the term was found in one of the histories written by Li Yanshou, the Tang historian. When describing the history of the Southern Liang dynasty (502–557), Li tells a story about Lü Sengzhen, a model and modest official. One of the examples showing his modesty was that, per Li's record, Lü never raised his chopsticks from the table and ate the food at imperial dinners with the emperor.[30]

[29] See Zhen Jun, *Tianzhi ouwen* (Legends of the heavenly realm) (Beijing: Beijing guji chubanshe, 1982), 22–25. Though the text was written in the late nineteenth century, Zhen (1837–1920), a learned Manchu, recorded many traditional customs of his people in earlier centuries.

[30] According to the historical text, Lü only used chopsticks to eat a dessert offered by the emperor while he was a bit drunk. His unusual behavior cracked up the emperor. See Li Yanshou, "Biography of Lü Sengzhen," in *Nanshi* (History of the southern dynasties) – "Lü Sengzhen" (Biography of Lü Sengzhen), HDWZK, 1396. A search in ZJGK finds that the phrase *juzhu* appeared 561 times in various texts from the Tang to the Qing periods.

Lü Sengzhen's behavior is portrayed as exceptional because few can resist food, especially when it is bestowed by the imperial court.

Over time, what Lü Sengzhen did became exemplary of appropriate table manners as well as of good moral character. Gao Chu (1574–1655) was a Ming scholar-official known for his sympathy toward the poor. When he witnessed a famine, seeing dead bodies on the road, he wrote: "Who could wield his chopsticks [and eat the food] and not cry to Heaven, yet Heaven was so high, hardly hearing [the cry]."[31] Overcome by his sorrow, Gao was unable to hold up his chopsticks for food – a figurative description underscoring his compassion and humanity. Yet in real life, whether and how one should wield one's chopsticks in front of food could be a serious matter. For example, it is expected in China that when invited to a meal, a polite guest would not be the first one to grab the chopsticks and dig into the food; it is better to wait until the host or the senior first puts his/her hand on the chopsticks. To demonstrate hospitality, conversely, a host needs to raise his/her chopsticks to gesture and urge, sometimes repeatedly, others to eat. This tradition is also observable in other cultures. When eating at home, for example, it is customary that a senior first apply his/her chopsticks and start eating before anyone else does. According to a Ming text, wielding one's chopsticks without invitation was a disorderly social behavior during that era. It could become even worse if the person also put down the chopsticks and left the table after gulping down his food while others were still working on theirs.[32]

If a minister could display his modesty by not touching his chopsticks in front of food, then an emperor could also show his humility towards, or bestow his kindheartedness onto, his counselor by holding chopsticks for him. One such case happened in the fifth century during the Northern Wei dynasty (386–557), a regime of the Xianbei people who invaded and unified North China after the Han. Cui Hao (381?–450), a brilliant strategist credited with the success, received such treatment from Emperor Taiwu (r. 424–452), the dynasty's third ruler. As they were quite close, historical records suggest, the Emperor often called on Cui at his residence, sometimes during his mealtime. Instead of asking Cui to stop eating, the Emperor often picked up the chopsticks and gave them to Cui, encouraging him to finish the meal. The Emperor's unusual gesture suggested his eagerness for Cui's advice and his openhandedness toward

---

[31] Gao Chu, *Jingshan'an ji*, ZJGK, 282.
[32] This was referred to as "*shiqujiu*" (lit. lost manners), see Lu Ji, *Gujin shuohai* (Sea of stories of the past and present), in ZJGK, 490–491.

Cui, for few emperors in China would act the same way in treating a minister. However, by accepting the Emperor's exceptional graciousness, Cui Hao, in stark contrast to Lü Sengzhen's prudence, also unveiled his vanity. And he paid a hefty price in the end; implicated falsely in a conspiracy, Cui was later put to death by the Emperor.[33]

Besides *juzhu*, or to raise, hold and wield chopsticks for food, Chinese authors also wrote stories involving *touzhu*, or dropping and tossing chopsticks, suggesting such a practice had a long history. As mentioned in Chapter 2, together with the spoon, chopsticks made an early appearance in Chen Shou's *History of the Three Kingdoms*. Startled by Cao Cao's remarks, Liu Bei dropped both his spoon and chopsticks. Since then, *touzhu* has become a stock phrase to help describe someone's fear, shock and/or surprise. In the wake of the Tang dynasty's fall in the tenth century, several military strongmen vied for control of China proper. Gao Jixing (858–929), an ambitious general who rose to power through the ranks, was one of them. While collaborating with the Late Tang dynasty (923–937), Gao planned to invade Sichuan but was unsure if it was the right move. While he hesitated, another army quickly took Sichuan. The news came when Gao was just about to eat his meal. Upon hearing it, Gao "dropped his spoon and chopsticks," as one historical text puts it, regretting his earlier indecision. In the end, Gao only managed to establish a small kingdom, without ever seizing Sichuan.[34]

One could drop one's utensils out of shock or fear, one could also intentionally toss or put down one's chopsticks to express certain feelings – happiness, unhappiness or mixed emotions. The chopstick-tossing custom at wedding ceremonies is an illustration of this; the bride who tosses her chopsticks on the wedding day might want to express at once her sadness for leaving her parents behind and her happiness at beginning a new life. As losing one's chopsticks is generally regarded as inauspicious, even foreboding, in literary tropes, *touzhu* is often depicted as an unusual and unnatural act, associated with anxiety, frustration and angst. That is,

---

[33] Sima Guang, *Zizhi tongjian* (A comprehensive mirror of aid in government) – "Cui Hao" (Biography of Cui Hao), HDWZK, 1330.

[34] The case that Gao Jixing dropped his spoon and chopsticks upon hearing about Sichuan is recorded in the *Shiguo chunqiu* (Spring and autumn annals of the ten kingdoms), a historical text by Wu Shichen, in *juan* 1, ZJGK, 741. "Dropping utensils" seems a standard usage in describing one's surprise and other high emotions. One such usage is found in Zhang Tingyu, *Mingshi* (Ming history) – "Wen Tiren" (Biography of Wen Tiren). It records that after Wen, a manipulating Grand Secretariat, lost the trust of the emperor and was dismissed from his position, "Wen, who was just about to eat, dropped his spoon and chopsticks." HDWZK, 7936.

touzhu connotes that someone deliberately and forcefully puts down the chopsticks to express a strong emotion. The *History of the [Liu] Song dynasty* (Songshu), written by Shen Yue (441–513), a historian-cum-writer, offers an early example. The dynasty was ruled by several despotic rulers and plagued with internecine warfare. One such disturbance occurred in 476 when Prince Liu Jingsu (452–476) was involved in an attempt to challenge the reigning emperor, a teenage boy with an erratic and violent temper. But the challenge failed and Liu was killed in the fight. After his death, one of his associates petitioned the court, then under a new emperor, in defense of Liu's political loyalty. The petitioner cited an instance to show that Liu had been a filial son to his mother: whenever he found his mother was not eating, he would "instantly put down his chopsticks and stop eating too." Then the petitioner asked: "How could such a filial son be disloyal to the government?" In other words, a person who respected order and family hierarchy at home would not have committed any treasonous act against the government.[35] Putting down the chopsticks was used to strengthen the argument.

In later texts, *touzhu* is employed not only to characterize one's love for a family elder, but also to express compassion for others. The "Biography of Wu Yinzhi" in the *History of the Jin Dynasty* (Jinshu), an official history which appeared about a century later than Shen Yue's history, describes the early life of Wu Yinzhi (?–414), a highly respected official of that period, as follows:

When Wu Yinzhi was young, he lost his parents. As he had been quite close to his mother, Wu often sobbed when he thought of her. Overhearing his crying, Wu's neighbor, Mrs. Han, a kind lady, *put down her chopsticks, quit eating and wept tears*. She would then tell her son, Han Kangbo, who was then the Director of Protocols in the government, that "When you have a chance, you should promote a person like Wu." Several years later, Han became the Minister of Personnel. He followed his mother's advice and recruited Wu into the government [italics added].[36]

Instead of just stating that Mrs. Han stopped eating, the text includes the action of *touzhu* – her putting down the chopsticks – to emphasize how strongly she sympathized with Wu Yinzhi's loss.

---

[35] Shen Yue, *Songshu* (History of the [Liu] Song dynasty) – "Jianping Xuanjianwang Hong, zi Jingsu" (Biographies of Prince Xuanjian of Liu Hong and his son Liu Jingsu), HDWZK, 1864. *Touzhu* appears a total of 409 times in various texts in ZJGK.

[36] Fang Xuanling, *Jinshu* (History of the Jin dynasty) – "Wu Yinzhi" (Biography of Wu Yinzhi), HDWZK, 2341.

Li Bai (701–762), China's most celebrated poet, also used *touzhu* to convey and emphasize his sadness. In a well-known poem, "Difficult Departure" (Xinglu nan), Li describes how sad he felt in bidding farewell to his friends when he decided to leave Chang'an, the capital of the Tang dynasty where he had stayed for a brief period. The poem begins with a depiction of the extravagant farewell party his friends threw for him – delicious foods on jade plates and boundless wine in golden cups. Then Li expresses his emotion in these words: "I stopped drinking the wine and tossed down my chopsticks because I had no appetite. I drew out my sword, looking around, my mind was utterly absent." Here again, the phrase "putting down the chopsticks" is employed to accentuate Li Bai's sorrow at leaving behind his friends.[37]

Yet the acts involving chopsticks do not have to be associated with distress or angst. Rather, chopsticks can also help celebrate a happy occasion. For such a purpose, the phrase *jizhu* was coined, meaning "to strike the chopsticks" onto an object, be it a plate or a table. The purpose of *jizhu* is to make some sound, or even music if the person is so trained. Yet to do that is unusual, for etiquette forbids one to make noise with chopsticks. So *jizhu* only happens when one is overwhelmed with emotions, or in ecstasy. Bai Juyi, a Tang poet, depicts such an occurrence in his poem. When he met Liu Yuxi in 826, Bai described their meeting as follows: "When I was drinking, you raised your cup and poured me more wine; when you were singing, I struck my chopsticks on the plates to sound the beat." The scene seems indeed rather joyful: the two men, possibly half drunk, sang and chatted over drinks to celebrate their reunion. It was so delightful for them because their gathering was unexpected. Despite their successes as accomplished poets, they were both demoted and forced out of the Tang capital – then they ran into each other on the road![38]

Bai Juyi tapped his chopsticks on the plates spontaneously. But such an act is also depicted in other Tang poems, giving the impression that it was probably more common than one would think. Was there a custom in that period that people struck chopsticks at parties to sound the beat while they were singing? That *jizhu* often occurred with singing in Tang poems seems to suggest this.[39] In fact, records show that this phenomenon had occurred in earlier periods. Wang Chong (27–97? CE), a Han scholar, wrote that someone of his time used chopsticks to strike bronze bells and make music,

[37] Li Bai, *Xinglu nan*, ZJGK, 17.   [38] Cited in Liu, *Zhongguo zhu wenhuashi*, 243.
[39] *Jizhu* first appeared in Tang texts and was found a total of thirty-seven times in the texts in ZJGK.

which to him seemed odd because a mallet would be a better instrument.[40] But in the post-Han period, after trapezoidal dulcimers were introduced to China from Central Asia, Chinese musicians played on them with thin bamboo sticks, or chopsticks. It was said that Liu Yun (465–517), a musician and poet in the Southern Liang dynasty, could play a zither with either his chopsticks or his brush pen (usually made of the same material) to entertain his audience. Before him, the Chinese zither, or *qin* (stringed instrument), which is quite similar to a trapezoidal dulcimer, had been traditionally played with the fingers.[41]

The people in the Tang struck plates and bowls with chopsticks to make music because during the period most of the food utensils were made of ceramic and even porcelain, no longer bronze as in the Han and earlier periods. Thus legend has it that Wan Baochang (?–595), an indentured musician at the Sui dynasty court, performed this way at imperial dinners. On one occasion, someone asked Wan about music when he was just about to eat. For want of proper instruments, Wan instead used the chopsticks he was eating with to strike the bowls of various sizes, hitting all the notes for his explanation. His musicality impressed many, including the emperor; at the latter's invitation, Wan composed court music, though his status remained unchanged throughout his life. Then during the ninth century, a court musician named Guo Daoyuan demonstrated his virtuosity by tapping, again with a pair of chopsticks, various types of porcelain vessels that contained different levels of water to make beautiful music. Obviously, the difference in size and quality of the vessels, as well as the different levels of water in them, helped Guo to create the musical notes. He also mastered the skill of striking those vessels with chopsticks to create different musical tones as he intended.[42]

Besides describing how chopsticks were used on various occasions, historians, poets and scholars also commented on the varieties of chopsticks and assigned different values and meanings to them. The earliest and perhaps the most well-known example, of course, is Han Feizi's criticism of King Zhou's use of ivory chopsticks. As the case became well known, ivory chopsticks came to be associated with a profligate and decadent lifestyle in almost all textual references. But in real life, ironically, probably because of the association, the rich and well born coveted ivory chopsticks, and

---

[40] Wang, *Lunheng* – "Ganxu" (Ficticious influences), *juan* 5, ZJGK, 48.
[41] Li, *Nanshi* – "Liu Yun zhuan" (Biography of Liu Yun), HDWZK, 988.
[42] Li Yanshou, *Beishi* (History of the northern dynasties) – "Yishu xia" (Arts II), HDWZK, 2982. The case of Guo Daoyuan is in Liu, *Zhongguo zhu wenhuashi*, 197.

other ivory artifacts in general, as a way to show off their status, success and wealth. Compared with other varieties, ivory chopsticks are more fragile, and become cracked and stained rather easily if used with less care. Discoloring also takes place even if one does not use them on a daily basis. All this probably explains why ivory chopsticks were not well received from their first appearance in traditional Asia.

Gold chopsticks are also delicate. In fact, pure gold chopsticks are extremely rare because they are hard to make and, once made, they are as impractical and unusable as ivory chopsticks. However, it seems that gold chopsticks have a much better image, as shown in the following story. During the Tang dynasty, per the historical record, Emperor Xuanzong (r. 712–756) gave a pair of gold chopsticks to Song Jing (663–737), his then prime minister, at a banquet. Known for his high integrity, Song was at first quite reluctant to receive such an expensive gift because he did not know what the Emperor's intention was. Seeing his hesitation, the Emperor explained: "I give you the pair of chopsticks not because they are made of gold, but because they are as straight as you are [in giving me advice]." Song then thanked the Emperor and accepted the chopsticks. As one of the first instances of gold chopsticks recorded in history, Song Jing's earning of a gold pair of chopsticks was recited time and again in later texts.[43] As such, in contrast to ivory chopsticks, gold chopsticks were endowed with a positive moral connotation, associated with Song Jing's upright and straightforward character.[44] To follow the Tang example, imperial families of later dynasties collected gold chopsticks and occasionally also gave them as gifts to reward and commend loyal and worthy ministers. Two pairs of gold chopsticks, for example, were found among numerous pairs of gold-plated and silver chopsticks in Yan Song's (1480–1567) collection. Once a highly trusted Ming official, Yan obtained the two pairs of gold chopsticks from the imperial family. Zhang Juzheng (1525–1582), another powerful figure in the Ming government, also received a pair of gold chopsticks from the Grand Empress for his dedicated service.[45]

---

[43] Wang Renyu, *Kaiyuan tianbao yishi* (An unofficial history of Emperor Xuanzong's reign), available in ZJGK. From then on, *jinzhu* appeared 129 times in various texts in ZJGK, mostly recitations of Song Jing's story.

[44] Many Chinese writers and poets associated gold chopsticks with moral uprightness, shown in the texts in ZJGK. Korean scholars also did the same in their writings, seen in the texts in http://db.itkc.or.kr/itkcdb/mainIndexIframe.jsp.

[45] Few gold chopsticks have been unearthed in China yet the Palace Museum in Beijing has collected several pairs of gold and silver chopsticks, purchased by the imperial families of the Ming and Qing dynasties. See Liu, *Zhongguo zhu wenhuashi*,

Besides ivory and gold, other expensive materials are also used to make chopsticks. Some indeed are as rare and valuable as ivory, such as rhinoceros horn, deer antler and ebony, whereas others are expensive because they are mostly imports, such as certain wood like mahogany and narra (Malay padauk), which are native to Vietnam, Thailand and other parts of Southeast Asia and less seen in East Asia. Interestingly, few of these prized chopsticks seem to have the same immoral association as do ivory chopsticks. Of these valued varieties, silver chopsticks are relatively more affordable, as the metal is more common and more malleable than other metals. In fact, some gold chopsticks mentioned in historical texts were more likely made of a gold-silver alloy. Although susceptible to discoloring, silver chopsticks are also hardy and durable, hence popular as both a valuable collectible and a convenient utensil. As noted previously, archaeological digs have found many silver chopsticks in China and Korea, attesting to their enduring popularity over the ages. Surprisingly, perhaps because they are relatively common, mentions of silver chopsticks are not as frequent as those of their gold and ivory counterparts in Chinese texts. One of the earliest cases is in the *Famous Sites on the West Lake* (Xihu fansheng lu), an anonymous text likely from the thirteenth century. It records that up-market restaurants in Lin'an, the capital of the Southern Song dynasty (1127–1279), prepared food with silver utensils – the text mentions it perhaps because it was a bit unusual.[46] But apparently people did use silver chopsticks as an eating tool. In a poem, Tang Xianzu (1550–1616), a prominent playwright of the Ming, describes a sumptuous gala he attended, sighing: "It would not be hard for anyone to get drunk [when foods] were carried by silver chopsticks and gold spoons."[47] Silver chopsticks, paired with gold spoons, are metaphors for a comfortable, if also luxurious, life. But again, there is no outright moral condemnation.

Besides the precious chopsticks mentioned above, there is another valued material of which chopsticks have been made throughout the

428–429. Yan Song's collection is described by Liu Zhiqin in her *WanMing shilun* (Essays on Late Ming history) (Nanchang: Jiangxi gaoxiao chubanshe, 2004), 270. The mention of Zhang Juzheng's gold chopsticks is in Fu Weilin, *Mingshu* (Ming history), ZJGK, 1751.

[46] See Meng Yuanlao et al., *Xihu fansheng lu* (Beijing: Zhongguo shangye chubanshe, 1982), 17. Michael Freeman also noted that high-class restaurants in the Song supplied silver utensils to their customers. See his chapter, "Sung," in *Food in Chinese Culture*, 153.

[47] Tang Xianzu, "Yebo jinchi" (A night at Jinchi), *Yumingtang quanji* (Complete works of the Yuming Hall), ZJGK, 267.

ages, which is jade. From time immemorial, the Chinese, and to a certain degree Koreans too, have developed a fascination with jade. As early as the Paleolithic Age, (nephrite) jade was already being made into various objects for both utilitarian and ceremonial purposes, as shown in archaeological finds in China. Over time, jade became the "imperial gem" for the Chinese; as ritual objects, jade artifacts (vessels, ornaments, etc.) were indispensable in religious ceremonies at the state level. In traditional China, men and women also habitually wore jade as personal adornments, whereas skilled artisans crafted jade into *objets d'art*, which became collectibles for the rich. In some instances, the status of a piece of high-quality jade can exceed that of gold and silver in China. Naturally, the Chinese also made jade chopsticks. But once formed into thin sticks, they are easily breakable, hence few real examples of jade chopsticks have surfaced at historical sites.

In texts, however, jade chopsticks have made frequent appearances. The *History of the Southern Qi Dynasty* (NanQishu), authored by Xiao Zixian (487–537), provides an early example. In rhapsodic style, Xiao writes about jade chopsticks as follows:

As far as I could see, emperors and kings rose on simple and modest lifestyles while falling on debauchery and profligacy. Having followed good examples from the past, you, our Majesty, reside in a wooden room and sleep on a whitewood bed. When you eat, you use pottery utensils and gourd bowls. Indeed, when broken, jade hairpins and chopsticks appear no different from the dirt and when on fire, fur and silk clothes are as flammable as the grass.[48]

Here, the fragility of jade chopsticks becomes a metaphorical case for praising as well as for remonstrating with the emperor to exhibit the qualities of exemplary morality.

Like ivory chopsticks, jade chopsticks are delicate, less useful and less usable in real life. But this hardly stops literary writers from using them as allegories in their works. Around the time when Xiao Zixian mentioned them in his history, *yuzhu*, or "jade chopsticks," appeared recurrently in literary texts, especially from the Tang. In fact, the term seems to have a much larger appeal than the references to gold or silver chopsticks.[49] There are two reasons for writers and poets to mention jade chopsticks. One is to use them to symbolize good living associated with one's career success. A poem by Du Fu is an example: "As gold plates and jade chopsticks are

---

[48] Xiao Zixian, *NanQishu* – "Cui Zusi, Liu Shanming, Su Kan, Huan Rongzu" (Biographies of Cui Zusi, Liu Shanming, Su Kan and Huan Rongzu), ZJGK, 216.

[49] In the texts collected in ZJGK, *yuzhu* (jade chopsticks) appeared 2284 times whereas *jinzhu* (gold chopsticks) 129 times and *yinzhu* (silver chopsticks) only 54 times.

nowhere to find, let me just taste the cherry and live my new life." After he relocated from the Tang capital Chang'an to Chengdu, Du received some red cherries from his new neighbor. The friendly gesture of his neighbor reminded Du of the life he used to have in the capital, for back then he received cherries from the imperial court. The "gold plates and jade chopsticks" thus stand for the successful life Du once had enjoyed as a government official.[50]

The other reason for the frequent appearance of jade chopsticks is that as jade is usually light-colored or transparent, once formed jade sticks look like tears flowing down one's cheeks. As such, *yuzhu* conjures up the image of someone crying. Chinese writers and poets often employed the phrase to describe a weeping woman – a widow missing her late husband or an unhappy lady-in-waiting in the imperial harem. One poem in the *New Songs at the Jade Terrace* (Yutai xinyong), an important poetry collection probably by Xu Ling (507–583), depicts an unhappy court lady who saw her youth slip away as she waited for the prince: "gold hairpins were hanging loosely on the hair, just as her tears were flowing down onto the chest like jade chopsticks." In another poem, a wife is crying over her separation with her husband serving in the army: "Staring at Venus in the sky, my eyebrows scrunched together; overwhelmed with sorrow, my tears flowed down like jade chopsticks."[51] Li Bai, the Tang poet, also used the metaphor to describe a sad and lonely woman. He portrays a scene where the woman is writing a letter to her lover, express-ing her longing for their reunion. Then she looks in a mirror, seeing that her "tears were like two jade chopsticks, dropping down from her cheeks onto the mirror."[52] Instead of stating that she cried, Li suggests that the woman did not realize she was shedding tears until she saw herself in the mirror: her tears were already rolling down in two lines like jade chopsticks.

Not only can the color and shape of chopsticks be described literally and metaphorically, but their size and length can also be used in measurement. Du Fu, for instance, once praises the chives he received from a friend in such words: "A fresh bunch of green, their scapes are round and tall like jade chopsticks."[53] Over two centuries previously, Jia Sixie in his *Essential Techniques for the Peasantry* also compares the length of noodles to chopsticks. When he describes the height and shape of plants and

[50] Du Fu, *Du Gongbu ji* (Works of Du Fu), ZJGK, 195.
[51] Xu Ling (?), ed., *Yutai xinyong*, ZJGK, 46 & 52.
[52] Li Bai, *Li Taibai ji* (Poems of Li Bai), ZJGK, 143.   [53] Du, *Du Bongbu ji*, ZJGK, 107.

vegetables, he frequently measures them against those of chopsticks for comparison, presumably to make his text easily understandable to readers, or the peasantry.[54] Over time, as chopsticks became more and more a day-to-day item, such comparisons also became increasingly prevalent and were made quite creatively and humorously. One interesting, perhaps bizarre, case is in the *Water Margin*, a Ming novel. Instead of comparing jade chopsticks to tears, which by then had become an archaic usage, the author writes, perhaps for exaggerating a peculiar face, that someone's ears resemble a pair of "jade chopsticks" and his eyes bulge like two "golden bells."[55]

In sum, ever since they became a daily utensil in ancient China, chopsticks have been a beloved subject for writers, poets and philosophers. While scholars philosophize on their characteristics to offer political wisdom on sound governance, writers employ them as an effective metaphor to aid their descriptions of sadness, anxiety and astonishment. Chopsticks also appear in scientific and technical writings, as they are easy examples for approximating length, size and shape for illustration. Yet poets seem to have favored them the most. From ancient times to more or less this day, Chinese poets have continually written about chopsticks, commenting on their utility and characteristics and exploring their embedded cultural meanings, real and imagined alike. Some examples are given here to conclude this chapter.

Cheng Lianggui, a little known poet, arguably might be the first to have composed a poem specifically on chopsticks. It reads:

> Hardworking are the bamboo chopsticks,
> always the first to taste, bitter or sweet;
> Though nothing is eaten,
> they love to serve, back and forth.[56]

Chopsticks here are personified as a diligent and selfless worker, a popular and recurrent theme in poems about chopsticks. Yuan Mei (1716–1797), a well-known writer and connoisseur in the Qing, paints a similar image in his poem, with sympathy and a bit of humor:

> Busy as you are,
> taking and giving for the mouths of others;

---

[54] Jia, *Qimin yaoshu*, http://zh.wikisource.org/zh/齊民要術, *juan* 9, for example, when he compares the length of noodles to chopsticks; other comparisons are made throughout the book.

[55] Shi Nan'an, *Shuihu zhuan*, ZJGK, 113.

[56] Cited in http://bbs.culture.163.com/bbs/gufeng/170441342.html.

> Having tasted all, sour and salty,
> can you savor anything yourself?[57]

Another popular theme about chopsticks is their straightness, a quality with which a person's moral character is often compared and commended. During the early Tang, a writer was already praising the quality of metal fire-sticks, or *huozhu*, as both "straight and steady," expressing his high hopes for such behavior in government officials.[58] Two centuries later, Zhou Chi (?–1213), who served under the Yuan dynasty, elaborates these qualities in his poem:

> Shaped like shorter arrows,
> you are painted in solid red.
> Lining up your heads, you work together,
> as one cannot leave the other.
> In rest, you are next to the plates,
> at work, you are held by palm and fingers.
> Having picked out bones from steamed pork,
> then you draw noodles in oiled scallions.
> Badmouthed often in use,
> stay straight, you never let your work lapse.
> I wish one acts like you,
> in spite of the sorrow wider than a river.[59]

While offering sympathy for the chopsticks' hard and unselfish work, here Zhou Chi also compares their experience with his own in the government. Probably an upright official, Zhou might have offered his straightforward advice, only to be "badmouthed" by others. But encouraged and inspired by the exemplary role chopsticks play in life, he hopes to "stay straight" like them, not letting his work and his moral standard slacken and slip.

Since this chapter begins with a love story, perhaps it is fitting to end it with a love poem. The "inseparableness" of chopsticks has turned them into a much-loved object while writing love poems, past and present alike. Some of the poems are carved on the husband–wife chopsticks, not only to register the couple's love but also to wish for their shared happiness.[60] The poem below was written by a contemporary Chinese poet, and appeared in an online blog. It is somewhat unpolished, but touching and beautiful

---

[57] Yuan Mei, *Suiyuan shihua* (Stories of poems at Suiyuan), ZJGK, 45.
[58] Yang Qia, "Tie huozhu fu" (Rhapsody on iron [chop]sticks), see Liu, *Zhongguo zhu wenhuashi*, 226.
[59] Liu, *Zhongguo zhu wenhuashi*, 294.
[60] Some of the poems are available in Lan, *Kuaizi, buzhishi kuaizi*, 193–246.

nevertheless. The author comments on almost all the characteristics one can think of associated with chopsticks use – their sameness in length, their togetherness at work, their role in tasting and carrying the food, and even their "quietness" as objects – and uses them effectively to depict a couple's love:

> Our lengths are the same,
> Just as the sameness of our hearts;
> Bitter or sweet,
> we spend our life together.
> Having tasted it all,
> We always live side by side.
> One knows the other;
> our intimacy is so seamless,
> no space even for a single word.[61]

---

[61] http://bbs.culture.163.com/bbs/gufeng/170441342.html.

7

"Bridging" food cultures in the world

Real Chinese food is delicate and rare; supposed to be tasted rather than eaten, for the number of courses is stupendous. If really to the manner born, you reach into one general dish with your chop-sticks; it is a clean and delicate way to dine. Unless you go in for too much bird's nest soup and century-old eggs, the prices are reasonable. Bird's nest soup is delicious, but anyone can have my share of the heirloom hen fruit.

Harry Carr, *Los Angeles: City of Dreams* (New York, 1935)

If you do not take your courage in hand, click your chopsticks together a few times to satisfy sceptical Chinese dinners that you can operate them, and plunge head first, so to speak, into real Chinese food, you cannot say that you have understood and savoured the taste of China.

George McDonald, *China* (Thomas Cook guide book) (Peterborough, 2002)

Chopsticks are pronounced the same as "bridge" in Japanese, as mentioned previously. Since the mid-nineteenth century, after Asia became incorporated into the modern world, the eating tool has indeed played such a part in bridging food cultures in that continent and those around the globe. As Chinese food moves from "China to Chinatown," to borrow the title of J. A. G. Roberts's recent book, chopsticks have also traveled along the pathway to regions outside the chopsticks cultural sphere of Asia. For a non-Asian customer, using chopsticks to convey food, perhaps, is the culmination and crystallization of the dining experience in a Chinese/Asian restaurant. To cater to and cultivate such interest, many Chinese restaurant owners also use "chopsticks" to name their restaurants outside China, for example "Golden Chopsticks" and "Bamboo Chopsticks" are popular.[1] Of course,

---

[1] The finding is drawn on a keyword search in Google.

chopsticks are not only found in Chinese restaurants, they are also provided for customers at Japanese, Korean, Vietnamese and sometimes Thai restaurants. As such, chopsticks use adds to the global appeal of Asian foods. If chopsticks are a "bridge," they bring together food cultures not only between Asians and non-Asians but also among Asians.

In the modern world, chopsticks have a global image because they are readily noticeable for anyone traveling to the chopsticks cultural sphere in Asia. From the sixteenth century when Europeans began visiting Asia, they quickly discovered that chopsticks use was a unique way of eating food among the Chinese and their neighbors and duly recorded the custom in their journals and travelogues. One of the earliest mentions of chopsticks appears in the journal written by Galeote Pereira, a Portuguese mercenary who went to South China via India between 1539 and 1547. Pereira's account updated Europeans' knowledge about China after Marco Polo's legendary book of the thirteenth century. (Marco Polo, incidentally, did not to mention the Chinese use of chopsticks, just as he omitted their drinking of tea.) Pereira finds the Chinese dietary custom both clean and civil, for their use of chopsticks. He writes:

All the people of China, are wont to eat their meat sitting on stools at high tables as we do, and that very cleanly, although they use neither table-cloths nor napkins. Whatsoever is set down upon the board, is first carved, before that it be brought in: they feed with two sticks, refraining from touching their meat with their hands, even as we do with forks, for the which respect, they less do need any table-cloths.[2]

Since chopsticks users did not touch food with their hands, the Europeans noticed, Asians did not even need to wash their hands before meals. Louis Fróis (1532–1597), a Portuguese Jesuit, and Lourenço Mexia, his traveling companion to Japan at the time, came up with a list of things they observed that differentiated Asians from Europeans. Asians, or the Japanese whom they encountered in this case, not only ate rice instead of bread, but their eating habits also diverged: "We wash our hands at the beginning and at the end of the meal; the Japanese, who do not touch their food with their hands, do not find it necessary to wash them."[3] This was because, observed Francesco Carletti (1573–1636), an Italian merchant visiting Japan in the later part of the century, "With these two sticks [chopsticks], the Japanese are able to fill their mouths with marvelous swiftness and agility. They can

[2] Boxer, *South China in the Sixteenth Century*, 14.
[3] Quoted in Donald F. Lach, *Japan in the Eyes of Europe: The Sixteenth Century* (Chicago: University of Chicago Press, 1968), 688.

pick up any piece of food, no matter how tiny it is, without ever soiling their hands."[4]

Thus, when first encountering chopsticks, Europeans were quite curious and intrigued (Plate 17). They found dining with chopsticks neat and clean, for the food would not dirty the hands. This might suggest that while forks and knives were believed to be already in use among Europeans by that time, there were still occasions when they transported foods with fingers, hence the need for napkins and tablecloths. In those early days of discovery, Matteo Ricci (1552–1610), the founding figure of the Jesuit mission to China, gave the most positive impression of chopsticks use. Compared with the accounts of his contemporaries, Ricci provides the most detailed descriptions of the dietary customs in Ming China for Europeans. While others simply called chopsticks "two sticks," he describes how the eating device was made: "These sticks are made of ebony or of ivory or some other durable material that is not easily stained, and the ends which touch the food are usually burnished with gold or silver." Ricci also comments that in China banquets were "both frequent and very ceremonious," because the Chinese considered the banquet the "highest expression of friendship." And at banquets, observes Ricci,

They [the Chinese] do not use forks or spoons or knives for eating, but rather polished sticks, about a palm and a half long, with which they are very adept in lifting any kind of food to their mouths, without touching it with their fingers. The food is brought to the table already cut into small pieces, unless it be something that is soft, such as cooked eggs or fish and the like, which can be easily separated with the sticks.[5]

Though impressed by their usefulness, Matteo Ricci did not mention whether he had tried to dine with chopsticks and, if he had, whether he used them as adeptly as did the Chinese. Indeed, of the various accounts left by European missionaries and other travelers from the sixteenth to the nineteenth centuries, few recorded if they were curious and tempted enough to try to use chopsticks, despite the otherwise quite adventurous spirit displayed in their accounts. The difficulty in wrapping their fingers around chopsticks and learning to use them might have thwarted their attempts.

Yet to some Europeans, while the ability to use chopsticks was striking, this eating style remained unappealing, for it was seen at times as

---

[4] Quoted in Giblin, *From Hand to Mouth*, 44.
[5] Matteo Ricci, *China in the Sixteenth Century: The Journals of Matthew Ricci: 1583–1610*, trans. Louis J. Gallagher (New York: Random House, 1953), 66, 64.

unrefined. Martin de Rada (1533–1578), a Spanish Augustinian who went to Asia from Mexico and landed first in the Philippines and later in South China, also noticed that the Chinese ate meals with chopsticks, which rendered tablecloths and napkins unnecessary. Yet unlike Galeote Pereira and Matteo Ricci, de Rada is less impressed by the custom. "At the beginning of a meal they eat meat without bread," he writes, "and afterwards instead of bread they eat three or four dishes of cooked rice, which they likewise eat with their chopsticks, even though somewhat hoggishly."[6] It appeared hoggish to him perhaps because the Chinese lifted the rice bowl and pushed the rice into the mouth, as a way to prevent rice grains from falling from the chopsticks.

Peter Mundy (1600–1667), an English traveler who went to South China from India in the seventeenth century, was equally impressed with the skillful handling of chopsticks by the Chinese he encountered. Yet his description of the dining method also smacks of disapproval. In his multivolume book, which details his trips to several Asian regions as well as to continental Europe, Mundy provides an illustration, portraying how the Chinese used chopsticks to eat a meal, in which the man raised the bowl close to his mouth and thrust the food into it hastily. Mundy's description goes as follows:

Hee [a boatman on the Grand Canal] taketh the stickes (which are about a foote longe) beetweene his Fingers and with them hee taketh uppe his Meat, being first cut smalle, as saltporcke, Fish, etts., with which they relish their Rice (it being their common Foode). I say first taking upp a bitt of the Meatte, hee presently applies to his Mouth a smalle porcelane [bowl] with sodden Rice. Hee thrusts, Crammes and stuffes it full of the said Rice with the Chopsticks in exceeding hasty Manner until it will hold No more. . . . The better sort eat after the same Manner, butt they sitt at tables as we Doe.

Mundy also mentions that "Then brought they us some henne cut in smalle peeces and Fresh porcke Don in like Manner, giving us Choppsticks to eat our Meat, butt wee knew not how to use them, soe imployed our Fingers."[7] Though amazed by the deftness of the Chinese in using chopsticks, which he was unable, possibly also unwilling, to imitate, Mundy did not approve of their eating style in general; he was a bit surprised by the fact that the upper-class Chinese dined in the same style.

---

[6] Boxer, *South China in the Sixteenth Century*, 287.
[7] Richard Carnac Temple, ed., *The Travels of Peter Mundy, in Europe and Asia, 1608–1667* (Liechtenstein: Kraus Reprint, 1967), vol. 3, 194–195. The illustration is on 165.

Though unimpressed by the Chinese use of chopsticks, Peter Mundy might be the first Englishman who recorded "chopsticks" as the name for the utensil. ("Chopsticks" also appeared in Martin de Rada's earlier account but it was a translation; de Rada might have simply used "*palillos*" or "sticks" as chopsticks are called in Spanish today.) Could Mundy claim the credit for coining the term in English? It is possible but it is also likely that someone else did it before him. The word's etymology reveals that "chopsticks" are pidgin Chinese English, combining "chop" ("quick" in Cantonese) as a prefix with "sticks." It was probably the result of some collaboration between an English person and a Cantonese-Chinese. When Mundy described their use, it sounded as if the term already existed in his time.

About three decades later, William Dampier (1651–1715), another English traveler who circumnavigated the world three times, mentions chopsticks in his *Voyages and Descriptions* (1699): "They [the utensil] are called by the English seamen Chopsticks." It was during the course of the seventeenth century, therefore, that "chopsticks" became coined in English to refer to the dining tool. By comparison, the term "sticks" has persisted in other European languages. Chopsticks, for example, are known as *baguettes* in French and *palillos* in Spanish (as in de Rada's account), both meaning "sticks." In German, chopsticks are called *Eßstäbchen*, or "eating sticks," whereas in Italian, *bacchette per il cibo*, and in Russian, *palochki dlia edy*, both meaning "sticks for food." An interesting exception is that in Portuguese, chopsticks are referred to as *hashi*, the same as in Japanese, reminding one of the Jesuit mission in Asia back in the sixteenth century.

From the eighteenth century, buoyed by the growth of capitalism, Europeans' overall interest in Asia increased notably, as the continent was perceived as a potential market for manufactured European goods. Yet their interest in Asian civilization and culture, and in the custom of chopsticks use in particular, declined. Lord George Macartney (1737–1806), the English diplomat who led an official embassy to pry open China's doors from the tight grip of the Qing dynasty (1644–1911), expressed the wish that the Chinese would soon learn to adopt the use of forks and knives instead. While in China, Macartney was greeted by two Chinese officials, or "mandarins," whom he described as "intelligent men, frank and easy in their address, and communicative in their discourse." Upon his invitation, he wrote, "they sat down to dinner with us, and though at first a little embarrassed by our knives and forks, soon got over the difficulty, and handled them with notable dexterity and execution upon some of the good things which they had brought us."[8]

If Macartney was complimentary about the Chinese mandarins, his compliment perhaps had more to do with the fact that, in his mind, the English eating custom was superior, or more civilized; as such, he hoped the Chinese would follow suit. Compared with his fellow countryman Peter Mundy over a century earlier, Macartney was little interested in, much less impressed by, the fact that the Chinese, and the Manchus (whom he called Tartars), were able to employ chopsticks to transport food. Contrary to the previous missionaries' accounts, Macartney made the following observation about the dietary practice in Qing China:

At their meals they use no towels, napkins, table-cloths, flat plates, glasses, knives nor forks, but help themselves with their fingers, or with their chopsticks, which are made of wood or ivory, about six inches long, round and smooth, and not very cleanly.

In other words, the Chinese eating customs were less civilized as they did not use a set of cutlery and other accessories as Europeans did. Even if they did use chopsticks, these were not so clean. "Our knives and forks, spoons," Macartney wrote with hope and pride, "and a thousand little trifles of personal conveniency were singularly acceptable to everybody, and will probably become soon of considerable demand ..."[9]

Lord Macartney failed in his mission to open China's doors to European trade; his requests were rejected outright by the Qing Emperor Qianlong (r. 1735–1796) because the Emperor upheld the traditional notion that China was the "Middle Kingdom" and the hub of all civilizations in the world. However, only about half a century after Lord Macartney's failed visit, the English succeeded in forcing the Qing dynasty to come to terms with them. In the aftermath of the Qing's defeat in the Opium War (1839–1842), the dynasty signed the Treaty of Nanjing, which for the first time allowed Europeans and Americans to reside and trade in China. A watershed moment, the Opium War ushered in a new era in history in that European and Asian cultures were to come into contact with each other on a much more frequent basis.

Yet Macartney's hope that the Chinese, or East Asians in general, were to turn to the use of forks and knives as did Europeans failed to materialize.

---

[8] George Macartney, *An Embassy to China: Being the Journal Kept by Lord Macartney during His Embassy to the Emperor Ch'ien-lung, 1793–1794*, ed. J. L. Cranmer-Byng (London: Longmans, republished, 1972), 71.

[9] Ibid., 225–226.

In fact, through the nineteenth century, as more and more European merchants went to China, perhaps swayed by the hospitality and insistence of their local hosts, they found themselves more and more attracted and adaptive to Asian food and the Asian dining style. Indeed, just as Peter Mundy had been asked by the Chinese to learn to use chopsticks, Western merchants in nineteenth-century China often had a similar experience. Prior to the outbreak of the Opium War, foreign merchants needed to sell their merchandise through their Chinese counterparts. As such, they worked with Chinese merchants and officials. W. C. Hunter, an American businessman, recalled that he and his fellow merchants on occasion were treated to "chopsticks dinners" by their Chinese partners. As the name indicates, these dinners were in the Chinese style, or as Hunter puts it, "no foreign element would be found in it." Since "these feasts," in Hunter's words, "were very enjoyable," one could imagine that he and other Westerners probably also tried using chopsticks to eat the food.[10]

After the Treaty of Nanjing, China became more and more accessible to Westerners, who traveled there from both Europe and America. When invited by the locals to use chopsticks, some adventurous travellers began to experiment with the eating device. Laurence Oliphant (1829–1888), a British author, traveler and diplomat who served as private secretary to the Earl of Elgin, the British plenipotentiary to China in the mid-nineteenth century, was an early example. Oliphant records such an experience in these words:

> We refreshed ourselves after the fatigues of our exploration at a Chinese restaurant, where I made my first experience in Chinese cookery, and, in spite of the novelty of the implements, managed, by the aid of chopsticks, to make a very satisfactory repast off eggs a year old preserved in clay, sharks' fins and radishes pared and boiled into a thick soup, *bêche de mer* or sea-slugs, shrimps made into a paste with sea-chestnuts, bamboo roots, and garlic, rendered piquant by the addition of soy and sundry other pickles and condiments, and washed down with warm samshu in minute cups. Dishes and plates were all on the smallest possible scale, and pieces of square brown paper served the purpose of napkins.[11]

As these words reveal, Oliphant obviously enjoyed the exotic Chinese dishes at the restaurant. Moreover, he appeared quite delighted that he managed to employ chopsticks in transporting them. So much so that

---

[10] W. C. Hunter, *The "Fan Kwae" at Canton: Before Treaty Days, 1825–1844* (London: Kegan Paul, Trench, & Co., 1882; reprinted in Taipei, 1965), 40–41.

[11] Laurence Oliphant, *Elgin's Mission to China and Japan*, with an introduction by J. J. Gerson (Oxford: Oxford University Press, 1970), vol. 1, 67–68.

when he had another dining experience in China, invited that time by a Chinese local official, Oliphant makes the following comments, in which he states that the Chinese eating custom was "more elegant," as chopsticks were "refined" whereas the knife and fork were "rude":

I was glad to have an opportunity at Shanghai of renewing my acquaintance with the Taoutai [Daotai, Intendant], whom I found to be a person of considerable intelligence and enlightenment. One day I dined with him, and partook not of a flimsy refection, such as those usually offered on such occasions, but of a good substantial repast, beginning with bird's-nest soup, followed by shark's fins, *bêche de mer*, and other indescribable delicacies, as *entrées*, then mutton and turkey, as *pièces de resistance*, carved at a side-table in a civilised manner, and handed round cut up into mouthfuls, so that the refined chopstick replaced throughout the rude knife and fork of the West. We may certainly adopt with advantage the more elegant custom of China in this respect; and as we have ceased to carve the joints in dishes, make the next step in advance, and no longer cut up slices of them in our plates.[12]

In contrast to Lord Macartney, Laurence Oliphant perhaps was one of the earliest Europeans who considered the Chinese use of chopsticks a more civilized eating manner. He too was impressed by the fact that the Chinese prepared food items in bitable morsels, readily delivered by chopsticks.

It is hard to imagine, though, that Oliphant was the only Westerner then who took on the challenge of dining with chopsticks in China. In 1935, an American woman named Corrinne Lamb published one of the first recipe books on Chinese cookery in English, *The Chinese Festive Board*. While offering fifty recipes of Chinese dishes, Lamb, who apparently had extensive traveling experience in China, also comments aptly and candidly on the dietary customs and eating etiquette as well as a number of proverbs relating to food and food culture in the country. At the outset of the book, by way of proving her expertise on Chinese food, Lamb corrects some of the well-known misconceptions possibly held by her readers, such as that rice was the only grain staple for the Chinese and that rat was consumed by them on a daily basis. She points out that in addition to rice, which was eaten by two fifths of the people, wheat, barley and millet were staple grains for the rest of the population. As for rat, she writes that the Chinese in South China did eat snake, but not rat.

Like Oliphant and others, Lamb notes that all food served in China was previously "sliced, carved, minced or reduced to proportions which need

---

[12] Ibid., 215.

no further dissection." As a result, chopsticks alone become quite sufficient in carrying food items, and effective. Lamb describes:

In the first instance, the service of food involves none of the complications of foreign table etiquette. What we know as chopsticks are really called in China *k'uai tzu* [*kuaizi*], which, in turn, may be freely translated as "quick little boys." This term is applied to them on account of their nimbleness and speed when once in action and it is a most appropriate name. One pair of *k'uai tzu* constitutes the entire cutlery equipment per person, unless by some chance a small porcelain spoon is available or called for to contend with a soup or other thin liquid. One bowl per person completes the table service. Many weary American house-wives might well wish that their dishwashing worries could be reduced to such a minimum. Table linen there is none, thus eliminating another unnecessary item.[13]

From her enthusiastic endorsement, it is easy to see that Lamb herself might have mastered the skill of using chopsticks, just as she did of cooking the Chinese dishes described in her book. Using chopsticks to eat Chinese food, indeed, was recommended for the patrons of Chinese restaurants in the United States, for "it is a clean and delicate way to dine," so stated a 1935 pamphlet about the city of Los Angeles.[14]

What is interesting is that Corrinne Lamb's enthusiasm for chopsticks use came at a time when the Chinese themselves began to reflect critically on the dietary custom. Through the course of the twentieth century, the Chinese made consistent efforts to modernize their society. Some of the Chinese took the name "Sick Man of the East," by which their country was disparagingly referred to at the time, to heart and tried to improve the health of their compatriots. In Japan, similar attempts had been made from the late nineteenth century. For instance, the idea of "hygiene" was first introduced to Japan and dubbed *eisei* 衛生 by the Japanese. Borrowing an existing term from ancient Chinese texts, these two Chinese compound words connote the meaning of "guarding life," which emphasizes the importance of hygiene for people. The Chinese have also used them, pronounced *weisheng*, to discuss the idea of "hygiene," despite some reservations.[15] It seems that they had strong reasons to adopt the Japanese translation because

[13] Corrinne Lamb, *The Chinese Festive Board* (Hong Kong: Oxford University Press, 1985; originally published in 1935), 14–15.
[14] Quoted in Roberts, *China to Chinatown*, 151.
[15] See Ruth Rogaski, *Hygienic Modernity: Meanings of Health and Disease in Treaty-Port China* (Berkeley: University of California Press, 2004), 104–164; and Sean Hsiang-lin Lei, "Moral Community of *Weisheng*: Contesting Hygiene in Republican China,"*East Asian Science, Technology and Society: An International Journal*, 3:4 (2009), 475–504.

during the 1930s a tuberculosis crisis occurred in China, making "guarding life" an imminent task. Both Chinese and Western medical professionals attributed the quick spread of the disease in the country partly to the unhealthy daily habits among the Chinese. One of those habits, lo and behold, was that "Food is taken from a common bowl, with the chopsticks conveying it to the individual mouth."[16]

In fact, during the early twentieth century, the Chinese needed to combat not only tuberculosis, but also other gastrointestinal diseases.[17] To prevent the spread of these epidemics, Chinese medical professionals advocated changing the daily habits among their compatriots. This amounted to a challenging task in that cultural traditions and social customs cannot be transformed overnight, for it often takes a long time for them to develop and be accepted among the populace. Granted, the Chinese, and other Asians in general, traditionally were conscientious about the food they consumed; this was also the general impression many Westerners had developed while traveling to the continent. In Chinese tradition, food was regarded as having medicinal effects on the human body, hence deserving high attention. This idea was also accepted and practiced among Koreans, the Japanese, the Vietnamese and other Asians. Yet at the same time, observed some Western missionaries, the Chinese lacked knowledge of "sanitary science," even though their lifestyle was by and large healthful. Indeed, though the Chinese were aware that certain diseases could be contagious and had developed various measures to prevent their spread, they were less concerned about food-sharing as a source of such contagion.[18]

Several years after Corrinne Lamb praised the Chinese use of chopsticks in carrying food, W. H. Auden (1907–1973) and Christopher Isherwood (1904–1986), two British writers, went to wartime China in 1938 and offered a rather colorful description of how primary chopsticks were for the Chinese:

One's first sight of a table prepared for a Chinese meal hardly suggests the idea of eating, at all. It looks rather as if you were sitting down to a competition in

---

[16] Quoted in Sean Hsiang-lin Lei, "Habituating Individuality: The Framing of Tuberculosis and Its Material Solutions in Republican China," *Bulletin of the History of Medicine*, 84:2 (Summer 2010), 262.

[17] Ka-che Yip, *Health and National Reconstruction in Nationalist China* (Ann Arbor: Association for Asian Studies, Inc., 1995), 10.

[18] Rogaski, *Hygienic Modernity*, 103. And Angela Ki Che Leung, "The Evolution of the Idea of *Chuanran* Contagion in Imperial China," *Health and Hygiene in Chinese East Asia*, eds. Leung & Furth, 25–50.

water-colour painting. The chopsticks, lying side by side, resemble paint-brushes. The paints are represented by little dishes of sauces, red, green, and brown. The tea-bowls, with their lids, might well contain paint-water. There is even a kind of tiny paint-rag, on which the chopsticks can be wiped.

These vivid words show that Auden and Isherwood were quite impressed by the use of chopsticks – they also write that while in China, they tried using chopsticks in conveying food, declining the knives and forks offered to them by their hosts. These two English authors also liked the custom that before a meal, everyone was offered a hot moistened towel to wipe their hands and faces, which in their recommendation should be introduced to the West.[19]

However, their beautiful depiction of the Chinese dietary practice is not so flattering as it appears on first sight. One thing is apparent: as everyone competes with each other for getting food, little concern is shown about passing their germs on to the communal dishes with their chopsticks. Corrinne Lamb also observes in her book that in China once food is put on the table, it is "prey to all present." "There ensues," she continues, "a simultaneous dive of chopsticks into the various dishes, the diners suiting their own fancy as to what they desire to concentrate upon after liberal sampling of the various offerings."[20]

Thanks to the education by medical professionals and government interventions, awareness of the importance of personal and public hygiene has been on the rise in modern China. This awareness helped draw attention to the drawbacks of the age-long practice of communal eating. Wang Li (1900–1986), a renowned Chinese linguist, coined a term *jinye jiaoliu* (exchange of saliva) to describe the fondness of the Chinese for sharing food dishes in the communal eating style. Using gallows humor, he writes as follows:

The Chinese are harmonious towards one another, thanks to the exchange of saliva [in dining]. While there are some who have advocated eating separately, there are always others who would like to share food as much as possible. For instance, when a soup is just brought on to the table, a host often first uses his own spoon to stir and sip it. He will do the same to a dish, with his chopsticks. As for inviting guests to eat, the host does not seem to care if he exchanges his saliva with all the others. ... Before I sat down at the table, I happened to notice that there was too much saliva in the host's mouth. When he opened his mouth to speak or eat, I could see a web of

[19] W. H. Auden & Christopher Isherwood, *Journal to a War* (New York: Random House, 1939), 40. Hot moistened towels are still offered to customers in restaurants in today's China.

[20] Lamb, *Chinese Festive Board*, 15.

saliva forming between the two rows of his teeth. He then used his chopsticks, which had been in and out of the web many times, to clasp and deliver foodstuff into my plate, all deferentially. I could not believe my own tongue: Why did the same sautéed chicken which had been so tasteful when I put it in my mouth by myself become so distasteful when it was delivered by his chopsticks? I must be really unworthy of the host's hospitality.[21]

Full of sarcasm, Wang's description was perhaps not completely divorced from reality in China; it is likely that his description draws on many of his personal experiences. Indeed, before the custom of using serving chopsticks and spoons was introduced to China in the late twentieth century, it had been normal for the Chinese, for showing their kinship, hospitality and generosity, to grasp food contents from the communal dishes and deliver them to others, be they younger family members or invited guests. Yet attacks on such communal dining habits had begun already in the early part of the century. Wang Li's sarcastic criticism of how the Chinese "enjoyed" exchanging saliva is but one example. Many published essays criticized the age-old yet now deemed unhygienic customs practiced among the Chinese. Some identified "communal eating" (*gongshi*) as the number one unhygienic habit on the list, whereas others have sought ways to modify it, such as urging the use of serving chopsticks (*gongkuai* or "public chopsticks" in Chinese).[22]

Yet to forsake communal eating was by no means easy; as discussed in Chapter 5, sharing food with chopsticks in a common bowl or a pot, such as eating a hot pot, had become an entrenched dining habit in China and beyond. And communal eating remains in practice among many Chinese, Vietnamese and Koreans today. When invited to a familymeal in Vietnam, for instance, everyone is given a pair of chopsticks to eat the dishes common for all; it remains quite rare for the Vietnamese to use serving chopsticks. Rice, however, is served into one's own bowl by a female member of the host family using a serving spoon.[23] In Korea, a Chinese visitor finds with surprise that some people use both their spoons and chopsticks to partake of food items in the communal dishes at public

---

[21] Wang Li, "Quancai" (Feeding), www.hanfu.hk/forum/archiver/?tid-1695.html.

[22] Zhang Yichang, "Guoren buweisheng de exi" (The unhygienic habits of my country-men), *Xinyi yu shehui jikan* (Journal of new medicine and society), 2 (1934), 156. Tao Xingzhi (1891–1946), a modern educator, asked students in the schools he founded in the 1930s to learn the practice of using a serving pair of chopsticks. Lan, *Kuaizi, buzhishi kuaizi*, 173.

[23] Nir Avieli, "Eating Lunch and Recreating the Universe: Food and Cosmology in Hoi An, Vietnam," *Everyday Life in Southeast Asia*, eds. Kathleen M. Adams & Kathleen A. Gillogly (Bloomington: Indiana University Press, 2011), 218.

gatherings. He notes that on such occasions the Chinese are more likely to use only chopsticks to take food from the common dishes, and apply the utensil rather carefully.[24]

So, a compromise had to be made. Some medical professionals attempted it in the early twentieth century, before the Chinese public was educated about the health risks involved in communal eating. In the late 1910s, Wu Liande (1879–1960), a Cambridge-trained doctor, introduced what he called a "hygienic dining table," otherwise known as the "lazy Susan," to the Chinese, claiming that it was his invention. The most hygienic way to consume a meal, Wu admitted, is to eat individually – everyone only eats the foods served (or self-served using a serving utensil) to his/her own plates or bowls. But this was not the best way to enjoy a Chinese meal, he argued. Then the other way was to let everyone pick up food items in common plates, but ask them to employ a pair of serving chopsticks to first bring the food to his/her rice bowls. To do so, however, could be cumbersome and confusing (some may just forget about switching between the personal and serving chopsticks), killing the fun of eating. Using a lazy Susan, Wu believed, presented a better solution, for it could balance the traditional desire among the Chinese to sample various dishes at a meal and their newly acquired interest in hygienic dining. More specifically, according to Wu's direction, one should place either a serving spoon or a pair of serving chopsticks next to every dish on the platform, reminding diners to use them as they rotate the platform and pick up food from the dishes. That is, using the lazy Susan this way allows diners to continue sharing and savoring the variety of the dishes but at the same time, it stops them from passing their saliva on to the common dishes.[25]

In 1972 US President Richard Nixon paid a historic visit to China. As this was an epoch-making event, it was well covered in the Western media, allowing the outside world to take a peek into how the Chinese had lived on the mainland after the Communists took over power in 1949. The coverage included, interestingly, details of how President Nixon prepared for his trip, such as how he practiced using chopsticks.[26] The time he spent on practicing seems to have paid off, as shown in Margaret Macmillan's description of the banquet the Chinese hosted for the visit:

[24] Tang Libiao, "Han'guo de shili" (Eating etiquette in Korea), *Dongfang shiliao yu baojian* (Food medicine and health care in the East), 9 (2006), 8–9.
[25] Lei, "Habituating Individuality," 262–265.
[26] Ann M. Morrison, "When Nixon Met Mao," Book Review, *Time*, December 3, 2006.

The band played the Chinese and US national anthems, and the banquet began. The Nixons and top-ranking Americans sat with Chou En-lai [Zhou Enlai, China's Premier] at a table for 20; everyone else was at tables of ten. Each person had an ivory place card embossed in gold English and Chinese characters and chopsticks engraved with his or her name.

The Americans had been briefed on how to behave at Chinese banquets. Everyone had been issued chopsticks and urged to practice ahead of time. Nixon had become reasonably adept, but national-security adviser Henry Kissinger remained hopelessly clumsy. CBS News anchor Walter Cronkite shot an olive into the air. . . .

The lazy Susans spun, laden with duck slices with pineapple, three-colored eggs, carp, chicken, prawns, shark fin, dumplings, sweet rice cake, fried rice, and in a nod toward Western tastes, bread and butter.[27]

Wu Liande's effort to introduce the so-called "hygienic dining table," or lazy Susan, therefore, was not in vain. Over time, the Chinese have indeed realized the importance of adopting a hygienic eating style. While few families, save for some wealthy ones, have a lazy Susan on their dining table, it is quite common to find this round, rotatable platform in restaurants in today's China and across Asia. At formal or state dinners, such as the occasion described at which US President Nixon and his entourage were entertained, a lazy Susan is almost indispensable in that it best displays the variety of the dishes the Chinese have prepared for the guests to sample and savor. Banquets remain "very ceremonious" in China, just as Matteo Ricci discovered in the late sixteenth century.

Despite the detailed description, the Western media did not specify whether or not the Nixons and US officials, while eating at lazy Susans, were provided with a serving spoon or a pair of serving chopsticks to first bring food to their plates. Probably they were not because it was a dignified occasion and waiters would most likely have served the food to their plates; the guests just needed to use their own chopsticks to move the food from the plates to their mouths. But today, most Chinese dining in public would follow Wu Liande's advice, using a serving spoon or a pair of serving chopsticks, or *gongkuai*, to first transport the food items to their own bowls before bringing them to their mouths. Indeed, not only do they

---

[27] Margaret MacMillan, "Don't Drink the Mao-tai: Close Calls with Alcohol, Chopsticks, Panda Diplomacy and Other Moments from a Colorful Turning Point in History," *Washingtonian*, February 1, 2007. Here MacMillan tries to compliment Nixon's adeptness in using chopsticks, but his success seems to be on relative terms. In his memoir, Dirck Halstead, an American photographer who witnessed the occasion, recalls instead that "We watched as President Nixon made a painful attempt to use his chopsticks on his Peking Duck." "With Nixon in China: A Memoir," *The Digital Journalist*, January 2005.

use *gongkuai* while eating out, but they also use them while entertaining their guests at home. Chopsticks users are now highly aware of the need to practice hygienic dining, even though this means that they have to remember the separate roles (public vs. private) assigned to the chopsticks.

Hygiene awareness has not only modified the communal eating tradition, but it has also changed people's attitudes toward restaurant chopsticks. As mentioned in previous chapters, various sorts of public eateries (inns, lodges, tea-houses, restaurants, etc.) had existed in China for centuries, beginning as early as in the Han period – Ōta Masako actually believed that the tradition for the Chinese to eat out had started during the Warring States period (475–221 BCE) and that it also helped promote chopsticks use among them.[28] If this were the case, then one could expect that as they were inexpensive and easy to make, it would not take long for chopsticks to be offered at those dining places for the convenience of customers. However, since the notion of hygiene was by and large absent in traditional societies, the sanitary condition of those public utensils varied tremendously. Isabella Bird (1831–1904), an English writer and globe-trekker, went to Asia in the second half of the nineteenth century. Her journal records her negative impression of the unsanitary conditions in China. Having witnessed poor laborers (whom she called "coolies") eating meals at a roadside eatery, she writes: "On each table a bunch of malodorous chopsticks occupies a bamboo receptacle. An earthen bowl with water and a dirty rag are placed outside for the use of travellers, who frequently also rinse their mouths with hot water."[29] Clearly, those chopsticks appeared squalid because they were not cleaned on a regular basis.

As people's concern about food hygiene increased, so did their demand for clean chopsticks at public eateries. To meet the demand, restaurants seem to have two solutions. One is to develop a regime to sanitize regularly the chopsticks placed in the receptacles and the other is to let customers use disposable, or one-time-use, chopsticks made of cheap wood. In the latter case, each customer is given a new pair of chopsticks every time s/he comes to eat a meal and these are thrown away after use. As of today, both methods are popular, though disposable chopsticks seem more favored simply because they look new, unused before by others. Disposable chopsticks are usually prepackaged in a paper or plastic sleeve, with two sticks connected together – users need to snap them apart before use. For many,

[28] Ōta, *Hashi no genryū o saguru*, 229–246.
[29] Isabella Bird, *The Yangtze Valley and Beyond* (Boston: Beacon Press, 1985), 193–194.

this requirement ensures that the chopsticks are new and clean. In Chinese, disposable chopsticks are called *yicixing kuaizi* (one-time-use chopsticks), but they are also referred to as *weisheng kuai* (hygienic chopsticks), suggesting they are perceived as sanitary by the public. By comparison, one can always question the cleanness of the chopsticks given by restaurants, even if they look clean, not "malodorous" as Isabella Bird found a century or so earlier.

Disposable chopsticks are a Japanese invention. As described in Chapter 4, the earliest chopsticks found in Japan were made of wood and were discarded, as scholars suspect, after use by construction workers at some ancient sites. According to Isshiki Hachirō, disposable chopsticks, or *waribashi*, first appeared in some seafood restaurants in the mid-Tokugawa period, or the eighteenth century. The name *waribashi* (lit. split chopsticks) describes how they are connected at one end, requiring their users to split them into two sticks before putting them into use. Made usually of wood, sometimes also of bamboo, disposable chopsticks are generally shorter than the reusable ones, such as lacquered wooden chopsticks and, in more recent years, plastic chopsticks. Compared with the reusable varieties, disposable chopsticks are far more popular in Japan; they are present in almost all kinds of eateries, be it a classy restaurant or a street food stand. Throwing away wooden chopsticks after use registered Shintoist influences, as discussed in Chapter 6, but the heightened hygiene awareness of modern times has also reinforced the practice, turning it into a powerful and prevalent trend in Japanese society today.

Over time, the tendency to use disposable chopsticks in public eateries has spilled over to Japan's neighbors; first to South Korea and Taiwan and, from the late 1980s on, to China and, more slowly, Vietnam. Yet the degree of their popularity varies notably. While in Japan disposable chopsticks are used at restaurants of almost all levels, outside Japan, disposable chopsticks tend to be found in smaller cafés and restaurants, such as fast-food chains and takeout places. As of today, disposable chopsticks have the least appeal to the Vietnamese who prefer instead the reusable variety, such as those made of plastic or bamboo. Thanks to the tradition of using metal utensils, Koreans also use fewer disposable chopsticks than do the Japanese and Chinese.[30]

---

[30] This seems to be the experience of Rachel Nuwer, a *New York Times* reporter who writes: "if you are in the mood for Vietnamese food, you'll probably be dining with the plastic variety [of chopsticks], while Korean restaurants tend to go with metal." "Disposable Chopsticks Strip Asian Forest," *New York Times*, October 24, 2011.

But in China, disposable chopsticks have become ubiquitous. China is also the leading exporter of disposable chopsticks in the world. This ought not to be so surprising, for since the late 1970s when the country reopened its doors to the outside world, it quickly became the "factory of the world," manufacturing almost all the products one can think of and exporting them to countries around the world. The period from the late 1970s onward also witnessed a growing trend among the Chinese to adopt the custom of using disposable chopsticks at restaurants. Disposable chopsticks have also become more commonly found at company and school canteens, dining halls and cafés than their reusable cousins, made either of wood, bamboo or plastic. Needless to say, this switch from reusable to disposable chopsticks reflects the rising interest in hygienic dining among their users. To fight the spread of disease, the Chinese government at once also encouraged the use of disposable chopsticks. The purchase of disposable chopsticks thus skyrocketed in a country where only a few decades ago the reusable variety had been the most common. "Throwaway chopsticks," states one observer, "are now used in all but the poorest and the most expensive restaurants throughout China. The poor ones reuse bamboo chopsticks after cursory washing. The expensive ones prefer sanitized, lacquered-wood chopsticks. All the rest use disposable wooden chopsticks."[31]

The demand for disposable chopsticks therefore is great, and growing. One estimate puts it that "Each year, the equivalent of 3.8 million trees go into the manufacture of about 57 billion disposable pairs of chopsticks in China." Of the 57 billion pairs, half of them are used in China; among the other half, seventy-seven percent are used by the Japanese, twenty-one percent by South Koreans and the remaining two percent by US consumers. Another estimate goes higher: in China alone, 45 billion pairs of disposable chopsticks are used and thrown away every year.[32] The highest figure is also the most recent, put out in March 2013, which states that as many as 80 billion pairs of one-time-use chopsticks are discarded in China every year![33]

Disposable chopsticks also play a major role in popularizing Asian foods, and Chinese food in particular, outside Asia. The global spread of

---

[31] Yang Zheng, "Chopsticks Controversy," *New Internationalist*, 311 (April 1999), 4.

[32] Nuwer, "Disposable Chopsticks Strip Asian Forest," and Dabin Yang, "Choptax," *Earth Island Journal*, 21:2 (Summer 2006), 6.

[33] Malcolm Moore, "Chinese 'Must Swap Chopsticks for Knife and Fork'," *The Telegraph*, March 13, 2013. The estimate was given at a speech by a delegate to the People's Congress who proposed to ban disposable chopsticks.

Chinese and Asian foods began when Asians emigrated to neighboring regions, first to parts of Southeast Asia and later, from the 1800s, to such faraway continents as Australia, Europe and North and South America. The initial reactions to Asian foods, which were usually found only in the Chinatowns then emerging in port cities (e.g. San Francisco which has the oldest Chinatown in the US), by non-Asians were apathetic and distrustful. But as time went on, especially after World War II, Asian and Chinese foods found more acceptance, serving not only immigrant communities of Asians, but also non-Asians. From the 1960s, according to J. A. G. Roberts, a trend of globalization of Chinese food began to occur – Chinese food gained an unprecedented popularity among consumers in Europe and America.[34] Since then, the trend has not only continued but has risen steadily. In the United States, while the number of authentic Chinese restaurants has increased notably in major cities, small takeout places have also popped up in towns throughout the country, whether they are in New York or New Mexico, Connecticut or Colorado. And when customers pick up their order, a pair or two of disposable chopsticks in paper sleeves are usually stuck inside the food bag. Indeed, in tandem with that in Asia, it has been a growing trend for Asian restaurants around the world to provide disposable chopsticks to their customers. The popularity of Chinese food is also shown in movies and TV series. In such popular hits as *Seinfeld, Friends, ER* and *Grey's Anatomy*, one often sees scenes in which characters eat Chinese food from takeout boxes, using disposable chopsticks. If chopsticks are a cultural "bridge" linking Asia to the world, the disposable kind ought perhaps to take the most credit.

However, the rising demand for disposable chopsticks around the world has caused some concern. Indeed, begun as a thrifty way to use wood scraps, disposable chopsticks are now perceived by some as an environmental hazard, causing deforestation not only in Asia but also around the world. According to a report by the United Nations in 2008, 10,800 square miles of Asian forest are disappearing each year. Manufacturers thus have turned to wood resources elsewhere. As early as in 2006, a subsidiary of Japan's Mitsubishi Group was reportedly cutting down centuries-old

---

[34] In the United States in 1960, there were over 6000 Chinese restaurants, which employed more workers than those working in laundries, the other traditional occupation for Chinese immigrants. By 1980, the number of Chinese restaurants in the United States and Canada had risen to 7796, constituting nearly thirty percent of all the ethnic restaurants. See Roberts, *China to Chinatown*, 164–165. As of today, the number of Chinese restaurants in the US is estimated at 40,000.

aspen groves in western Canada to make 8 million pairs of disposable chopsticks per day. In the United States, a company in Georgia is manufacturing and exporting large quantities of wooden chopsticks to Asia, using its native gumwood.[35]

The main appeal of disposable chopsticks is that they are seen as more sanitary than the reusable variety. Most Japanese, as put pithily by Yuki Komayima, former head of the Canadian Chopstick Manufacturing Company, simply "don't want a chopstick that has been used by someone else." This is both hygienic and spiritual because according to traditional Shinto belief, one's chopsticks carry one's spirit, which cannot be cleaned off by washing.[36] This is particular to traditional Japanese culture. But still, few chopsticks users would use chopsticks unsanitized. In China where concerns about food safety have run high in recent years, many Chinese do not trust restaurant chopsticks to have been washed thoroughly; they would rather choose the disposable type, believing it to be more sanitary.[37] Disposable chopsticks, however, are not always as clean as one thinks. When they are manufactured in factories, they are of course sanitized before being put into individual packages. But ironically, the problem arises in the sanitization process because the usual way to clean and sterilize the chopsticks once they are made is to apply various chemicals, which include paraffin, hydrogen peroxide and insect repellent. And to prevent the sticks from turning yellow, black or moldy, and to help them keep their brand-new look, some manufacturers also use sulfur dioxide to polish them. All these chemicals, needless to say, are harmful to human health, especially if applied without proper supervision. The Chinese government has now set up production standards, forbidding or curtailing the use of those chemicals. However, as disposable chopsticks are made of cheap wood, they need to be bleached and polished in order to have a presentable appearance. Using chemicals is the most economic way. Also, though disposable chopsticks are mass produced nowadays, this does not mean that they are always manufactured in large and well-managed factories that abide by government regulations. Instead, they are more commonly manufactured in

[35] Nuwer, "Disposable Chopsticks Strip Asian Forest" and "Life-Cycle Studies: Chopsticks," *World Watch*, 19:1 (January/February 2006), 2.
[36] Nuwer, "Disposable Chopsticks Strip Asian Forest" and "Life-Cycle Studies: Chopsticks." Citing a Japanese study, Wilson writes that the Japanese have a strong distaste for reusable chopsticks, even if they are cleaned. *Consider the Fork*, 200.
[37] Jane Spencer, "Banned in Beijing: Chinese See Green over Chopsticks," *The Wall Street Journal*, February 8, 2008.

small workshops with a problematic environment, at least according to news reports.[38]

While significantly contributing to the popularization of Asian foods around the world, disposable chopsticks therefore have their undeniable drawbacks: one is the issue about their cleanliness and the other is the environmental problem, or deforestation, to which their popularity may have contributed. There is not much dispute about how to ensure their sanitization; closely monitoring the manufacturers and making sure that a safe method is applied in the process is the best way. With respect to whether disposable chopsticks have exacerbated deforestation, however, there have been differing opinions. China has become the largest producer of disposable chopsticks because the disposable-chopsticks industry has contributed to the country's economic boom, employing over 100,000 people, mostly in Northeast China. "The chopsticks industry," says Lian Guang, founder and president of the Wooden Chopsticks Trade Association in Heilongjiang Province, "is making a great contribution by creating jobs for poor people in the forestry regions." Besides the economic benefit, Lian adds, the industry does not chop down valuable trees to make the chopsticks that are used and discarded within thirty minutes of a usual mealtime. Instead, disposable chopsticks are typically made from such fast-growing woods as birch and poplar, as well as bamboo, which is an abundant plant. In other words, like their predecessors in early Japan, today's disposable chopsticks are made of leftover wood that is not useful for other industries.[39]

Be that as it may, the environmental cost remains a concern for some because of the high demand for chopsticks around the world. Environmentalists estimate that if China (only) consumes 45 billion pairs of disposable chopsticks per year, 25 million trees must fall each year to meet the demand – not only birch and poplar but also cottonwood, spruce and aspen. Up till 2006, as the world's leading producer, China had shipped 180,000 tons of disposable chopsticks to other countries, with Japan being the most favored destination. Yet compared with Japan, which boasts a forest coverage rate of sixty-nine percent, the highest in the world, China is short of trees; its forest coverage rate is less than fourteen percent. Of course, the rapid pace of deforestation in China is

---

[38] Nuwer, "Disposable Chopsticks Strip Asian Forest"; "Life-Cycle Studies: Chopsticks"; and Yuan Yuan, "Yicixing kuaizi tiaozhan Zhongguo guoqing" (Disposable chopsticks challenge China as a country), *Liaowang zhoukan* (Outlook weekly), 33 (August 13, 2007).

[39] Spencer, "Banned in Beijing: Chinese See Green over Chopsticks."

caused by the country's overall modernization; it cannot and should not be attributed solely to the making of disposable chopsticks. But the ubiquity of disposable chopsticks in the country has spurred some of its citizens, including a few pop stars, to action, calling for a return to the reusable type. Other green activists have started the BYOC (Bring Your Own Chopsticks) movement, asking consumers to use their own utensils while eating out. A similar campaign – "Let's Carry Our Own Chopsticks" – is being waged simultaneously in Japan. The Chinese government imposed a tax on wooden chopsticks in 2007.[40]

At the end of 2011, hoping to raise public awareness of timber waste in making disposable chopsticks, 200 college students in China who were members of Greenpeace East Asia collected 82,000 pairs of them and made a "disposable forest" that consisted of four large trees, each sixteen feet high. These chopsticks trees stood in a busy shopping mall, while the students asked for signatures from spectators on a petition for banning the disposable utensil nationwide – such major cities as Shanghai and Beijing have already asked their restaurants to replace disposable chopsticks with reusable ones. In Japan, many restaurant owners nowadays no longer automatically provide disposable chopsticks to their customers; instead they are only given when asked for. And if eating in, customers are encouraged to use the reusable variety, stashed in a receptacle on the table. Japanese companies' canteens have also gradually replaced throwaway chopsticks with the reusable type.[41]

At the same time, serious attempts are made among Asians to recycle throwaway chopsticks. As they are made of wood, disposable chopsticks, once collected, can be turned into other useful items. Several Japanese companies are doing exactly that by making paper, facial tissues and particleboard from throwaway chopsticks.[42] Some scientists have experimented with ways to gasify waste disposable wooden or bamboo chopsticks to generate synthesis gas and hydrogen energy. Others have attempted to extract glucose from them to help produce ethanol as well as to recycle their fiber into making polylactic acid (PLA), a widely useful polyester in industry and medicine. At present, these

[40] Moore, "Chinese 'Must Swap Chopsticks for Knife and Fork'"; Nuwer, "Disposable Chopsticks Strip Asian Forest" and "Life-Cycle Studies: Chopsticks."

[41] Spencer, "Banned in Beijing: Chinese See Green over Chopsticks"; "Chopped Chopsticks," *The Economist*, 316:7665 (August 4, 1990); and Nuwer, "Disposable Chopsticks Strip Asian Forest."

[42] Nuwer, "Disposable Chopsticks Strip Asian Forest."

ideas have not gone beyond the experimental stage.[43] But they are certainly noteworthy and with significant potential. As 1.5 billion people use chopsticks to convey food on a daily basis and many of them (still) use the disposable type, there is no shortage of chopsticks to industrialize any of the experiments, benefitting people in Asia and around the world. Once that happens, or once ways of reusing waste chopsticks are effectively and broadly adopted, our story of chopsticks will come full circle: through history, chopsticks have become a popular dining tool because they are convenient and economical. They can retain and expand on these two essential features to better serve people in the years to come.

---

[43] Kung-Yuh Chiang, Kuang-Li Chien & Cheng-Han Lu, "Hydrogen Energy Production from Disposable Chopsticks by a Low Temperature Catalytic Gasification," *International Journal of Hydrogen Energy*, 37:20 (October 2012), 15672–15680; Kung-Yuh Chiang, Ya-Sing Chen, Wei-Sin Tsai, Cheng-Han Lu & Kuang-Li Chien, "Effect of Calcium Based Catalyst on Production of Synthesis Gas in Gasification of Waste Bamboo Chopsticks," *International Journal of Hydrogen Energy*, 37:18 (September 2012), 13737–13745; Cheanyeh Cheng, Kuo-Chung Chiang & Dorota G. Pijanowska, "On-line Flow Injection Analysis Using Gold Particle Modified Carbon Electrode Amperometric Detection for Real-time Determination of Glucose in Immobilized Enzyme Hydrolysate of Waste Bamboo Chopsticks," *Journal of Electroanalytical Chemistry*, 666 (February 2012), 32–41; Chikako Asada, Azusa Kita, Chizuru Sasaki & Yoshitoshi Nakamura, "Ethanol Production from Disposable Aspen Chopsticks Using Delignification Pretreatments," *Carbohydrate Polymers*, 85:1 (April 2011), 196–200; Yeng-Fong Shih, Chien-Chung Huang & Po-Wei Chen, "Biodegradable Green Composites Reinforced by the Fiber Recycling from Disposable Chopsticks," *Materials Science & Engineering: A*, 527:6 (March 2010), 1516–1521.

Conclusion

To end this book, I would like to share a personal story. When I was four or five, my mother, who has been a busy career woman all her life, sat me down one afternoon, asking me to practice the correct use of chopsticks. Of course, as a child growing up in China, I had been using chopsticks, along with a spoon, to eat before then. But my mother thought that I had reached the right age to learn to use chopsticks the right way. She taught me the correct method and asked me to clasp and move my toy wooden blocks spread on the table. What a long and grueling afternoon! I did not, initially, feel natural holding and using the chopsticks in the way she taught me. But in the end, I got used to it. And I have been using the utensil this way ever since.

I assume my experience was not uncommon among my generation, for as I was growing up, I saw many people use chopsticks the same way. Of course, I also saw some others who used the utensil in their own self-developed ways. Honestly, I must say that I find my way, or the way I learned from my mother, both more elegant and effective. In more recent decades, as an academic, I have traveled extensively across Asia. I have seen that most Japanese, Vietnamese and Koreans hold chopsticks in the same way that I do. How is this so? Did they have similar childhood experiences? Why do so many people in the region, or in the chopsticks cultural sphere, bother to learn to use the implement to convey foods?

I do not think I have found all the answers to these, and other related questions readers might have, in researching this book. For instance, I have not been able to locate a book – a manual or an instruction guide – from the past that teaches people how to use chopsticks correctly. I guess the way my mother taught me was also how she had learned to use chopsticks herself from her parents when she was young. I have no idea how early this seemingly universal method for chopsticks use was developed and adopted among chopsticks users inside the zone. What I have found is as follows. There were multiple reasons why the Chinese and other Asians learnt to use chopsticks in carrying food to their mouths, even though it requires more practice than using a spoon, a fork and a knife. The first, perhaps also the most obvious reason, was in order to eat cooked food. In 1964, Claude Lévi-Strauss (1908–2009), the legendary French anthropologist, published a seminal work, *The Raw and the Cooked*, in which he analyzed the part cooking played in bridging the worlds of humans and nature, or culture and nature. To him, this was a universal stage of civilizational development across the globe. In the book, Lévi-Strauss cited several cases from different cultures and concluded that cooking, even a symbolic act of cooking, became a way to transform a person, changing him/her into a new phase of physiological development, or from "raw" to "cooked." "The conjunction of a member of the social group with nature must be mediatized," Lévi-Strauss observed, "through the intervention of cooking fire, whose normal function is to mediatize the conjunction of the raw product and the human consumer, and whose operation thus has the effect of making sure that a natural creature is at one and the same time *cooked and socialized* [italics in the original]." Interestingly, the French scholar also noted that utensils played "a mediatory function" between nature and culture.[1]

The "raw" (*sheng*) and the "cooked" (*shu*) were two concepts, or signifiers, frequently used in ancient China to mark different levels of civilizational development in their known world. That is, a civilized society, such as their own as the Chinese believed, was "cooked" in contrast to barbaric or "raw" societies who were usually located on the margins of their cultural realm. The word for China in Chinese is *Zhongguo*, which is customarily rendered in English as the "Middle Kingdom." Yet the term also denotes the center/periphery binary in geography, as the cradle of Chinese civilization was traditionally believed to be in North China, located roughly in the center of mainland Asia. When they described the differences between their society and that of the inhabitants away from the center, the Chinese applied the two terms raw and cooked, or *sheng* and *shu*, quite literally and considered eating cooked or raw food a demarcation of cultural differences. The phrase *rumao yinxue* (literally

---

[1] Claude Lévi-Strauss, *The Raw and the Cooked: Introduction to a Science of Mythology: 1*, trans. John & Doreen Weightman (New York: Harper & Row, Publishers, 1969), 334–336.

meaning eating haired – or raw – animal meat and drinking fresh blood), therefore, became a standard expression, indiscriminately used by the ancient Chinese in North China to accentuate the barbarity of the other groups, regardless of whether they were the nomads from the Mongolian Steppe or the mountain people south of the Yangzi River. Indeed, for the Chinese, comments Frank Dikötter, "The consumption of raw food was regarded as an infallible sign of savagery that affected the physiological state of the barbarian."[2]

The Chinese preference for cooked food was also extended to drinking water: many of them prefer boiled or warm water instead of cold water. By the Tang period, tea had become a popular beverage throughout the land. In subsequent centuries, tea also spread to the neighboring regions in East Asia and beyond. If the Chinese believed that eating cooked food distinguished their culture from their neighbors', then drinking boiled water flavored by tea leaves, instead of the unboiled – "raw" – water, would certainly achieve a similar effect. Tea drinking, as mentioned in the Introduction, played its part in facilitating the wide use of chopsticks as an eating tool in Asia.

Drawing on Claude Lévi-Strauss's thesis, cooking food and boiling water thus help transform humans from nature to culture. In this process, utensils use also played a part. This is the second observation I have made in this book. The example given by Lévi-Strauss was the contrast between roasting and boiling. Both were/are popular ways of cooking, of course. But to Lévi-Strauss, there are differences: "the roast can be placed on the side of nature, and the boiled on the side of culture," for boiling entails the use of a receptacle, "which is a cultural object." In other words, though roasting and boiling both use fire, the former exposes food directly to fire, a form of nature, whereas the latter works through a cultural mediation.[3] The Chinese, too, considered the use of utensils in handling food a cultural, or cultured, sign. During the Tang period, contacts between the Chinese and outsiders, some from as far as Central Asia, were quite frequent; Buddhism, which entered East Asia no later than the second century, played a role in facilitating such cultural exchanges. Not only did Chinese Buddhists make pilgrimages to India and other Buddhist kingdoms in South and Southeast Asia, but Korean and Japanese

---

[2] Frank Dikötter, *The Discourse of Race in Modern China* (Hong Kong: Hong Kong University Press, 1992), 9.

[3] Claude Lévi-Strauss, *The Origin of Table Manners: Introduction to a Science of Mythology*, trans. John & Doreen Weightman (New York: Harper & Row, Publishers, 1978), 479–480.

Buddhists and travelers also came to visit Tang China – some of them staying there for a long period of time. In Chinese travelers' accounts, many authors quickly noticed and recorded how the natives still used their hands to convey food to their mouths.[4] Yet thanks to Tang cultural influences, all this was about to change. From the seventh century onward, as I have detailed in this book, the chopsticks cultural sphere took shape; more and more people in the region adopted the dietary custom of eating with utensils.

If East Asians believe that using utensils to convey foods amounts to cultured behavior, using chopsticks in particular is a result of the changing food production, preparation and consumption in the region. The fact that cooked rice, one of the staple grains in the zone, can be carried in lumps (thanks to its consistency) with a pair of chopsticks, facilitated the implement being widely used for transporting both grain and nongrain foods. This is a dietary custom commonly seen in East and Southeast Asia today but which goes back as early as at least of the eleventh century. Yet the real push for chopsticks use, I suggest, came from the growing appeal of floured wheat products, which occurred in China from the first century and elsewhere in the continent from a later period. In particular, eating noodles and dumplings rendered the spoon, which had been the primary eating implement across the area, less useful. In other words, the changing ways of food production and preparation exerted a major impact on the choice of utensils by their users. Chopsticks became a ubiquitous eating device because of the grain staples people grew and consumed in the region.

Compared with other eating tools, chopsticks have an obvious advantage – they are economical and easy to make from many common materials. So the popularity of chopsticks use by and large followed a bottom-up route: the instrument was more readily adopted as the sole eating device by people of the lower social strata than those of the upper echelon; the latter clearly had other tools available to them. Yet at the same time, chopsticks gained ground at the expense of other eating implements also because of the development of table manners and rudimentary concern for food cleanness and hygiene. Although I have not located a manual on using chopsticks in history, there is a sizable body of literature on dining

---

[4] My discussion here draws on a keyword search, using *bizhu*, in the *Siku quanshu* (Complete Library of the Four Treasures) database, the largest collection of texts on imperial China, which shows that the Chinese usually noted that other Asians outside their cultural realm did not use utensils for meals.

etiquette, habits and customs, originating as early as the age of Confucius, or the fifth century BCE. The eating instructions given by those compendia were mostly targeted at keeping up appearances and maintaining politeness toward others, which also reflected, perhaps indirectly, an interest in keeping the food clean and hygienic. Whether one is rich or poor, these are legitimate concerns regarding food consumption. Given their nimbleness and slim shape, chopsticks have enabled their users to pick up whatever they desire swiftly in the bowl or plate. Of course, to do so requires one to use chopsticks skillfully and to follow the customary chopsticks etiquette. As we have seen, this etiquette shares many similar characteristics across the chopsticks cultural sphere. One thing is quite clear: chopsticks are not an enabler for "double dipping" in food, as many outside the zone might believe on first sight. On the contrary, I would like to argue, their proper use actually helps people to alleviate concerns, perhaps most economically in a pre-modern age, about contaminating food while sharing it with others. In a modern age, despite the concerns about deforestation, disposable wooden chopsticks have become a convenient means for people to eat foods hygienically, for using disposable plastic utensils (which are harder to break down than wood) as an alternative might be environmentally more damaging.

Lastly, I now believe I understand the reason why instructions for chopsticks use went unwritten for many centuries. For among their users, this instrument has been interwoven, naturally and seamlessly, into the basic fabric of their daily lives. Using it to convey foods is an essential experience of how one grows up in the chopsticks cultural sphere. Given how indispensable they are, chopsticks thus become much more than a mere eating tool. That the Japanese call the utensil "the sticks for one's life" is a case in point, for chopsticks are, for the Japanese as well as for other Asians, a symbol for life. This is suggested by the great number of folktales, fables, fairytales, myths and legends about chopsticks and their use that have appeared in the region. While growing up, children not only learn how to hold the sticks correctly with their fingers, they are also told these stories by their parents and grandparents until they remember them by heart and can retell them to their children in future years. In sum, having accompanied and served the people in regions of East and Southeast Asia for several millennia, chopsticks and their use have become a living tradition. This tradition lives on with life itself.

Glossary

baigu	百谷
baxianzhuo	八仙桌
bi	匕
bing	餅
bizhu	匕箸
cai	菜
char kway teow	炒粿條
chengre chi	趁熱吃
chhá-kóe-tiâu	炒粿條
chi	吃
chi	匙
chifan	吃飯
chirirenge	散り蓮華
chizhu	匙箸
chōjubashi	長寿箸
damifan	大米飯
dianxin	點心
ding	鼎
eisei	衛生
enjubashi	延寿箸
enmeibashi	延命箸
enmusubibashi	缘結び箸
fan	飯
fangzhuo	方桌
fenshizhi	分食制
fu	釜

fu	賦
fukujubashi	福寿箸
fun	粉
geng	羹
gohan o taberu	ご飯を食べる
gongkuai	公筷
gongshi	公食
gongyi zhu	工藝箸
Guanzhong	關中
hakurai no hashi	舶來の箸
harenohashi	晴の箸
hashi	橋
hashi	箸
hashisugi shinkō	箸杉信仰
hashiwatashi	橋渡
heshizhi	合食制
honzen ryōri	本膳料理
Houji	後稷
hu	胡
hua	滑
huangliang	黃粱
hubing	胡餅
huchuang	胡牀
huiyu zhu	回魚箸
huntun	餛飩
huren	胡人
ichizen	一膳
itadakimasu	いただきます
ji	稷
jia	梜/筴
jiaochuang	交牀
jiaozi	餃子
jikabashi	直箸
jinye jiaoliu	津液交流
jinzhu	金箸
jiugu	九谷
jizhu	擊箸
juzhu	举箸
kagezen	陰膳

kaiseki-ryōri	懷石料理
kang	炕
kangzhuo	炕桌
katakuchibashi	片口箸
kenohashi	褻の箸
Kentōshi	遣唐使
Kenzuishi	遣隋使
kodama	木靈
kogei bashi	工芸箸
kuaile	快樂
kuaizi	筷子
kuaizi shen	筷子神
lamian	拉麵
li	鬲
liang	梁
liuchi	流匙
liugu	六谷
luodi	落地
luodi	落第
ma	麻
maifan	麥飯
makurameshi	枕飯
manabashi	真魚箸
mantou	饅頭
mayoibashi	迷い箸
meimeizen	銘銘膳
mi	米
mianbing	麵餅
miancha	麵茶
miotobashi	夫婦箸
nabemono	鍋物
namidahashi	涙箸
Nanyue	南越
neburibashi	舐り箸
nenshitsumai	粘質米
nuo	糯
nuribashi	塗り箸
ohashi	御箸
ohashizomeishiki	お箸初め式

oiwaibashi	お祝い箸
okuizomebashi	お食い初め箸
qin	琴
quangeng	犬羹
reibashi	霊箸
rikyūbashi	利休箸
rou	肉
rumao yinxue	茹毛飲血
ryōkuchibashi	両口箸
saguribashi	探り箸
saibashi	菜箸
seimei no tsue	生命の杖
shan	膳
shao	勺
shaobing	燒餅
sheng	生
shi	食
shi'an	食案
shinhashi	神箸
shinjin kyōshoku	神人共食
shirakibashi	白木箸
shizhi	食指
shu	黍
shu	熟
shuanyangrou	涮羊肉
shuifan	水飯
si	柶
su	粟
tairikufū	大陸風
tangchi	湯匙
tangfan	湯飯
tatebashi	立て箸
tōfū	唐風
toribashi	取り箸
touzhu	投箸
tungeng	豚羹
utsuribashi	移り箸
waribashi	割り箸
weiqi	圍棋

weisheng	衛生
weisheng kuai	衛生筷
wending	温鼎
wugu	五谷
xiafan	下飯
xian xiami, xian chifan	先下米，先吃飯
xiangzhu	象箸
xiaomifan	小米飯
xiaoshi	小食
xifan	稀飯
xinggeng	铏羹
Xiyu	西域
yanggeng	羊羹
yan	甂
yanxi	宴席
yicixing kuaizi	一次性筷子
yinzhu	銀箸
yizi	椅子
yu	鬻
Yue	越
Yuenan	越南
yunzi	雲子
yuzhu	玉箸 / 玉筯
zen	膳
zeng	甑
zhan	饘
zhima	芝麻
zhima shaobing	芝麻燒餅
Zhongguo	中國
zhou	粥
zhu	箸/筯/櫡
zhubing	煮餅
zongzi	粽子

Bibliography

Primary source databases

CTP (Abbreviation in footnotes). Chinese Text Project (http://ctext.org). This is a web-based e-text system that presents ancient Chinese texts, particularly those relating to Chinese philosophy, with a cross-referencing feature. Translations of some of the texts were done by James Legge (1815–1897).

DB of the Korean Classics (http://db.itkc.or.kr/itkcdb/mainIndexIframe.jsp). This database contains "Classic Translation Series," "Korean Literary Collection in Classical Chinese," "Original Editions of Korean Studies," "Annals of the Chosen Dynasty," "Diary of the Royal Secretariat," and "Records of Daily Reflection."

HDWZK (Abbreviation in footnotes). Hanji dianzi wenxian ziliaoku 漢籍電子文獻資料庫 (Scripta Sinica) (http://hanchi.ihp.sinica.edu.tw/ihp/hanji.htm). Begun in 1984, Scripta Sinica contains over 670 titles and 444,800,000 characters, including almost all of the important Chinese classics, especially those related to Chinese history.

Siku quanshu. 四庫全書 Compiled by imperial fiat in the late eighteenth century, this was the largest collection of Chinese texts before the twentieth century. It contains a total of 3503 books, organized by such bibliographic categories as *jing* 經 (classics), *shi* 史 (history), *zi* 子 (philosophy) and *ji* 集 (literature). The database was created on the Wenyuan'ge 文淵閣 version.

ZJGK (Abbreviation in footnotes). Zhongguo jiben gujiku 中国基本古籍库. This is hitherto the largest database of Chinese texts in China, three times the size of the Siku quanshu 四庫全書 compiled in the Qing period. Created by the Beijing Airusheng Digitization Research Center and published by Huangshan Shushe (Hefei, Anhui) in the early twenty-first century, it contains over 10,000 books with a total of 1.6 billion characters, covering the period between the eleventh century BCE and the early twentieth century CE.

Printed works

Anderson, E. N. "Northwest Chinese Cuisine and the Central Asian Connection," *Di 6 jie Zhongguo yinshi wenhua xueshu yantaohui lunwenji* (Proceedings of the 6th academic symposium on Chinese food and drink culture) (Taipei: Zhongguo yinshi wenhua jijinhui, 1999), 171–194.

Anderson, E. N. *The Food of China* (New Haven: Yale University Press, 1988).

Auden, W. H. & Isherwood, Christopher. *Journal to a War* (New York: Random House, 1939).

Avieli, Nir. "Eating Lunch and Recreating the Universe: Food and Cosmology in Hoi An, Vietnam," *Everyday Life in Southeast Asia*, eds. Kathleen M. Adams & Kathleen A. Gillogly (Bloomington: Indiana University Press, 2011), 218–229.

Avieli, Nir. "Vietnamese New Year Rice Cakes: Iconic Festive Dishes and Contested National Identity," *Ethnology*, 44:2 (Spring 2005), 167–187.

Barber, Kimiko. *The Chopsticks Diet: Japanese-Inspired Recipes for Easy Weight-Loss* (Lanham: Kyle Books, 2009).

Barthes, Roland. *Empire of Signs*, trans. Richard Howard (New York: Hill and Wang, 1982).

Bird, Isabella. *The Yangtze Valley and Beyond* (Boston: Beacon Press, 1985).

Boxer, C. R., ed. *South China in the Sixteenth Century* (London: Hakluyt Society, 1953).

Bray, Francesca. *Science and Civilization in China: Biology and Biological Technology. Part 2, Agriculture* (Cambridge: Cambridge University Press, 1986).

Bray, Francesca. *The Rice Economies: Technology and Development in Asian Societies* (Berkeley: University of California Press, 1994).

Brook, Timothy. *The Confusions of Pleasure: Commerce and Culture in Ming China* (Berkeley: University of California Press, 1998).

Brüssow, Harald. *The Quest for Food: A Natural History of Eating* (New York: Springer, 2007).

Ch'oe Pu, *Ch'oe Pu's Diary: A Record of Drifting across the Sea*, trans. John Meskill (Tucson: The University of Arizona Press, 1965).

Chang, K. C., ed. *Food in Chinese Culture: Anthropological and Historical Perspectives* (New Haven: Yale University Press, 1977).

Chang, Te-Tzu. "Rice," *Cambridge World History of Food*, eds. Kenneth F. Kiple & Kriemhild C. Ornelas (Cambridge: Cambridge University Press, 2000), vol. 1, 149–152.

Chen Mengjia 陳夢家. "Yindai tongqi" 殷代銅器 (Bronze vessels in the Shang dynasty), *Kaogu xuebao* (Journal of archaeology), 7 (1954).

Clunas, Craig. *Superfluous Things: Material Culture and Social Status in Early Modern China* (Urbana: University of Illinois Press, 1991).

Confucius. *Confucian Analects, The Great Learning and The Doctrine of the Mean*, trans. James Legge (New York: Dover Publications, Inc., 1971).

Cui Daiyuan 崔岱远, *Jingweier* 京味儿 (Beijing taste) (Beijing: Sanlian shudian, 2009).

Dawson, Raymond S., ed. *The Legacy of China* (Oxford: Oxford University Press, 1971).

Dikötter, Frank. *The Discourse of Race in Modern China* (Hong Kong: Hong Kong University Press, 1992).

Dong Yue 董越. *Chaoxian zalu* 朝鮮雜錄, in *Shi Chaoxian lu* 使朝鮮錄 (Records of Chinese embassies to Korea), eds. Yin Mengxia & Yu Hao (Beijing: Beijing tushuguan chubanshe, 2003), vol. 3.

Ennin. *Ennin's Diary: The Record of a Pilgrimage to China in Search of Law*, trans. Edwin Reischauer (New York: Ronald Press, 1955).

Fernandez-Armesto, Felipe. *Food: A History* (London: Macmillan, 2001).

Francks, Penelope. "Consuming Rice: Food, 'Traditional' Products and the History of Consumption in Japan," *Japan Forum*, 19:2 (2007), 147–168.

Giblin, James Cross. *From Hand to Mouth, Or How We Invented Knives, Forks, Spoons, and Chopsticks and the Table Manners to Go with Them* (New York: Thomas Y. Crowell, 1987).

Golden, Peter B. "Chopsticks and Pasta in Medieval Turkic Cuisine," *Rocznik orientalisticzny*, 49 (1994–1995), 73–82.

Goody, Jack. *Cooking, Cuisine, and Class: A Study in Comparative Sociology* (Cambridge: Cambridge University Press, 1982).

Goody, Jack. *Food and Love: A Cultural History of East and West* (London: Verso, 1998).

Goody, Jack. "The Origin of Chinese Food Culture," *Di 6 jie Zhongguo yinshi wenhua xueshu yantaohui lunwenji* (Proceedings of the 6th symposium of Chinese food and drink culture) (Taipei: Zhongguo yinshi wenhua jijinhui, 2003), 1–9.

Han Kyung-koo. "Noodle Odyssey: East Asia and Beyond," *Korea Journal*, 66–84.

Harada Nobuo 原田信男. *Riben liaoli de shehuishi: heshi yu Riben wenhua* 日本料理的社会史: 和食与日本文化 (A social history of Japanese cuisine: on Japanese food and Japanese culture), trans. Liu Yang (Hong Kong: Sanlian shudian, 2011).

He Julian 贺菊莲. *Tianshan jiayan: Xiyu yinshi wenhua zonghengtan* 天山家宴: 西域饮食文化纵横谈 (Dining on Mt. Tianshan: discussions of food cultures in the Western regions) (Lanzhou: Lanzhou daxue chubanshe, 2011).

Ho, Ping-ti. "The Loess and the Origin of Chinese Agriculture," *American Historical Review*, 75:1 (October 1969), 1–36.

Hu Zhixiang 胡志祥. "XianQin zhushi pengshi fangfa tanxi" 先秦主食烹食方法探析 (Study of the ways staple [grain] food were cooked in the pre-Qin period), *Nongye kaogu* (Agricultural archaeology), 2 (1994), 214–218.

Huang, H.T. "Han Gastronomy – Chinese Cuisine in *statu nascendi*," *Interdisciplinary Science Reviews*, 15:2 (1990), 139–152.

Hunan Sheng Bowuguan (Hunan Museum) 湖南省博物馆. *Changsha Mawangdui yihao Hanmu* 长沙马王堆一号汉墓 (The first tomb of Mawangdui, Changsha) (Beijing: Wenwu chubanshe, 1973).

Hunter, W.C. *The "Fan Kwae" at Canton: Before Treaty Days, 1825–1844* (London: Kegan Paul, Trench, & Co., 1882; reprinted in Taipei, 1965).

Iryŏn 一然. *Samguk yusa* 三國遺事 (Memorabilia of the Three Kingdoms), annotated by Sun Wenfan (Changchu: Jilin wenshi chubanshe, 2003).

Ishige Naomichi 石毛直道. "Filamentous Noodles, '*Miantiao*': Their Origin and Diffusion," *Di 3 jie Zhongguo yinshi wenhua xueshu yantaohui lunwenji*

(Proceedings of the 3rd academic symposium on Chinese food and drink culture) (Taipei: Zhongguo yinshi wenhua jijinhui, 1994), 113–129.

Isshiki Hachirō 一色八郎. *Hashi no Bunkashi: Sekai no Hashi Nihon no Hashi* 箸の文化史：世界の箸・日本の箸 (A cultural history of chopsticks: world chopsticks and Japanese chopsticks) (Tokyo: Ochanomizu Shobō, 1990).

Itō Seiji 伊藤清司. *Kaguya-hime no tanjō: Kodai setsuwa no kigen* かぐや姫の誕生：古代說話の起源 (The birth of the bamboo girl: origins of ancient legends) (Tokyo: Kōdansha, 1973).

Jeong Inji 鄭麟趾 et al. *Goryeosa* 高麗史 (History of the Goryeo dynasty) (Taipei: Wenshizhe chubanshe, 1972).

Kim Ch'on-ho (Jin Tianhao). "Han, Meng zhijian de roushi wenhua bijiao" (A comparative study of meat consumption cultures between the Koreans and the Mongols), trans. Zhao Rongguang & Jiang Chenghua, *Shangye jingji yu guanli* (Commercial economy and management), 4 (2000), 39–44.

Kim Pu-sik 金富軾. *Samguk sagi* 三國史記, annotated by Sun Wenfan (Changchun: Jilin wenshi chubanshe, 2003).

Knechtges, David R. "A Literary Feast: Food in Early Chinese Literature," *Journal of the American Oriental Society*, 106:1 (January–March, 1986), 49–63.

Knechtges, David R. "Gradually Entering the Realm of Delight: Food and Drink in Early Medieval China," *Journal of the American Oriental Society*, 117:2 (April– June 1997), 229–239.

Kosegi Erino 小瀬木えりの. "'Osoroshii aji': taishū ryori ni okeru Chuka no jyuyou sarekata: Filipin to Nihon no rei wo chūshinni" '恐ろしい味'：大衆料理における中華の受容のされ方－フィリ⊠ンと日本の例を中心に ("Terrible Taste": the acceptance of Chinese food as a daily food in the Philippines and Japan), *Di 6 jie Zhongguo yinshi wenhua xueshu yantaohui lunwenji* (Proceedings of the 6th academic symposium of Chinese food and drink culture) (Taipei: Zhongguo yinshi wenhua jijinhui, 1999), 225–236.

Lach, Donald F. *Japan in the Eyes of Europe: The Sixteenth Century* (Chicago: University of Chicago Press, 1968).

Lamb, Corinne. *The Chinese Festive Board* (Hong Kong: Oxford University Press, 1985; originally published in 1935).

Lan Xiang 藍翔. *Kuaizi, buzhishi kuaizi* 筷子、不只是筷子 (Chopsticks, not only chopsticks) (Taipei: Maitian, 2011).

Lan Xiang 藍翔. *Kuaizi gujin tan* 筷子古今谈 (Chopsticks: past and present) (Beijing: Zhongguo shangye chubanshe, 1993).

Lefferts, Leedom. "Sticky Rice, Fermented Fish, and the Course of a Kingdom: The Politics of Food in Northeast Thailand," *Asian Studies Review*, 29 (September 2005), 247–258.

Lei, Sean Hsiang-lin. "Habituating Individuality: The Framing of Tuberculosis and Its Material Solutions in Republican China," *Bulletin of the History of Medicine*, 84:2 (Summer 2010), 248–279.

Lei, Sean Hsiang-lin. "Moral Community of *Weisheng*: Contesting Hygiene in Republican China," *East Asian Science, Technology and Society: An International Journal*, 3:4 (2009), 475–504.

Leung, Angela Ki Che. "The Evolution of the Idea of Chuanran Contagion in Imperial China," *Health and Hygiene in Chinese East Asia*, eds. Leung & Furth, 25–50.

Leung, Angela Ki Che & Furth, Charlotte, eds. *Health and Hygiene in Chinese East Asia: Policies and Publics in the Long Twentieth Century* (Durham: Duke University Press, 2010).

Lévi-Strauss, Claude. *The Origin of Table Manners: Introduction to a Science of Mythology*, trans. John & Doreen Weightman (New York: Harper & Row, Publishers, 1978).

Lévi-Strauss, Claude. *The Raw and the Cooked: Introduction to a Science of Mythology: I*, trans. John & Doreen Weightman (New York: Harper & Row, Publishers, 1969).

Li Hu 黎虎, ed. *HanTang yinshi wenhuashi* 汉唐饮食文化史 (A history of food and drink culture during the Han and Tang dynasties) (Beijing: Beijing shifan daxue chubanshe, 1998).

Li Ziran 李自然. *Shengtai wenhua yu ren: Manzu chuantong yinshi wenhua yanjiu* 生态文化与人：满族传统饮食文化研究 (Ecological culture and humans: study of Manchu traditional food and drink culture) (Beijing: Minzu chubanshe, 2002).

Lin Hong 林洪. *Shanjia qinggong* 山家清供 (Simple foods at mountains) (Beijing: Zhongguo shangye chubanshe, 1985).

Liu Bing 刘兵. "Neimenggu Chifeng Shazishan Yuandai bihuamu" (Wall paintings in the Yuan tomb in Shazishan, Chifeng, Inner Mongolia), *Wenwu*, 2 (1992), 24–27.

Liu Pubing 刘朴兵. *TangSong yinshi wenhua bijiao yanjiu* 唐宋饮食文化比较研究 (A comparative study of food and drinking cultures in the Tang and Song periods) (Beijing: Zhongguo shehui kexue chubanshe, 2010).

Liu Yun 刘云. ed., *Zhongguo zhuwenhua daguan* 中国箸文化大观 (A grand view of chopstick-culture in China) (Beijing: Kexue chubanshe, 1996).

Liu Yun 刘云 et al., eds. *Zhongguo zhu wenhuashi* 中国箸文化史 (A history of chopsticks culture in China) (Beijing: Zhonghua shuju, 2006).

Liu Zhiqin 刘志琴. *WanMing shilun* 晚明史论 (Essays on Late Ming history) (Nanchang: Jiangxi gaoxiao chubanshe, 2004).

Longqiuzhuang yizhi kaogudui 龙虬庄考古队 (Archaeological team of the Longqiuzhuang ruins). *Longqiuzhuang: Jianghuai dongbu xinshiqi shidai yizhi fajue baogao* 龙虬庄：江淮东部新石器时代遗址发掘报告 (Longqiuzhuang: Excavation report on the Neolithic ruins in the east of Jiangsu and Huai River) (Beijing: Kexue chubanshe, 1999).

Lu Rong 陆容. *Shuyuan zaji* 菽園雜記 (Notes in the legume garden) (Beijing: Zhonghua shuju, 1985).

Macartney, George. *An Embassy to China: Being the Journal Kept by Lord Macartney during His Embassy to the Emperor Ch'ien-lung, 1793–1794*, ed. J. L. Cranmer-Byng (London: Longmans, republished, 1972).

MacMillan, Margaret. "Don't Drink the Mao-tai: Close Calls with Alcohol, Chopsticks, Panda Diplomacy and Other Moments from a Colorful Turning Point in History," *Washingtonian*, February 1, 2007.

Mencius. *The Works of Mencius*, trans. James Legge (New York: Dover Publications, Inc., 1970).

Meng Yuanlao 孟元老 et al. *Dongjing menghualu, Ducheng jisheng, Xihu laoren fanshenglu, Mengliang lu, Wulin jiushi* 東京夢華錄、都城紀勝、西湖老人繁勝錄、夢粱錄、武林舊事 (Beijing: Zhongguo shangye chubanshe, 1982).

Moore, Malcolm. "Chinese 'Must Swap Chopsticks for Knife and Fork'," *The Telegraph*, March 13, 2013.

Morrison, Ann M. "When Nixon Met Mao," Book Review, *Time*, December 3, 2006.

Mote, Frederick. "Yuan and Ming," *Food in Chinese Culture: Anthropological and Historical Perspectives*, ed. K. C. Chang (New Haven: Yale University Press, 1977).

Mukai Yukiko 向井由紀子 & Hashimoto Keiko 橋本慶子. *Hashi* 箸 (Chopsticks) (Tokyo: Hōsei daigaku shuppankyoku, 2001).

Mundy, Peter. *The Travels of Peter Mundy, in Europe and Asia, 1608–1667*, ed. Richard Carnac Temple (Liechtenstein: Kraus Reprint, 1967), vol. 3.

N. A. *XianQin pengren shiliao xuanzhu* 先秦烹饪史料选注 (Annotated pre-Qin historical sources of culinary practices) (Beijing: Zhongguo shangye chubanshe, 1986), 58.

Nakayama Tokiko 中山時子, ed. *Zhongguo yinshi wenhua* 中国饮食文化 (Chinese food and drink culture), trans. Xu Jianxin (Beijing: Zhongguo shehui kexue chubanshe, 1990).

Nguyen, Van Huyen. *The Ancient Civilization of Vietnam* (Hanoi: The Gioi Publishers, 1995).

Nguyen, Xuan Hien. "Rice in the Life of the Vietnamese Thay and Their Folk Literature," trans. Tran Thi Giang Lien, Hoang Luong, *Anthropos*, Bd. 99 H. 1 (2004), 111–141.

Nuwer, Rachel, "Disposable Chopsticks Strip Asian Forest," *New York Times*, October 24, 2011.

Ohnuki-Tierney, Emiko. *Rice as Self: Japanese Identities through Time* (Princeton: Princeton University Press, 1993).

Oliphant, Laurence. *Elgin's Mission to China and Japan*, with an introduction by J. J. Gerson (Oxford: Oxford University Press, 1970).

Ōta Masako 大田昌子. *Hashi no genryū o saguru: Chūkoku kodai ni okeru hashi shiyō shūzoku seiritsu* 箸の源流を探る：中国古代における箸使用習俗の成立 (Investigation into the origin of chopsticks: the establishment of the habit of chopsticks use in ancient China) (Tokyo: Kyūko Shoin, 2001).

Rebora, Giovanni. *Culture of the Fork*, trans. Albert Sonnenfeld (New York: Columbia University Press, 2001).

Ricci, Matteo. *China in the Sixteenth Century: The Journals of Matthew Ricci: 1583–1610*, trans. Louis J. Gallagher (New York: Random House, 1953).

Roberts, J. A. G. *China to Chinatown: Chinese Food in the West* (London: Reaktion Books, 2002).

Rogaski, Ruth. *Hygienic Modernity: Meanings of Health and Disease in Treaty-Port China* (Berkeley: University of California Press, 2004).

Shafer, Edward. "T'ang," *Food in Chinese Culture*, 85–140.

Shinoda Osamu 篠田統. *Zhongguo shiwushi yanjiu* 中国食物史研究 (Studies of Chinese food), trans. Gao Guilin, Sue Laiyun & Gao Yin (Beijing: Zhongguo shangye chubanshe, 1987).

Shū Tassei 周達生. *Chūgoku no Shokubunka* 中国の食文化 (Food culture in China) (Tokyo: Sōgensha, 1989).

Song Yingxing (Sung Ying-hsing) 宋應星. *T'ien-kung k'ai-wu: Chinese Technology in the Seventeenth Century*, trans. E-tu Zen Sun and Shiou-chuan Sun (University Park: Pennsylvania State University Press, 1966).

Spencer, Jane. "Banned in Beijing: Chinese See Green over Chopsticks," *The Wall Street Journal*, February 8, 2008.

Sterckx, Roel. *Food, Sacrifice, and Sagehood in Early China* (New York: Cambridge University Press, 2011).

Taylor, Keith Weller. *The Birth of Vietnam* (Berkeley: University of California Press, 1983).

Tomes, Nancy. *The Gospel of Germs: Men, Women, and the Microbe in American Life* (Cambridge: Harvard University Press, 1998).

Van Esterik, Penny. *Food Culture in Southeast Asia* (Westport: Greenwood Press, 2008).

Visser, Margaret. *Much Depends on Dinner: The Extraordinary History and Mythology, Allure and Obsessions, Perils and Taboos, of an Ordinary Meal* (New York: Grove Press, 1986).

Wang Chong 王充. *Lunheng* 論衡 (Discursive weighing) (Shanghai: Shanghai renmin chubanshe, 1974).

Wang Lihua 王利华. *Zhonggu huabei yinshi wenhuade bianqian* 中古华北饮食文化的变迁 (Changes in food and drink culture of North China during the middle imperial period) (Beijing: Zhongguo shehui kexue chubanshe, 2001).

Wang Mingsheng 王鳴盛. *Shiqishi shangque* 十七史商榷 (Critiques of seventeen histories) (Shanghai: Shanghai shudian chubanshe, 2005).

Wang Renxiang 王仁湘. "Cong kaogu faxian kan Zhongguo gudaide yinshi wenhua chuantong" 从考古发现看中国古代的饮食文化传统 (Traditions of food and drink culture in ancient China shown in archaeological finds), *Hubei jingji xueyuan xuebao* (Journal of Hubei economics college), 2 (2004), 108–112.

Wang Renxiang. "Shaozi, chazi, kuazi: Zhongguo jinshi fangshi de kaoguxue yanjiu" 勺子、叉子、筷子：中国进食方式的考古学研究 (Spoon, fork, and chopsticks: an archaeological study of the eating method in ancient China), *Xun'gen* (Root exploration), 10 (1997).

Wang Renxiang. *Wanggu de ziwei: Zhongguo yinshi de lishi yu wenhua* 往古的滋味：中国饮食的历史与文化 (Tastes of yore: history and culture of Chinese foods and drinks) (Ji'nan: Shandong huabao chubanshe, 2006).

Wang Renxiang. *Yinshi yu Zhongguo wenhua* 饮食与中国文化 (Foods and drinks in Chinese culture) (Beijing: Renmin chubanshe, 1994).

Wang Saishi 王赛时. *Tangdai yinshi* 唐代饮食 (Food and drink culture in the Tang) (Ji'nan: Qilu shushe, 2003).

White, Lynn. "Fingers, Chopsticks and Forks: Reflections on the Technology of Eating," New York Times (Late Edition – East Coast), July 17, 1983, A-22.

Wilson, Bee. *Consider the Fork: A History of How We Cook and Eat* (New York: Basic Books, 2012).

Wu Zimu 吳自牧 & Zhou Mi 周密. *Mengliang lu, Wulin jiushi* 夢梁錄、武林舊事 (Dreaming of Kaifeng in Hangzhou; History of Lin'an) (Ji'nan: Shandong youyi chubanshe, 2001).

Xiang Chunsong 项春松. "Liaoning Zhaowuda diqu faxian de Liaomu huihua ziliao" 辽宁昭乌达地区发现的辽墓绘画资料 (Paintings discovered in a Kitan tomb of the Zhaowuda area, Liaoning), *Wenwu* (Cultural relics), 6 (1979), 22–32.

Xiang Chunsong. "Neimenggu jiefangyingzi Liao mu fajue jianbao" 内蒙古解放营子辽墓发掘简报 (Concise report on the dig of the Liao-dynasty tomb in Jiefangyingzi, Inner Mongolia), *Kaogu* (Archaeology), 4 (1979), 330–334.

Xiang Chunsong & Wang Jianguo 王建国. "Neimeng Zhaomeng Chifeng Sanyanjing Yuandai bihuamu" 内蒙古昭盟赤峰三眼井元代壁画墓 (Wall paintings in the Yuan tomb in Sanyanjing, Chifeng, Zhaomeng District, Inner Mongolia), *Wenwu*, 1 (1982), 54–58.

Xinjiang Weiwuer zizhiqu bowuguan 新疆维吾尔自治区博物馆 (Uyghur autonomous district in Xinjiang). "Xinjiang Tulufan Asitana beiqu muzang fajue jianbao" 新疆吐鲁番阿斯塔纳北区墓葬发掘简报 (Brief report on the excavation in the tombs of northern Astana, Turpan, Xinjiang), *Wenwu* (Cultural relics), 6 (1960).

Xu Hairong 徐海荣. Ed. *Zhongguo yinshishi* 中国饮食史 (A history of Chinese food and drink culture) (Beijing: Huaxia chubanshe, 1999).

Xu Jing 徐兢. "Xuanhe fengshi Gaoli tujing" 宣和奉使高麗圖經 (Illustrated record of the Chinese embassy to the Goryeo court during the Xuanhe era), in *Shi Chaoxian lu* (Records of Chinese embassies to Korea), eds. Yin Mengxia & Yu Hao (Beijing: Beijing tushuguan chubanshe, 2003), vol. 1.

Xu Jingbo 徐静波. *Riben yinshi wenhua: lishi yu xianshi* 日本饮食文化：历史与现实 (Food culture in Japan: past and present) (Shanghai: Shanghai renmin chubanshe, 2009).

Xu Pingfang 徐苹方. "Zhongguo yinshi wenhua de diyuxing jiqi ronghe" 中國飲食文化的地域性及其融合 (Regions and cross-regional development in Chinese food and drinking culture), *Di 4 jie Zhongguo yinshi wenhua xueshu yantaohi lunwenji* (Proceedings of the 4th academic symposium on Chinese food and drinking culture) (Taipei: Zhongguo yinshi wenhua jijinhui, 1996).

Yang Dabin. "Choptax," *Earth Island Journal*, 21:2 (Summer 2006), 6–6.

Yang Zheng "Chopsticks Controversy," *New Internationalist*, 311 (April 1999), 4.

Yao Weijun 姚伟钧. *Changjiang liuyu de yinshi wenhua* 长江流域的饮食文化 (Food and drink culture in the Yangzi River region) (Wuhan: Hubei jiaoyu chubanshe, 2004).

Yao Weijun. "*Fojiao yu Zhongguo yinshi wenhua*" 佛教与中国饮食文化 (Buddhism and the food and drink culture in China), *Minzhu* (Democracy monthly), 9 (1997), 32–33.

Yao Weijun. *Zhongguo chuantong yinshi lisu yanjiu* 中国传统饮食礼俗研究 (Study of the dining etiquette and habits in traditional China) (Wuhan: Huazhong shifan daxue chubanshe, 1999).

Yi Sông-u, "Chōsen hantō no shoku no bunka" (Food culture on the Korean Peninsula), in *Higashi Ajia no shoku no bunka* (Food cultures in East Asia), eds. Ishige Naomichi et al. (Tokyo: Heibonsha, 1981), 129–153.

Yin Yongwen 尹永文. *MingQing yinshi yanjiu* 明清飲食研究 (Studies of food and drink in the Ming and Qing dynasties) (Taipei: Hongye wenhua shiye youxian gongsi, 1997).

Yip Ka-che. *Health and National Reconstruction in Nationalist China* (Ann Arbor: Association for Asian Studies, Inc., 1995).

Yu Ying-shih. "Han," in Chang, K. C. ed. *Food in Chinese Culture*, (New Haven: Yale University Press, 1977), 53–84.

Yuan Yuan 袁元. "Yicixing kuaizi tiaozhan Zhongguo guoqing" 一次性筷子挑战中国国情 (Disposable chopsticks challenge China as a country), *Liaowang zhoukan* (Outlook weekly), 33 (August 13, 2007).

Yun Kuk-Hyong. *Capchin Mallok*, Korean Classics Database (http://db.itkc.or.kr/itkcdb/mainIndexIframe.jsp).

Zhang Guangzhi (Chang K. C.) 張光直. "Zhongguo yinshishi shangde jici tupo" 中國飲食史上的幾次突破 (Several breakthroughs in the Chinese food and drink history), *Di 4 jie Zhongguo yinshi wenhua xueshu yantaohui lunwenji* (Proceedings of the 4th academic symposium on Chinese food and drink culture) (Taipei: Zhongguo yinshi wenhua jijinhui, 1996), 1–4.

Zhang Jiangkai 张江凯 & Wei Jun 魏峻. *Xinshiqi shidai kaogu* 新石器时代考古 (Neolithic archaeology) (Beijing: Wenwu chubanshe, 2004).

Zhang Jingming 张景明 & Wang Yanqing 王雁卿. *Zhongguo yinshi canju fazhanshi* 中国饮食餐具发展史 (A history of eating and drinking utensils in China) (Shanghai: Shanghai guji chubanshe, 2011).

Zhang Yichang, "Guoren buweisheng de exi" (The unhygienic habits of my countrymen), *Xinyi yu shehui jikan* (Journal of new medicine and society), 2 (1934), 156.

Zhao Rongguang. *Zhongguo yinshi wenhua gailun* 中国饮食文化概论 (Introduction to food and drink culture in China) (Beijing: Gaodeng jiaoyu chubanshe, 2003).

Zhao Rongguang. *Zhongguo yinshi wenhuashi* 中国饮食文化史 (A history of Chinese food and drink culture) (Shanghai: Shanghai renmin chubanshe, 2006).

Zhao Rongguang 赵荣光. "Zhu yu Zhonghua minzu yinshi wenhua" 箸与中华民族饮食文化 (Chopsticks and Chinese food and drink culture), *Nongye kaogu* (Agricultural archaeology), 2 (1997), 225–235.

Zhen Jun 震鈞. *Tianzhi ouwen* 天咫偶聞 (Legends of the heavenly realm) (Beijing: Beijing guji chubanshe, 1982).

Zhongguo shehui kexueyuan kaogu yanjiusuo 中国社会科学院考古研究所 (The Institute of Archaeology, Chinese Academy of the Social Sciences), *Tang Chang'an chengjiao Suimu* 唐长安城郊隋墓 (The Sui tombs near the Tang capital Chang'an) (Beijing: Wenwu chubanshe, 1980).

Zhou Xinhua 周新华. *Tiaodingji* 调鼎集 (Collection of food essays) (Hangzhou: Hangzhou chubanshe, 2005).

Index